child-menders

GEORGE H. WEBER

Foreword by LaMar T. Empey

child-menders

SAGE Publications   *Beverly Hills   London*

For information address:

SAGE PUBLICATIONS, INC.
275 South Beverly Drive
Beverly Hills, California 90212

SAGE PUBLICATIONS LTD
28 Banner Street
London EC1Y 8QE

Printed in the United States of America

International Standard Book Number 0-8039-1184-X

Library of Congress Cataloging in Publication Data

Weber, George, 1921-
   Child-Menders.

   Bibliography; p.
   1. Social work with delinquents and criminals.
2. Juvenile delinquency.   3. Juvenile corrections.
I. Title.
HV7428.W4   362.7'4   79-4244
ISBN 0-8039-1184-X

FIRST PRINTING

CONTENTS

ACKNOWLEDGMENTS

I am most appreciative to Dr. Gerald B. Suttles for his professional interest in and encouragement of this effort, to Marilyn T. Wilhelms for her assistance in commenting on and editing the vignettes, and to Pat Chicca and El-Marie Hamiltion for typing and retyping the manuscript. This work was carried out in my private capacity. No official support or endorsement by the U.S. Department of Health, Education, and Welfare is intended or should be inferred.

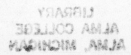

FOREWORD

In his introduction to the *Child-Menders,* George Weber says his book was written in the hope that it could inform youth care workers, budding professionals, and interested lay persons about the realities of work with delinquents in residential settings. Dr. Weber has more than achieved that goal. The story he unfolds is simultaneously moving and realistic. Its central characters—its children and its child-menders—could be found in any training school in the country.

Even more important is the disturbing theme which pervades the *Child-Menders.* I seriously doubt that the youth worker who has found a comfortable home in a bureaucracy, the enthusiastic novice, or the romantically inclined child-saver is fully prepared to confront its unmistakable message: the task of trying to redeem the children who have been swept to the backwaters of society is usually thankless and heartrending. It quickly proves unrewarding to the self-righteous; it reveals the easy corruptibility of the feckless; and, worst of all, it consumes the strong. Real winners are rare.

Such a message would have been difficult to accept in the best of times, but, at present, it is even more distressing. The reason is that the humane sentiments which have made a difficult task marginally tolerable now seem to be waning. The prevailing mood of the country may be switching from feelings of concern and sympathy for the young offal of society to feelings of disconcern and resentment.

For more than a century, there have always been highly visible groups of reformers who, though they were often painfully sanctimonious, were dedicated nonetheless to the task of reclaiming deviant or unattractive children.

To most of them, the stakes seemed unusually high. The thought that many youngsters might be left to an uncertain, even dismal future was not easy to bear; however maddening, unresponsive, or predatory they might appear. Something, it was always argued, could be done. Indeed, this sentiment toward children reflected a broader article of faith in the American credo which suggested that all humans are malleable and that most can be saved.

A NEW SENTIMENT

Today, by contrast, a new sentiment is growing—a narcissistic sentiment symbolized by the popular bumper sticker which reads, "If it feels good, do it." Threatened by accounts of youth crime and unrest, disillusioned by political chicanery and bureaucratic ineptitude, and pessimistic about the future, Americans have turned inward rather than outward in their search for purpose and gratification. More and more, personal satisfaction is said to come not from a sense of duty to others or from the rewards inherent in bringing richness to the lives of people less fortunate than oneself, but from one's own gratification and pleasure.

These individualistic and narcissistic sentiments have produced a curiously paradoxical situation for children. On the one hand, they have helped to foster a child-rights movement, suggesting that children should enjoy all the rights and privileges enjoyed by adults. No longer should children be treated as second-class citizens, fettered by rules which inhibit their own personal choice of domicile, school, work, sexual activity, or political participation. Anything that is permissible for adults should be permissible for children. And while this movement has by no means totally altered the status of children, it has produced some changes that are radical by traditional standards: the right to due process and counsel in legal proceedings; the right of free speech in the schools; the right to abortion without parental consent; or the reduction of legal controls over children for such status offenses as truancy, incorrigibility, sexual promiscuity, or running away from home.

On the other hand, it should come as no surprise that, as greater privileges have been granted to children, demands have been also made that they be held responsible for their acts. No longer is it permissible, for example, for courts to treat criminal children like status offenders. Instead, sharp distinctions between the two have been drawn. Such trends, as a result, are ominous for those "deep end" delinquents who populate our training schools, and on whom many parents, neighborhoods, and communities have already given up. In response to the emergence of new sentiments and practices, they have become young pariahs whose futures are doubly threatened.

Reflecting this very conclusion, the past two decades have witnessed a rapid erosion of faith in the concept of rehabilitation and in the optimistic beliefs on which it was constructed. An equivocal body of scientific findings on its effectiveness has been used by a new generation of neoclassical, utilitarian philosophers to propound a conclusion that is not only pessimistic, but nihilistic: *Nothing works!* However enlightened the method, however persistent the worker, however comprehensive or humane the approach, none has a desirable effect. Good intentions and costly programs are simply wasted on an undeserving and ungrateful few. The only justifiable alternative, therefore, is to insure that the community is protected by seeing that justice is done and that the lawbreaker is given his "just deserts."

This philosophy has also gained credence because it stresses a fundamental principle in human affairs to which most people subscribe so long as it is not applied to them; namely, that the individual should be held fully accountable for his own transgressions. But while the philosophy of rehabilitation suggests that one can eventually extract accountability and responsibility from transgressors by attending to and changing the factors which motivate their transgressions, the philosophy of retribution suggests that accountability should be meted out in proportion to the seriousness or repetitiveness of the *acts* which the transgressors commit. In short, we are back once again attending to acts rather than to people. As a result, punishment or incapacitation, not reformation, are said to be the primary factors on which our attention should be concentrated. Reformation may come as the by-product of a more punitive system of justice, but it should not be the primary goal of that system.

The limitations of such a classical approach for immature and often abandoned children would seem to be obvious. Our traditional concept of childhood has suggested that childhood and adolescence should be treated as transitional periods in the life cycle in which the young are granted greater license than adults to make mistakes. Since they are not capable of full responsibility, policies and practices should be avoided which would permanently impair their life chances. Thus, in philosophy at least, when a young person has violated the law, practices have been disfavored which would label and exile him permanently. Now, however, that philosophy is undergoing change and steps are being taken which could seriously impair the reentry of criminal children into the conventional trace that leads from childhood to adulthood.

JUST DESERTS

It would be surprising to me if George Weber ever anticipated that *Child-Menders* might be used to reflect on these kinds of issues. Yet, it does so in a most striking way. On the one hand, the frustrations and heartaches portrayed in the book clearly reveal the extent to which our efforts to "mend" children in the past have fallen short of the rehabilitative ideal. In a value context supposedly supportive of rehabilitation, places like Central State Training School have been inept and ineffective at best, and destructive and inhumane at worst. People who are unfamiliar with the inner workings of total institutions, therefore, will benefit greatly from the way that system is dramatized in this unusual natural history document.

On the other hand, to the degree that a resurgent philosophy of retribution gains a firm foothold in this country, conditions for children who are committed to institutions could become even worse. While one must strain to explain how this could happen, some reasons have already been given and others can be cited.

In the first place, if the license granted to adolescents to make mistakes is withdrawn, and granted only to younger children, then harsher and more rigid penalties will be the result. Indeed, steps in this direction have already been taken. Not only have some states lowered the age of accountability for criminal behavior, but one, the state of Washington, has passed a determinate sentence law which requires that juvenile court judges consider only prior offense history and the offender's current offense as the criteria for passing sentence. Only in rare instances, where "manifest injustice" might be done, can exceptions be made, and judges must carefully justify those. In short, the most fundamental premise of the traditional juvenile court—namely, that the court should treat children and not offenses—has been largely reversed.

Second, when offenses and not offenders become the focus of attention, "just deserts" become the central criterion for levying penalties. That too has happened. In passing its determinate sentence law, the Washington State Legislature ranked rehabilitation fifth or sixth on its list of priorities behind equal justice or community protection. In other words, it formally renounced rehabilitation as a high-ranking goal, and freed institutional superintendents and youth workers from pursuing it as their primary responsibility. One can only speculate as to what the ultimate result will be. But, as the *Child-Menders* reveals, since rehabilitation has only been haltingly pursued under the best of circumstances—that is, when it was hailed as the sole purpose of institutions—it is likely to become of even lesser concern to the degree that a retributive philosophy replaces it.

Finally, and perhaps most important, a cynical and retributive mood in the country tends to deflect attention away from the destructive impact on children of a place like Central State Training School. If rehabilitation is hopeless, and retributive justice becomes our first priority, then there will be less need for concern for the delinquents who are incapacitated in society's holding tanks. They ask for what they get, and they get what they deserve.

LIFE IN TOTAL INSTITUTIONS

But is this image an accurate one? What is the picture of delinquents that is painted in the *Child-Menders?* Are they psychopaths for whom only the most severe of controls are adequate?

Child-Menders makes it all too clear that there are no simple answers. Some of the boys at Central State Training School are manipulators, some are users of smuggled drugs, some are thieves, and some are tough exploiters who rule the inmate domain by force. But these boys are not all of a delinquent type. Many are also confused, lonely, and depressed boys for whom life, to say nothing of their present captivity, has been anything but rewarding and happy. Indeed, George Weber's vignettes raise serious questions about the efficacy of further punishment for them, since that has been about all they have known throughout their short and troubled lives.

Rick Brown epitomizes the type of boy found in every institution who is inclined to run away. "Rick's a funny kid," says Mr. Wellman, his cottage supervisor. "He doesn't seem to feel that he measures up. I don't know where he gets his super high standards. We've got quite a number like that here in Lexington [cottage] but I'd say he's the farthest out of the lot. He works hard around the cottage, [and] hits the books at school."

Why, then, does an apparent achiever like Rick run away? Why does he risk new offenses or virtually insure that his time in captivity will be extended, once he is caught? The answer is that he tries too hard. Motherless and the son of an impatient, demanding, and punitive father, he never feels that he measures up. Adding to his problems is the fact that his cottage supervisor, like his father, expects him to be better than anyone else. "We let him know that he's our best student in this unit and we expect him to come through," Mr. Wellman explains.

The trouble is that Rick cannot handle this well-intentioned but misguided pressure. First, he apparently freezes on an important test in school and is openly ridiculed by his teacher. Then he is further mocked by his peers. Finally, ridicule and mockery lead to a bloody fight. In response to it all, Rick runs away, taking some other boys with him. To the end, however, Mr. Wellman fails to understand why. "He's let us down," says the disgruntled supervisor. "There's no damned excuse for the kind of stuff he keeps pulling."

Timmy Stover is a similar boy, only when he runs away he makes his escape a permanent one: he hangs himself. A friendly, even pathetic individual, Timmy symbolizes the many boys who have been raised by the state because they are the children of uncaring parents. Timmy has written home several times, desperate for an answer. But none is forthcoming, either from his alcoholic father or from his mother who is now living with another man. Lacking any ratification for his worth as a person, therefore, Timmy thoughtfully gives his prized possessions to his surprised friends and quietly puts an end to his life.

Timmy's suicide in a shower stall is made no easier by the fact that his distraught supervisor has tried for weeks to get him out of the institution and into the home of his uncle, a farmer. But to no avail. The professionals in charge of such placements are so bound up in bureaucratic procedures and unreasonable standards that they fail to act. Their chief reason for delaying placement is that Timmy would be expected to do "sweaty," "smelly," and "dirty" work on his uncle's farm. Consequently, they procrastinate and Timmy dies.

Many other examples, movingly documented by Dr. Weber, could be cited, but these will suffice to illustrate two important points: (1) that delinquents are seldom totally evil persons, entirely bereft of human feeling or compassion; and (2) that the problems of correctional institutions are by no means the sole creations of their inmates. Even in instances in which drug use or systematic thievery are involved, staff members as well as inmates are sometimes involved.

In the case of drugs, for example, it is janitors who smuggle marijuana into the training school, not inmate ring leaders. Furthermore, in an ironic turn of events, pressure by a high-placed politician is put on the Central State's superintendent to reinstate these smugglers after they have been forced to resign. Meanwhile, impressionable but cynical young inmates are witness to a situation in which staff members avoid prosecution for their offenses, while they, the inmates, are punished.

In short, training schools are fractured not only by staff-inmate differences, but by intrastaff conflicts and sometimes by staff chicanery. To be sure, most staff members are well-intentioned and hard working, but even then, too many are ill-prepared, either by temperament or lack of experience, to deal with the unnatural character of total institutions. Membership in such places not only makes captives of delinquents, but in a very real sense makes captives of their keepers as well.

One person among those who does understand this fact is Jack Owens, Director of Group Life at Central. Patiently he tries to make sense of it all for both staff and inmates. But in this instance at least, he is destined to fail. Because he is forced to carry water in leaky buckets, he is like Gunga Din in Rudyard Kipling's famous poem: through his heroic efforts, Jack is able to carry just enough water to keep the troops alive; eventually, he comes to recognize that most will perish from causes worse than thirst. Ultimately, this knowledge becomes too heavy for Jack to bear. Depressed by his sense of failure and weary of the struggle, he perishes. Like Timmy, whom he tried to save, he dies alone, consumed by his own sense of inadequacy.

Given these outcomes, the events at Central State Training School leave us much to ponder. Not only must we wonder about the fate of society's "deep-enders," but about the fate of those who are their keepers. In a more simple, and perhaps more romantic time, a person like Jack Owens might have been hailed as a hero because of his selfless devotion to an unpopular cause. In the present day, however, his eventual status is more uncertain. To the extent that we have become cynical about child-mending and preoccupied with self, we will be tempted to view Jack as hopelessly naive and old-fashioned. What person, in his right mind, would take on the thankless role that Jack played, and in behalf of such a marginal group of children?

Only time will tell how this question will be answered, or which image of Jack will prevail.

—LaMar T. Empey

INTRODUCTION

I have written *Child-Menders* with two distinct audiences in mind. I have designed the book, first of all, for individuals working with delinquent youth in residential settings—most particularly youth care workers—and for persons who are preparing to work in this field. In addition to appealing to youth care practitioners and students, I have developed this book for the more general reader, both in terms of its subject matter and its form. *Child-Menders* focuses on the very human process of working with delinquents and is presented in the form of vignettes. I chose the vignette format because I am convinced that it has the capacity to convey to both categories of readers a sense of the many complexities involved in working with delinquents. Through such components as setting, characters, plot, and theme, the vignette format is able to deal with the perplexing and often insurmountable problems associated with the treatment of delinquents; including the seemingly intractable behavior of some delinquents, the rigidities of archaic institutional procedures, the ineptness of untutored staff efforts, and the lack of community understanding.

Though I have tried to get as close as possible to the world of the staff and their problems, this book is neither muckraking nor an apologia. In my effort to gain closeness, I have devoted attention to the influences and counterinfluences among staff members, among staff and delinquents, and the consequences of these for each concerned. Where relevant, I have related the actions of the staff and the delinquents to the impact of public opinion and vested interests, in the community and to the institutional and agency bureaucracies and the effects of their administrative routines and their fears of the political system.

The substance of the vignettes—their settings, plots, themes, and characters—is rooted in reality. However, in several instances the vignettes can be described as reality based; that is, their material is drawn from facts that are dealt with in ways that transpose the literal truth without fundamental accuracy being altered. To get down to specifics, Jack is a composite of two persons who had exceptionally similar ways of perceiving and dealing with delinquents. "Jack's Entrance," Chapter 1, contains elements of fiction, particularly the dynamics of Jack's upbringing. The basis for "Sex Education," Chapter 7, was modified from a small half-day meeting to a day-long workshop. "Jack's Exit," Chapter 13, is partly fiction, most specifically because I have exercised an author's license in describing the dreams associated with his death. The content comprising those dreams, however, had been described to me; hence, they are reality based, and the death was—as it always is, ultimately—real. The dialogue is consistent with the thrust of actual occurrences—expressed in my words—and with the reality of my experiences and those of my colleagues.

In addition to the vignettes, *Child-Menders* contains a Workshop, located at the back of the book and intended for youth care workers, prospective workers, and their instructors—be they college or university faculty or inservice instructors. The Workshop suggests a number of concepts and procedures that may be used in analyzing the material in this volume, a sample case analysis, and questions to aid discussion of the vignettes.

Most of the vignettes are open-ended in that they do not provide final resolutions to the problems they introduce, which may be somewhat perplexing to readers. However, not only does the open-endedness give the reader an opportunity to provide his own solutions, or at least next steps which might be taken on a case, but it corresponds to the general lack of solutions to delinquency treatment problems—one of the features (indeed, one of the most frustrating features) of the professional staff member's life at any institution such as Central State. This, however, is where the challenge stands.

The vignettes draw from three traditions: the short story, especially as it is grounded in actuality and objectivity; the case study used in social science; and the case method used in teaching human relations and law. I want to touch here on a small portion of the literature pertaining to these traditions.

Since the nineteenth century, the short story has had a variety of emphases, including a grounding in actuality. In the early 1830s, when Poe and Hawthorne were writing short stories in America and Poe was theorizing about them, Gogol was producing stories in Russia that combined objective and psychological considerations (*Nevsky Prospect* and *Diary of a Madman*, both 1835). At about the same time, Mérimée (*Mateo Falcone*, 1829) and Balzac, writing in France, also grounded their short stories in realism, though frequently of a sardonic and biting nature.

Later in the nineteenth century, Maupassant (*The House of Mme. Tellier*, 1881) in particular among the French writers emphasized the realism of hunger, fear, greed, envy, and sex. In the United States during the same period, writers sought objectivity in dealing with real places, events, and persons. The regionalist stories (particularly those by G.W. Cable, Mark Twain, Bret Harte, and Sara Orne Jewett) were of this tradition. Chekhov, writing in Russia during the latter part of the century and influenced by Gogol, concentrated on average men and women who could not seem to understand one another and so became lonely, isolated human beings (*Kashtaska*, 1887; *Ward No. 6*, 1892).

After World War I the short story flourished in Great Britain. Major novelists, including James Joyce, D. H. Lawrence, and Virginia Woolf, produced notable works. During this time Katherine Mansfield (*Bliss*, 1920) of Australia portrayed the importance of ordinary life incidents by using a stream-of-consciousness technique. Following World War II, Sillitoe (*The Loneliness of the Long-Distance Runner*, 1960) of England conveyed the rebellion of an institutionalized delinquent against the school administrators who sought to exploit his running talent.

As in Great Britain, the major twentieth-century American novelists—Willa Cather, F. Scott Fitzgerald, Ernest Hemmingway, William Faulkner, John Steinbeck, and Robert Penn Warren, for example—often wrote as skillfully in the short story form as in the novel. Like the regional American short story writers of the late 1800s, some twentieth-century short story writers in America attempted to grasp the objectivity of life at close range, and focused on regional themes, particularly the South (Faulkner, Warren, Porter, and Welty).

A second category of literature pertinent to *Child-Menders* is the case study or life history. Regarded as one of the oldest methods of portraying and analyzing personal experiences and human conduct, its roots are buried in fables, allegories, novels, short stories, and narratives of many kinds (Burgess, 1927; Young, 1949).

Though Le Play was probably the first to apply the case-study method systematically in his study of the family, Spencer is usually remembered for his early and extensive use of case material, perhaps because of his overly enthusiastic and uncritical efforts (Sorokin, 1928). In the area of crime and delinquency, William Healy (1915) was the first to extensively employ the case-study method to gain a psychiatric understanding of juvenile delinquents. After examining a thousand juvenile delinquents, he concluded that, unaided, "statistics never tell the whole story." Cyril Burt (1925) in London followed Healy in the use of the case-study method. However, it was Clifford Shaw's (1930 and 1938) case studies on delinquents which became preeminent. Using various data, including having a delinquent write his own story, Shaw sought insights into the behavior patterns, social relationships, and social circumstances of the delinquents. Shaw's documents—as in the case with other life histories—are not statistical social science data; however, they do present the complexities and subtleties of human behavior with clarity and sensitivity. During this same period, Edwin Sutherland collaborated with Chic Conwell in writing *The Professional Thief* (1937). Recent documents following this general style of investigation include the *Box Man* (King, 1972), *Hustler* (Williamson, 1965), and *Time Game* (Manocchio and Dunn, 1977).

While *Child-Menders* makes use of the traditions reflected in the foregoing descriptions of short story and case-study techniques, it also draws on the case methods used to teach case law in law schools (Landman, 1930), human relations (as they take place in day-to-day situations) in the social sciences (Baur, 1960; Donham, 1944; Cabot and Kahl, 1953; McCluggage, 1955); in child care, psychotherapy, and teaching (Beker, 1972; Standal and Corsini, 1959; Corsini and Howard, 1964); and in schools of business (McCluggage, 1958; McNair, 1954; Andrews, 1953).

In law, where the case method of teaching began, cases are made up of a legal situation or action from whose analysis the students gain both principles of law and practical training. In the area of human relations and social science, cases are descriptions of problem situations from which the students derive some understanding of the complex facts with which they may eventually have to deal in their work places. The method presents no pat formulas, but functions on the assumption that the individual will develop knowledge through the processes described, particularly as his understanding is sharpened through discussions with skilled teachers and interested peers. The method is unique because it permits the direct involvement of learners in realistic, though vicarious, problem situations. Along with learning from the content and procedures described in the cases, the student can learn to seek the solutions to problems, rather than merely seeking someone on whom to place the blame. This can be done much less painfully in a classroom learning, rather than a sudden, real-life situation.

In summary, *Child-Menders* presents a set of cases in the form of vignettes modeled on the short story format concerning the treatment of institutionalized delinquents—particularly the function of youth care workers. I am hopeful that this approach will serve as an effective vehicle for shedding light on the intricate process of delinquency treatment.

REFERENCES

Sources Used on the Short Story

Bates, H. E. *The Modern Short Story*, a critical survey. Boston: The Writer, 1956.

Brooks, C. & Warren, R. P. (Eds.). *Understanding Fiction*. New York: Appleton-Century-Crofts, 1959.

Current-Garcia, E. & Patrick, W. R. (Eds.). *American Short Stories*. Glenview, Il: Scott, Foresman, 1962.

West, R. B., Jr. *The Short Story in America 1900-1950*. New York: Arno, 1952.

Sources Used for Case Study and Case Methods

Andrews, K. R. (Ed.). *The Case Method for Teaching Human Relations and Administration*. Cambridge, MA: Harvard University Press, 1953.

Baur, E. J. "A student guide for interpreting case material." *International Quarterly Journal,* 1960, Summer, 104-108.

Beker, J. *Critical Incidents in Child Care: A Casebook.* New York: Behavioral Publications, 1972.

Burgess, E. W. "Statistics and case studies as methods of sociological research." *Sociology and Social Research* 1927, 12, 114.

Burt, C. *The Young Delinquent,* New York: Appleton-Century-Crofts, 1925.

Cabot, H. & Kahl, J. A. (Eds.). "Introduction," in *Human Relations,* Vol. 1. Cambridge, MA: Harvard University Press, 1953.

Corsini, R. J. & Howard, D. D. (Eds.). *Critical Incidents in Teaching.* Englewood Cliffs, NJ: Prentice-Hall, 1964.

Donham, W. B. *Education for Responsible Living.* Cambridge, MA: Harvard University Press, 1944.

Healy, W. *The Individual Delinquent.* Boston: Little, Brown, 1915.

King, H. *Box Man,* ed. B. Chambliss. New York: Harper & Row, 1972.

Landman, J. H. *The Case Method of Studying Law.* New York: G. A. Jennings, 1930.

McCluggage, M. M. "Teaching sociology by the case method." *Midwest Sociologist,* 1955, 17, 37-38.

――― "Human relations―a statement of objectives." *University of Washington Business Review,* 1958, 18, 29-36.

McNair, M. P. (ed.). *The Case Method at the Harvard Business School.* New York: McGraw-Hill, 1954.

Manocchio, A. and Dunn, J. *Time Game.* Beverly Hills, CA: Sage, 1977.

Shaw, C. T. *The Jack Roller,* Chicago: University of Chicago Press, 1930.

――― *Brothers in Crime.* Chicago: University of Chicago Press, 1938.

Sillitoe, A. *The Loneliness of the Long-Distance Runner.* New York: Alfred A. Knopf, 1960.

Sorokin, P. *Contemporary Sociological Theories.* New York: Harper & Row, 1928.

Standal, S. W. & Corsini, R. J. (Eds.). *Critical Incidents in Psychotherapy.* Englewood Cliffs, NJ: Prentice-Hall, 1959.

Sutherland, E. H. *The Professional Theif.* Chicago: University of Chicago Press, 1937.

Williamson, H. *Hustler,* ed. R. L. Keiser. Garden City, NY: Doubleday, 1965.

Young, P. V. *Scientific Social Surveys and Research.* New York: Prentice-Hall, 1949.

1

JACK'S ENTRANCE

Meet Jack Owens—Director of Group Life at Central State Training School. He is the central character in most of the vignettes you will be reading. They will tell you about Jack and his work with the School's cottages—especially the cottage supervisors—and, even more importantly, with the boys. You will also become acquainted with the various roles which the other staff members—including the superintendent, school principal, teachers, psychiatrists, social workers, psychologists, and maintenance workers—play in the life of Central State. But the spotlight will return again and again to focus on Jack.

How would you know Jack? His appearance in no way set him apart from his fellow workers. Of medium height, with brown eyes, a wrinkled brow, and sandy hair, he wore the unofficial uniform common to cottage supervisors: polyester trousers, a short-sleeved sport shirt, with a tie added on days when major staff meetings were held. When visitors were scheduled to come to the School, he might even wear a coat, but this added formality clearly made him appear awkward. It was often slung over his arm or draped on the back of a chair, ready to be hurriedly donned when necessary. Jack's characteristic neatness and attention to his wardrobe suffered when he was under pressure: his shoes would go unshined, a pair of trousers would be worn a day or two too long, and neckties and coats would be discarded when boys ran away or cottage supervisors were upset or quitting. Jack's posture was typically erect, yet he appeared relaxed. He spoke hesitantly but well; pauses gave him a chance to observe the impact he was having on people. Perhaps it was the defensiveness of certain chronically overwrought cottage supervisors or the thin-skinned personalities of particular boys that nurtured this habit. At any rate, it not only made Jack better able to tune in on the people he was talking with, but somehow helped him get across whatever points he most wanted to make. Plain language spiced with concrete illustrations and subtle humor characterized his talk.

In addition to his undistinguished appearance, Jack did not create—at least initially—the impression of a strong person. His politeness and reserve implied to some that he was shy, and to others that he was aloof. The opinion of an experienced psychiatrist who knew him casually could stand as typical: "He's rather unassuming, friendly but not outgoing. From what I've observed, I'd judge he is agreeable but probably not a decisive, strong-willed person—not much of an innovator and pretty much apt to go along with whatever is required. Yet I don't feel that I really know him. For example, I don't know what's going on with him when he gets caught up in a problem. Then he'll look intently into your eyes as he talks, suggesting that he's thinking deeper thoughts than his usual manner expresses." A probation officer, after visiting the training school, commented, "Oh yes, we were told about the School and shown around by . . . I can't recall his name; anyway he's the man in charge of the cottages. He was accommodating but quite reserved. That's what makes me doubt that they've got very much going in their cottage program. I must say I couldn't figure him out. At times he seemed overly modest about the program. At other times he seemed proud and almost condescending as he talked with me." Jack had developed a somewhat different image with the staff of the training school. While they were aware of his friendliness, kindliness, and unassuming manner, they tended to focus on his stability, his capacity to work effectively under pressure, his ingenuity in modifying faulty child-care techniques, and his fantastic sensitivity in grasping what might be involved in a problem.

Now the spotlight turns to focus on Jack's background: what were his own boyhood and young adulthood like? The town where he grew up and the people who made up his world will shed some light on the question.

Jack grew up in Lawnwood, a midwestern town in a region regarded as primarily agricultural. Though Lawnwood was the county seat of White County, its population was only 900. It served as both the commercial and political center of the county. From Lawnwood, it is an easy morning's ride on the interstate to Capital City, the state capital and the site of Central State Training School for Boys.

Tourists passing through Lawnwood saw it as similar to many of the other small towns which dotted White County. New Englanders who first settled

Lawnwood following the Civil War set the pattern for the town: a clean place with a meticulously kept town square, complete with courthouse, small colonial-style shopping center, freshly painted white frame houses, manicured lawns, and tree-lined streets.

In the 1890s emigrants from Germany and Poland joined the New England settlers in Lawnwood and surrounding lands as part of the last waves of emigration from northern and western Europe. Though the customs, traditions, and value systems of the newcomers stood in contrast to those of the established residents, they were welcomed. There was work to be done and the country remained to be developed.

Immediately on arrival, the new ethnic groups began the process of making a place for themselves in the organized life of Lawnwood—involvement in school affairs, town and county politics, and church and town activities. This is not to suggest that the New Englanders, who were cautious and convinced of their own superiority, always reached out to accept the newcomers. In fact, at times they kept themselves isolated as much as possible from these "foreign influences." Nor is it suggested that the Germans and Poles, rooted in European customs and fierce competition, always sought the advice of the original settlers or saw them as models after which they should pattern their own lives. Nevertheless, the fact that they were now neighbors and were interacting in business, in their concerns about schools and roads, in their working together feverishly at times of crisis such as snowstorms and the flooding of the nearby James River, brought them together. Moreover, their common values of thrift and hard work served to bond them together.

This group of heterogeneous people—second generation transplanted New Englanders and recent European immigrants—ushered in the twentieth century at Lawnwood. Initial poverty gave way to a good, though hard living, which turned to prosperity and peaked with the boom of World War I. The people of Lawnwood and the surrounding area suffered during a brief national depression that followed the war, but by 1923, farming, the major enterprise of the area, was thriving again and the town's economy was bolstered by the addition of a flour mill, a creamery, and a small box factory. These major changes were related to the production of the gasoline engine; soon the movement of cars around Lawnwood became a common sight and mechanized farm machinery increased agricultural efficiency. Some farmers sought more acreage and succeeded in enlarging their operations. Others were less successful and either continued to farm on a marginal basis or left for factory work in the cities.

The spotlight turns again, this time to focus on the influence of Jack's parents on his boyhood and young adulthood. It was during this period of postwar fervor and development that the Owens were married. Mr. Owens' parents were from the original New England settlers, while Mrs. Owens' parents were among the Germans who came to homestead farmland around Lawnwood. Mr. Owens' father had established the general store which Mr. Owens now operated. Like many other men in the town and surrounding countryside, Mr. Owens was a man of great energy and perseverance; a driving man, yet tolerant and gentle. He unloaded merchandise from delivery trucks, stored it, unpacked it, and placed it on the store's shelves. He kept an inventory of his stock, handled the ordering from wholesalers, and kept the books which included the accounts of his many credit customers.

This work was basic and time consuming; however, it was only a small part of Mr. Owens' business activity. Selling merchandise took most of his time and was the activity he most enjoyed, whether across the counter or from a shed about twenty yards from the back of the store where small farm machinery and animal feed were stored. Mr. Owens enjoyed visiting with his customers—learning about their families, discussing the town's problems, and talking state politics. He provided a place in one corner of his store where they could visit comfortably with one another, and furnished it with five or six cast-off rockers, about an equal number of straight-backed chairs, and a small table. The visiting area was especially popular with the farmers' wives on Wednesday and Saturday afternoons, when they came into town to do their shopping. The men gathered together in a less comfortable area in the back of the store: in space given over to hardware—kegs of nails, wire, farm tools—Mr. Owens provided a few old chairs for some while others sat on kegs and unpacked crates. During the week, town people, especially retired farmers, would take over these areas for visiting, and different groups kept different hours. While the retired farmers gathered there during the afternoons, the town's business leaders congregated in the mornings.

Mr. Owens' "office," an area partitioned off by shipping crates and boxes of unpacked goods, was the special meeting room of Lawnwood's business leaders: Mr. Beall, the banker; Mr. Zink, owner of the hardware store; Doc Arnold West, the town's physician; Mr. Godbey from the drugstore; and a number of others. They met regularly at about 9:30 each morning to have a cup of coffee brewed in a dark-stained pot and to talk about what was happening in town. Gravity and levity mingled as the significant and insignificant were hashed over: the number of farmers coming to town to do their "trading," the condition of the crops, the need for rain, the quality of teaching in the schools, the need for road work, the possibility of holding a Fourth of July celebration, and the illness or death of one of Lawnwood's citizens.

If a matter requiring the expenditure of town funds came up, such as regraveling Main Street or replacing the engine pump at the town well, one of the group, usually Mr. Beall, the banker, would pull an advertisement or a used envelope from the heap lying on the old table in the corner of Mr. Owens' office and do some figuring. If the subject of road repairs came up, the group would turn to Mr. Zink for his reactions. Or, if a matter of sanitation or health came into the conversation, Doc West and Mr. Godbey would be consulted.

Relaxed on an odd assortment of chairs and an old horsehair couch, the men prepared themselves to discuss these matters with the formal groups in town—the town council, the county commissioners, the school board—of which they were members. So, while this informal group did not have any official capacity, it did have genuine influence by means of the power of its members. Yet these men had no thought of building their morning sessions into a power base; rather, they had unwittingly found a unique mechanism for facilitating their daily work and social life.

An equal influence on Jack's life was his mother. While Mrs. Owens shared many of her husband's characteristics—a steadiness and firmness that came from a commitment to maintain their family in the community, help develop it, and raise their children within the Protestant ethic of "hard work and good deeds as the way to a good life and salvation"—she was a cheerful person with a subtle sense of humor. These qualities and the community's knowledge of her basic commitment to carry out the prescribed family duties of a mother—cooking, washing, cleaning the house, and caring for the children—made acceptable her forwardness, outspokenness, and activities in the community. To have worked less at home and with her children would have made her efforts in Lawnwood unacceptable—indeed meddlesome and out of place for a woman.

Once the children were of school age, Mrs. Owens began helping out at the store, clerking on Wednesday and Saturday afternoons and evenings when most of the farmers came to town to do their shopping. At first, the children were left in the capable hands of Mrs. Owens' older, widowed sister, who came to town especially to lend this assistance, usually with her own two youngsters. As the Owens children moved into adolescence, one after another joined the family work force at the store during busy periods. Though pressed for time, Mrs. Owens was active in church affairs—especially the Ladies Aid, which visited members of the congregation who were sick or bereaved.

Considerable informal visiting with neighbors and relatives took place in the Owens' home, particularly during the winter months. The practice of "dropping in" was welcomed by the Owens, who were warm and hospitable hosts. Sundays were reserved for the family, and Sunday afternoons often included a drive into the countryside.

Alert and intelligent, Mrs. Owens was a keen observer of the community and of her husband's activities. Though deferent to his expertise in business matters and his final authority in the family, she discussed with him at length matters of the community. These discussions, however, occurred in the home; for to have spoken with her husband on equal terms at the store would have been interpreted by the community as in bad taste. But at home conversations were exceptional in their spontaneity and rare in their rapport. These discussions included Jack and his younger brothers and sisters, especially as they developed the capability to participate. Mrs. Owens enjoyed tossing out controversial problems for debate at the dinner table, stimulating energetic responses. Often arguments developed and the atmosphere became tense, but these disagreements did not run deep. The children developed an avid interest in social issues and the necessary skills to exchange ideas well.

The common bonds of work and a well-developed sense of responsibility brought the Owens together as a family. Not only did the children have their regular chores at home; they were introduced to work at the store at an early age. Jack, being the oldest, was the first to spend after-school hours and Saturdays helping his parents. While stocking shelves, sacking and delivering groceries, and running a number of errands, he had an opportunity to view many aspects of community life and to watch his father at work.

From his observations, Jack sensed that consideration and appreciation of others were especially important in interpersonal relations. Moreover, he grew to view tolerance for opposing, even offensive opinions as not only important in allowing others their human rights, but he saw such tolerance as the basis for discussing and perhaps influencing another's point of view.

Jack observed that his father's gentle and indirect manner with customers was shaded with considerably more assertiveness when he dealt with the men gathered in his office for their morning coffee, and with substantially greater directness when he did business with salesmen. Thus, Jack perceived that relationships were not only influenced by the issues at stake, but also by the circumstances and persons with whom one was dealing. Moreover, he learned the importance of perseverance through watching his father talk, listen, cajole, and argue over a period of several years in the interest of developing Lawnwood's city park, improving its sewage system, and raising the teachers' pay.

Mrs. Owens' influence on Jack's development took the form of her consistency, adaptability, and optimism. Her interest in education, shared with her husband, led Jack to see it not only as a means of self-improvement, but also as a means of improving society. Perhaps Mrs. Owens' major contribution to Jack's value system was her empathy with the poor and disadvantaged.

Encouraged by his parents, Jack looked forward to starting school. And he did well, achieving a strong B average in his subjects. However, friends and activities were his major interests in both grade school and high school. His high school days were generally uneventful, though a minor family crisis emerged when Jack decided to drop debate. His parents urged him to continue, explaining that it would teach him how to think on his feet and how valuable he would find it if he decided.to become a lawyer some day. Jack agreed that he needed experience in developing quick thinking, but he countered that he was interested in talking effectively with people in a less formal way than debate—in a common-sense way, listening to what others have to say and responding in a natural, off-the-cuff manner. He must have learned his debate lessons well, for they reluctantly agreed to let him go his way.

Supported by his parents, Jack's decision to attend the state university proved a wise one. After exploring the subject matter of several fields, he chose education as his major. He maintained a B average, participated in several student activities, and became the typical, well-adjusted, man-on-campus. His classmates voted him "most likeable" during his senior year, but Jack felt he ran far behind living up to this exalted label.

The most notable event in his senior year, however, was not related to the university. Rather, it was the discovery by the family physician that his father had an advanced cancer. Following the discovery midway during fall semester, Jack made frequent trips home. Stricken with pain and frustrated by weakness and inactivity, Mr. Owens unwittingly made Jack feel responsible for providing him some relief. In conversations with his son, he reminisced about the times when they had worked together in the store. In fact, their last conversation ended in Mr. Owens' tearful regret that he had not taken time off from work periodically to spend with Jack.

As Mr. Owens approached death, he was tortured by constant pain so that when he finally died, the community reacted with a combination of relief and sorrow. Jack was perceptibly disturbed by the tragedy of his father's death. Not only did he feel sad about his loss but also guilty that he had not spent more time with his father during those final months. On his return to school following the funeral, Jack's friends observed that he was more quiet and serious than before. The experience seemed to have a lasting effect on him; Jack often thought about his final conversations with his father, especially when he was under stressful circumstances. In later years those conversations helped Jack sort out the issues of a problem when he was under pressure, and enabled him to place value where he thought it ought to be placed—on people's concerns and feelings.

Jack completed his work at the university that year, and even though his mother wanted him to return to Lawnwood and take charge of the store, he took a teaching and coaching job in a small high school. Before making his decision, however, he went through some trying moments. His mother acknowledged the "good sense" of his plans to teach, but at the same time indicated her strong need for him to return to Lawnwood. In addition to describing her interest in having him return, she stressed the idea that taking over the store would give him "a chance to follow in the footsteps" of his father. This message aroused an appalling guilt in Jack. His mother's clear expectation that he would decide to stay in Lawnwood drove him to walk through the countryside for hours each afternoon for a week. He agonized over his rejection of the opportunity to run the family store, and on a number of occasions he came close to giving up his newly acquired teaching job in its favor. However, the longer he mulled over his dilemma, the more he became convinced of the soundness of his decision to leave Lawnwood.

The week before he left Lawnwood saw both Jack and his mother in a better mood. In fact, once his decision was made firm, calm prevailed. In a letter during that week to his new superintendent, Jack opened with, "I am looking forward, more than ever, to the beginning of the school year. I am planning to see you on the morning of September 1."

How did Jack respond to the world of professional work? Even while getting settled in his new community, Western City, Jack's job totally engrossed him and gave him much satisfaction. In a September letter to his mother, he wrote, "The teaching is great fun and tremendously stimulating." There can be no doubt about the impression the students made on him. In another letter to his mother he noted, "Even those who by no measure could be called students have something worthwhile to contribute to the class. I'm glad to have them all."

Without plans beyond being a classroom teacher, however, Jack's career was interrupted by World War II. He esimated that his draft number would come up during the summer following his first year of teaching. After considering the several services, he enlisted in the Navy. His enlistment was not an enthusiastic act of patriotism, but a necessary one, and he accepted it with a sense of quiet resignation. However, once he had completed boot camp, Jack began to enjoy the camaraderie of the Navy.

After the defeat of Germany, and while Japan's capability to continue the war was doomed by the atomic bomb, Jack began to plan his return to civilian life. While serving aboard an aircraft carrier and waiting for his discharge, he recalled his teaching in Western City with fondness. Yet, he felt that after four years in the Navy he ought to aspire to a principal's or assistant principal's job. He pursued this course after his discharge and became the principal of a junior high school.

His initial enthusiasm for administrative work, however, began to decline after several years, especially as the central office coordinating the junior high schools made excessive demands on his time for meetings and reports, all of which seemed to have little significance or consequence—at least for the students. Having made a commitment to himself to develop the program at his junior high, Jack dutifully carried out his responsibilities in spite of the heavy emphasis on administrative ritual.

In contrast to his own negative assessment of the administrative aspects of his job, most of Jack's associates felt he had "made it." To be sure, his salary was good and his responsibilities important, but after three years during which inconsequential administrative detail grew by leaps and bounds, Jack began to explore other job opportunities. He talked with his friends about other job possibilities within the system, perhaps at another junior high school. However, he soon learned that his job problems were common to the whole system and that transferring to another school would not solve them.

A chance conversation at a teachers' convention with Mr. Graves, superintendent of Central State Training School for Boys, opened a new world for Jack. Vaguely aware of the training school as a place which took delinquent boys from the court for behavior which the community didn't feel it could control, Jack was surprised at the rather elaborate program Mr. Graves described: a detailed diagnostic study for all of the boys when they were admitted to the school, and their careful assignment to a variety of activities gauged to help them. He had imagined an austere program aimed at containing the boys until they could be sent back to the community.

After a long visit with Mr. Graves and a subsequent visit to the programs of Central State, Jack was offered the position of principal, a possibility he had not considered. He was reluctant to think about it seriously because he had had his fill of administrative work and was not seeking to duplicate his junior high experience. Yet the setting and tasks were significantly different. Moreover, it was the top educator's job at the school. Jack would report directly to Mr. Graves. He decided to take it.

A curious aspect of their agreement was that Jack would join the training school staff in June, and for a period of two months would work with the institution's cottages to help them develop their recreational activities, familiarizing himself with the boys and the staff.

How did Jack approach his new role and responsibilities? After reporting to Central State, he began working with uncommon effort and dedication. In meeting with cottage supervisors, conducting a number of activities, having cottage supervisors carry out others, and scheduling trips out into the community, Jack ignored the usual forty-four hour week—working as many as sixteen hours a day. Informally, and often at odd hours, Jack worked especially hard to help the cottage supervisors organize recreation in their living units. He helped them plan activities and taught them specific skills in arts, crafts, and games so that they in turn could teach the boys. Then Jack followed up with informal visits to the units to help them implement the activities or to encourage the supervisors to carry out their newly acquired skills. He was able after a month of long, busy days, to develop an effective activity program. The boys became involved with constructive activities and the supervisors became more relaxed and helpful. Jack felt a heady sense of achievement.

As August approached, Jack began to plan for the school year. The curriculum required a thorough review and updating, class schedules had to be arranged, books and supplies had to be checked, and plans for beginning to work with his teachers had to be developed.

It was with these thoughts in mind that Jack responded to Mr. Graves' request of a meeting to see him. In shirt sleeves and perspiring heavily from his work on the ball field, Jack appeared at Mr. Graves' office. Relaxed and in a cordial mood, Mr. Graves asked Jack how he was feeling about his first two months at Central State. As Jack described some of his unusual experiences— some of which now made him chuckle—Mr. Graves chimed in with similar experiences of his own. After this exchange, Mr. Graves moved the focus of their discussion to the importance of the cottage program. "Group living" he called it. Mr. Graves observed, in a general way, that Central State needed leadership in that aspect of the program. Jack recognized that he and Mr. Graves had shifted from swapping stories to talking about the institution's program. He agreed enthusiastically with Mr. Graves' observation about the need for strong leadership and made some supporting comments based on his summer experiences. However, he did not feel that the discussion had any reference to him personally until Mr. Graves said, matter-of-factly, "Jack, I would like you to consider giving up the school principal's job and taking on the job of heading the cottage program."

And so the persuasion began. After several conferences during the following week, Jack assumed the job of Director of Group Life. The salary was the same as that of the principal's job, but the hours would be longer. The features of the job which Mr. Graves emphasized were its difficulties and consequent challenges. Not one to forget the attraction of rewards, he spoke about the need for an assistant superintendent at Central State, which would be open to Jack if he succeeded in the Group Life job.

2

HE KEEPS ASKING
THE SAME QUESTION

Facing the mall, Jack's office on the first floor of the Administration Building
afforded him a full view of Central State: the educational building, gymnasium, repair shops, and greenhouse, all clustered at the far end of the campus;
twelve cottages facing one another on opposite sides of the long rectangular
mall; the Commissary on one side of the mall and the clinic on the other,
linking the cottages to the Administration Building. The architectural design
of the buildings, the arrangement of buildings around a mall, and the
well-ordered landscaping gave the institution the appearance of a small, idylic
college.

Central State was, of course, no college, but a state institution for
delinquent boys. Through the years the staff had attempted to help the boys
and had tried to cope with them at the same time. The program had varied
over the years—at one time it emphasized the military, at another a work
program, and finally it was emphasizing therapy. All of the past programs had
been well-intentioned and in vogue in their day, but in light of critical
reflection they appeared largely inefficient and ineffective. Whether the
current program of therapy would look any better to evaluators in the future
remained an open question.

Teachers, shop and work supervisors, a few administrators, and cottage
supervisors had been the backbone of the institution over the years. Psychologists had been on the scene for a number of years, first testing the boys' IQs
and educational aptitudes, then acting as guidance counselors, and finally as

therapists. Their latest role coincided with the entry of other professionals—social workers and psychiatrists—during the past ten to fifteen years. Initially, all of these professionals plied their skills with the boys during formal office interviews, giving them reassurance and encouraging them to verbalize their problems with the hope that, once aired, the problems could be worked on more effectively.

Mr. Graves, through skillful negotiation, moved the program from an initial domination by these professionals to one where other members of the team, especially teachers and cottage supervisors, had something to say about decisions concerning the boys. At the same time, he urged cottage supervisors to be active in responding to the boys' personal problems, especially by spending time with them, talking with them, being supportive of them, and following up on their problems.

For Jack, this orientation meant working with his cottage supervisors and helping them plan activities for the boys within the cottage environment. Jack coordinated inservice training for his staff; he also spent considerable time talking with cottage supervisors about their experiences with new boys, and in light of these experiences he planned with them ways new boys could be helped by the program. In following this new program, Jack made a practice of dropping in on the living units, and his staff became accustomed to these spontaneous visits. Jack encouraged, supported, and taught them in his low-key, comfortable way; over coffee or relaxing in the dayroom they sometimes talked about sports or politics, but always about the boys. Runaways, fighting, homosexuality, shyness, and weird behavior were discussed. Woven into these conversations were the pertinent questions: "What is really the matter with him?" and "What can we do about it?"

In some of his cottage supervisors Jack was fortunate. One in particular, Mr. William Blake, proved capable from the day he was hired. A tall, slender man in his early fifties, he had applied to the school out of interest rather than the need for a secure preretirement position sought by other men his age. He was unusual in another respect: he was financially independent. As the exceptionally successful owner of a small hardware store, Mr. Blake had been able to turn over the business to his son and, in his words, "look for something worthwhile to do."

Because Mr. Blake had expressed a desire to work in the cottages, Jack talked with him at length about the realities of working with the boys: the long days; being called back to work on occasions; the boys' teasing, fighting, depressions, jumpiness, anger, and sexual behavior. Jack also talked a little about the satisfactions of the work—the good feelings one gets from helping boys in trouble—but he was careful not to overdo it, knowing that inexperienced applicants tend to be overly optimistic about what they might accomplish with the boys. Wanting both to select an able supervisor and to protect Mr. Blake from making an unwise decision, Jack arranged for him to observe the cottage program during several evenings. Challenged by what he saw, Mr. Blake's interest only increased, and Jack was convinced that Central State was the right place for him. Within eight months Mr. Blake took over as senior cottage supervisor, and a strong working relationship grew between the two men, stimulated partly by personal compatibility and partly by mutual dedication to improving the cottage program.

One Tuesday morning Jack came to his office early so he could clear his desk and see a number of supervisors about their work. After reviewing a stack of case folders, he leaned back to stretch and, looking out across the grounds, suddenly realized that two hours had passed while he had been working. Having just finished the case folder on Dick Jones, a boy recently admitted to Mr. Blake's charge in Frontier Cottage, Jack decided to start his rounds there.

Frontier was a 20-year-old, three-storied building which housed boys the psychologists had labeled emotionally disturbed; that is, those with serious personal problems, as distinct from other boys at Central State who were emotionally hardened and brazen, shallow and exploitative, or hyperaggressive. Although the emotionally disturbed boys kept much of their anxiety and guilt to themselves, they often became agitated and more than occasionally lashed out and attacked one another. There were always a number of docile, depressed, beaten-down boys in the cottage who were the safe and therefore the favorite punching bags. However, whatever the means of expressing their tension, the boys occupying Frontier had exceptionally little skill at denying or concealing their problem behavior. When in trouble or about to get into trouble, they would suddenly act casual or very secretive, and the staff would be warned by the obvious shift in their behavior.

That Tuesday Jack turned onto the sidewalk leading to the cottage, picking his way through a haphazard network of bicycles. The dayroom was quiet, which meant the boys were in school, but a faint rustle told him where to find Mr. Blake. As Jack entered the reading room, Mr. Blake looked up from his task of picking up newspapers that lay scattered all over the floor.

Jack laughed. "That's the kind of exercise a young man needs."

In the same genial mood, Mr. Blake returned, "With that kind of spirit I should expect some help from you with these papers!"

"I need some exercise all right," Jack agreed, "but it looks like you've got everything under control."

"Look," Mr. Blake said, slightly more serious, "since you're not much on picking up papers, maybe I can try you on something else."

They settled into chairs opposite one another.

"You know, there are a couple of kids I've got to talk with you about." Mr. Blake paused and then asked with a trace of anxiety, "Do you know Dick Jones? He came in yesterday from Dolan."

Jack nodded his head. "Only what I've read in his folder."

"Well, I don't know what it says there but in real life he's as wild as a March hare."

"Is he tense or what?"

"Is he tense?" Mr. Blake exclaimed. "You bet he is! And he's trying to run it off. Jack, he's always running off to do something . . . but then there are other things about him . . ."

"How do you mean?" Jack asked.

"He's sad, or at least he looks sad, especially in the evenings when he's not running around. He really looks down. . . . I feel sorry for him."

"I know he's had a hard time of it," Jack explained. "Got caught in a lot of fighting between his folks. Some of it was pretty rough. Father's been in and out of the family. I think he left again just before Dick got into stealing groceries out of some restaurant's warehouse up in Dolan."

"I got some of that from Miss Smith in Social Services; she talked to me about him before he came."

"So in addition to doing a lot of running around, how is he getting along?" Jack asked.

"That's what gets me. He's about to drive me crazy by asking me the same questions—over and over again. I bet I've told him two dozen times about how his program will be set up. You know, all about the testing, interviewing, and staff meeting routines that have to run their course. Also, I've gone over the daily and weekly schedules here in the cottage with him a dozen times, telling him what was coming up. . . . I've explained all of these things over and over. Besides, I told him he didn't have anything to worry about."

"But you sense he is worrying."

"Oh, yes, about something; there's something worrying him. He's terribly anxious, tense—kind of wild. He's so upset, he's beside himself. He never walks, or hardly ever. He runs every place he goes. When he does sit down, like at the end of a day, he'll go into a corner of the dayroom by himself and a terribly sad expression comes over his face. Another thing, I know he's not putting me on. He's really in bad shape!"

It was obvious that Mr. Blake was upset—he was beginning to repeat himself.

"What else have you noticed about Dick?" Jack encouraged.

"Well, along with this panicky behavior when he's either running all over the damned place or asking all of these pleading questions, he's always very restless. I know he doesn't sleep well because the night supervisor has told me. Besides forgetting and not hearing directions—or whatever—he's generally absentminded. The only other thing I've noticed about him is that he uses the can a lot! He's in there urinating constantly."

"He sure sounds upset," Jack concurred, rubbing his forehead. "How have you been handling all this?"

"Like I said, at first I filled him in detail on all his questions. You know, I went through it all with him in detail about two dozen times. After that I changed my tune. For awhile, then, I didn't pay much attention to him. I figured that I had already answered his questions and if I kept answering them he'd keep asking. . . . But that didn't work out because he kept right on badgering me with his questions. So I've shifted again. Now I'm routinely giving him answers. You know, easy like. I don't lecture him. My idea is that if I'm steady, it may steady him."

"Is what you're doing now doing him any good?" Jack asked hopefully.

"Yes, yes it is," Mr. Blake responded optimistically, then his voice lowered with doubt. "But the improvement doesn't last long. Whatever I tell him usually seems to satisfy him for a short while—maybe half a day at the most—and then he comes right back to me with the same old questions. Like I said, we've gone around the track many times on his questions . . ."

As Mr. Blake calmed down, Jack commented, "You know, I'm wondering if he's not too scared to really hear you. His intelligence is high enough, at least as I remember his record. I don't remember his *medical* record. Maybe I'm jumping to conclusions about his being too scared; it could be that he actually doesn't hear you."

"He's okay medically because he is hearing me. No doubt about it, because he responds to what I say and what *he* says is on target, but I figure he's so upset that he keeps forgetting, or if he remembers, he just keeps wanting to hear all these specific things to tie down the new world he's in. It sounds a little crazy, but I think what I'm saying is right." He paused to take a breath. "To make it worse, the kids have been teasing him. They've nicknamed him Pete and Repeat. You know, he's been putting them through this same thing. I've gotten on them and I think the teasing has eased up, but I wouldn't be surprised to see that nickname stick. I would hate to see that happen, but it just might. It's catcy and it's just close enough to the truth to make it real."

"Talk with the kids. See if you can appeal to their sense of fair play," Jack suggested. "See if you can get them to cut out giving him the Pete and Repeat treatment."

"I'll have a session with them . . . but we've got to do more than that."

"Ordinarily with this kind of problem, the things you've been doing would have had some greater effect," Jack reasoned. "You ought to be seeing some of his question-asking drop off. But since it hasn't, you need to do two things: make sure that his schedule is just as certain as you can make it and continue to give him all the information he asks for."

"Jack, I've *done* all that," Mr. Blake insisted impatiently. "So what do I do now?"

"You just have to continue it. Be patient. When Dick gets into a fuller schedule—you know, enrolled in school and all—this may pass. Or at least most of it."

"Okay, okay," Mr. Blake assented, but with dissatisfaction. "It just seems like we're asking time to take care of a lot of things, a lot of things it may never do. More than time is needed!"

"Time will help, and so we need to get time on our side," Jack said somewhat defensively. "Remember, it's not the only thing we're trying to take advantage of here: we want the program and its routine to have a chance to influence him. The regularity of the routine and the relationships with the staff and hopefully with the kids will start to give him some security. Once these influences have had a couple of weeks to work on Dick, I predict we *will* see some changes in him."

Mr. Blake nodded his agreement; however, his expression was still troubled.

Jack paused, then said in a lighter tone, "You still think there's something more we should be doing?"

"That's right," Mr. Blake nodded. "Either us or somebody else. Incidentally, I did explain all of this to Miss Smith in Social Services. She said to just keep working with Dick the way I have been. She feels that his questions and his running all over the place come from anxiety. You know, he's jet propelled by anxiety. She's not sure, but she hopes he'll settle down after a week or so. Miss Smith has seen him a time or two, but she says he clams up when he comes to see her."

Jack pondered his next comment for awhile before voicing it. "Well, if you would like to pioneer a little, I suggest we figure out a way to ask Dick what's bothering him."

"Right, I think we should," Mr. Blake agreed enthusiastically. "I really think we should. There's more to his being upset than his being committed to Central State."

"Okay, so how are you going to ask him? What are you actually going to say?"

Mr. Blake looked blank.

"Gee, I don't know," he said slowly. "I don't have any particular way of approaching him mapped out. . . . I'll just have to feel my way. Maybe when he gets me into one of his question-asking barrages, I can begin to open up my concern about him. After I answer some of his questions, I should be able to move in to asking him some questions in return."

"Good," Jack said. "Let's carry our conversation a little further. The more we talk now about what you're going to say, the better prepared you'll be when you open this thing up with Dick. Our talk can serve as a bit of a warm-up."

Mr. Blake shifted in his chair again, and ventured, "Whatever I ask him will have to have a soft touch to it or it will scare him."

Jack thought for a moment and said, "Okay, let's say that after you've answered a number of his routine questions, you'll be in a position to ask about how things have gone for him in the cottage. In order to make the shift, find a pause in the conversation and try to shift the mood of your talk too, if you need to, so he'll know you've moved to a subject that he's worried about."

Mr. Blake nodded, so Jack continued. "You begin with something like, 'You know, I've answered your questions about the routines many times. Is there something else bothering you?' He may hedge around a bit but let's assume he comes through and begins to tell you about some of his troubles. So listen closely and let him talk. He may tell you some things you don't want to hear about your cottage program!"

Mr. Blake got up from his chair, paced the floor a few times, then sat down again. "Anything he's got to say, I'll be glad to hear" he said, his voice strained.

"Well, the point I'm trying to make—and making it poorly—" Jack apologized, "is not to get defensive about any criticism he may make about the cottage or the school. In addition to helping him let off steam, his complaints might be useful in shaping up the program."

"I've got you," Mr. Blake agreed.

"Okay." Jack continued, "Also, pay special attention to the feelings he expresses while he's talking. He'll emphasize what's really important to him by the way he stresses it."

"So I should encourage him to talk while I listen."

"Right. After he runs down—assuming he talks a lot—you should be in a good position to ask him, gently, about whatever he has cued you in on as important—like the teasing. Maybe the kids have not only teased him but have kicked him around and treated him badly in general. Remember, you're setting up a situation in which you have a chance to learn more about what has been happening to him *as he sees it.* And even more importantly, you're giving him a chance to pour out some of the feelings that he must be having about his troubles."

Mr. Blake looked at him doubtfully. "Look, you're throwing more at me than I can handle."

"Not really," Jack reassured him. "Don't worry about trying to cover all of his troubles. You obviously can't do that. Zero in on one or two. That's all anyone could be expected to do."

"I get you," Mr. Blake acceded. "Now I need you to get more specific about questions I should ask him to get into talking about his *family* problems. I think I can get at his cottage problems all right."

"There are two routes to that area. You can either approach it via Dick's problems here, or you can approach it directly. The questions for the first route have to lead from problem areas here to comparable problem areas at home. Questions like, 'Dick, you've had more than your share of problems in getting along with others here. What was it like for you at home?' The questions for the second route might be like 'You know, we ought to talk a bit about your life at home in order to understand how you look at things here.' On either route you'll want to key the questions to the circumstance you're in."

"Tell me more about the first route," Mr. Blake suggested. "How will I know if a problem has its roots in his earlier experiences? Give me an example."

"Okay, let's say that Dick says, 'Nobody is looking out for me when the kids are giving me a bad time.' First talk that out with him, and then follow through with, 'Tell me what it's been like for you in the past in this connection.' "

Jack paused, lit a cigarette, and then continued on a serious level, one he wanted to emphasize aside from strategy, technique, or procedural matters. "Now in all of this, you're going to have to remember the total boy," Jack cautioned. "These maneuvers we've been talking about are simply tools that can help us to get at what we suspect is lurking someplace in his mind. We don't know what is really involved. We don't know how complicated it is. And we don't know how explosive it is. So, along with paying attention to your technique, that is, what you say and do, keep a very careful eye on the boy. If we're right that his anxiety and confusion are rooted in his past, then you can bet his past has been pretty stormy, and your asking him the kinds of questions we've been talking about is apt to lead him into memories that store the painful details of those experiences. So you'll want to watch carefully and tread easily, with your focus being to guard against doing any harm."

Jack's cigarette burned unsmoked as he outlined an approach to Dick's problems, until suddenly he flinched, dropped the butt, then hastily retrieved it. He lost his concentration for only a moment before continuing.

"Bill, you should know that the typical approach to getting at this type of problem is to let sleeping dogs lie. What I mean is, while we might suspect the kinds of things we've been talking about, the usual strategy is to leave the boy alone rather than probing to find what's bothering him. And along with leaving the youngster alone, planned psychological supports are thrown around him. So the avoidance of what is underneath, even if well-intentioned, turns out to be a cop-out."

As Jack moved away from talking about specific techniques and focused on the intricacy of working to get at underlying problems, Mr. Blake looked increasingly uneasy.

"It's complicated work," Jack said bluntly, letting the sentence dangle.

After fidgeting in his chair, Mr. Blake said, "I don't know about all this; you're throwing too much at me. I'm beginning to wonder whether I ought to try uncovering what's behind Dick's behavior. I hate to chicken out, but it sounds like it may be beyond me. Even more than that, I surely don't want to do anything that might make him worse."

"Besides your interest, there are several reasons in favor of your going ahead if you want to," Jack reassured. "First, you've got a good relationship with the boy—I expect the closest of anyone at the school. Second, the kid is in misery and what we've been doing hasn't done him much good. It may be too early to tell, but the program clearly hasn't done him much good up to this point. Then too, there's the avoidance problem, when everybody so consistently avoids disturbing the boy that we let him make some kind of low-level—and often a very, very low-level—adjustment. Sometimes a youngster goes all the way through his stay here without getting any significant help. It might be the same with Dick."

Jack paused and reflected a little on what he had been saying. "I don't mean to be talking *at* you, but these are some of the reasons why I think you should give it a try."

Mr. Blake nodded his head. "I think I understand. I'd like to see what I can do."

"Remember above all else that you must be a useful listener. Be patient and try to listen for the meaning behind what Dick is saying."

Jack and Mr. Blake seemed to be in agreement and the room was suddenly quiet. After several moments, Jack broke the silence and concluded, "Let me know what happens. I've got to be getting back to the Administration Building now."

Mr. Blake hurriedly added, "Look, this isn't all. I've got another kid I need to talk with you about. He's different from Dick but I really need help with him, too. It's Larry Higgins. You know, he's got trouble and then some."

"I have a meeting coming up that I can't miss," Jack explained as he got up from his chair. "I'm going to be staying late this afternoon. Why don't we have supper together? Let's eat late, say around six-thirty. Most people will have eaten by then so we'll be able to talk. In the meantime, you may have a chance to work with Dick. But don't push it; wait for the right opportunity to come up."

Late that afternoon Mr. Blake came into Jack's office. He took a chair near the desk and sat down slowly and rather heavily. After a few moments of silence, Jack said, "You're very quiet."

"Well, let me tell you," Mr. Blake began, "I've had an eye-opening experience."

"I'd like to hear about it," Jack said encouragingly. "Are you referring to Dick?"

"Right," Mr. Blake replied. "Remember, we figured the boy was so anxious about his personal problems that he wasn't hearing, at least wasn't remembering, what was being told to him. Well, right after you left, he came back from school. He immediately charged up to me all excited and wanted to know what his schedule was going to be for the rest of the week, for his whole stay at the school, when he could go home for a visit, and a whole string of other questions. Since I had answered them all before, I asked him to come into the reading room. I told him I wanted to talk with him. I tried to set a relaxed atmosphere, so I asked him, gentle-like, to sit down. I settled myself in a calm posture and said something like, "Dick, I've been trying very hard but I can't figure out why you keep asking me the same questions over and over again."

" 'Well,' he said, down-at-the-mouth-like, 'there's nothing to do around here and I keep hoping something good will be on the schedule. I get tired of nothing to do, and the boys won't let me in on what they're doing. Besides,' he complained, 'they're beatin' up on me.'

"I was really surprised that he talked right to the subject. So I said, 'The program *is* dull, but I've not been aware of the boys beating up on you. I've not seen it. Tell me more about what's happening.'

"After talking more with him—and he continued to talk right up—it came out that the boys weren't actually beating on him, though they were threatening to as a way of keeping him out of their hair. Actually, Jack, any threats of physical beatings by a gang of boys are pretty idle in my cottage. If I had the Venture or Anchor Cottage boys, I would worry about such beatings, but not with my kids.

"After his complaining ran down, I talked with Dick about how to go about getting 'in' with the other boys. One thing we talked about for quite awhile was how these kids get themselves into closely knit groups and how a new boy in the cottage has to bide his time about getting with them. I stressed that the one thing he has to be careful not to do—and this is what Dick was doing—is to push and nag."

"Then what happened?" Jack asked.

"Things began to move," Mr. Blake said with a smile. "I got a break—and was able to recognize it as one from the coaching you had given me this morning. Anyhow, at one point he said without any forewarning, 'It's when there's nothing to do that you get lonesome.'

"I had been talking with him like a father before—you know, matter-of-factly, kind of father-son talk," Mr. Blake continued. His enthusiasm now carried with it a strong tone of seriousness. "But when he said 'lonesome,' I decided to answer a little more like a counselor. So I spoke to what I thought he was feeling. I said, 'Dick, I have wondered whether you've been feeling lonesome.'

"It just seemed so obvious," Mr. Blake explained, "and he had given me the cue. I didn't mean to come on strong, but Dick didn't like my comment one bit. No sir! He turned away and said in an angry, choked way, 'I'm not lonesome.' Then he hung his head and stopped talking.

"He sat like that for awhile—maybe two or three minutes. When he put his head up, he turned it to the side away from me. His eyes filled with tears. I sat looking at him, getting very uncomfortable. I got a funny feeling on the back of my neck and felt sad for him. My first notion was to tell him that everything would be okay, but I figured that was a weak pill for the situation—and it wasn't even true.

"I began to speak to his feelings again. I was only able to get out, 'There is something sad . . .' but it sure opened up the flood gates. He sighed and then moaned with great suffering and then began to cry, really cry like his heart was breaking. He kept it up for what seemed like ten to fifteen minutes. At first he cried out in a shrieking voice, 'I don't know where she is! I don't know where she is! I don't know where she is!' After the crying finally let up a little, he shrieked it out less often. Finally he stopped. After a long pause, he said, 'You know, I don't know where she is!'

"I sat there looking at him sympathetically, trying to keep my cool until he decided to go on. He didn't say anything, so I asked, 'Is it your mother you're worrying about?'

"To this he was able to nod and then began crying in deep sobs. I figured it was good for him to cry and get some of that grief out of him, though I must say it made me uneasy, uneasy as the devil. To help him get the grief out, I tried to help his crying along. So when he was crying pretty hard, I said sympathetically, 'You do feel bad.' It made me feel better, at least at that moment, to say that, too. It seemed to give me some relief from the tension and sadness that I was feeling. But less than a minute later, I wished to God I hadn't said anything because he really let go and sobbed even harder. Jack, I'm telling you that his crying and grieving made me feel awful—really awful! To tell the truth, I thought a couple of times *I* was going to cry, foolish as it seems as I sit here and tell you about it now."

Mr. Blake paused, pulled his handkerchief out of his back pocket, and wiped his eyes. He looked at Jack, embarrassed, but continued when his emotion received a smile of support.

"At any rate, I held back, got control of myself, and when I got a little used to his crying, I had a chance to collect my thoughts. So, when he let up, I was all set to go again.

"I said then, 'I think this is important enough for us to talk about.' And with that, he started blurting out, 'I—I—I never saw her after the police picked me up at home. She never came to the Detention Center. She never came to court. I haven't gotten a single letter from her since I've been here. I—I don't know what't happened to her.'

"White and still trembling, Dick was a sad sight. I'm telling you. I wasn't all that sure what to say, but since I was in it with him, I knew I had to go ahead. So I asked him in a sympathetic voice where he thought she was now.

"He struggled to quit crying and finally he did—but, I'm telling you—it was hard, really hard for him to stop. And you have to remember that he wasn't putting on a show for my benefit. Well, like I said, after some huffing and puffing and deep sighs, Dick did quit. After getting his breath, he began talking in a low, sad voice, hoarse-like. 'Maybe she's not even in Dolan any more.'

"After saying that, he stopped, letting his head drop down even further than it had been before. I waited and waited but he didn't say anything. I asked, 'Where do you think she might be?'

"He chewed on his lip to hold in more tears. Then he repeated, 'Maybe she's not in Dolan anymore.'

"I tried to respect his sad, sad feelings and his slow pace, so I waited a few moments before saying, 'Yes . . . What do you suppose has happened?' This may have been the wrong thing to say, but I thought I was where his problems were, and I was trying to help him express himself. Anyway, a nervous shivering came over him and he began to cry and moan again. He got up from his chair, his face livid with emotion and folded or more or less wrapped his arms around himself. It seemed like he was trying to hold himself together. I swear to God that's exactly what it looked like to me—like he was trying to hold himself together! And then he began to walk, or really more nearly stumble around that dayroom, crying like he had earlier—a real, real deep cry like his heart was breaking."

Mr. Blake, who had become tense with emotion, stopped, took a deep breath, and then continued. "God, it was awful to watch him but he was there and I was there. I had to sweat it out! He started chewing his lip, and to make it worse, kept that up. And to make it still worse, he kept his head lowered and kept wrapping and unwrapping his arms from around himself. And all the while he kept on crying.

"Finally he began to mix some mumbling with his crying. I had a hard time picking up what he was saying but I finally figured it out."

Caught up in the tension of the story, Jack interrupted. "What was he saying? What was he mumbling?"

"He mumbled it out in bits and pieces. Anyway, what I put together was that his stepfather and his mother had got into a big Donnybrook—a real knock-down, drag-out fight about a week before Dick's stealing episode down at the warehouse. Well, Dick's mother not only got beaten to a pulp, but had her furniture, what little she had, wrecked—much of it was thrown out on the street by the s.o.b.! Then to top it off, that bastard left."

Jack murmured, "No wonder the boy has problems."

Mr. Blake was not to be deterred. Nodding emphatically, he continued, "As Dick was telling me this stuff I could see he was getting mad—really mad.

His face and the back of his neck had gotten beet-red, and he began to cuss out the 'man.' The 'man' stuff passed and he began to shout, 'That son-of-a-bitch, I'm gonna get him! That son-of-a-bitch! He beat her up until her nose and mouth were bleeding!'

"As Dick got wound up, he got carried away by his own intense fury. He really seemed to be out of his mind. He was screaming, 'That son-of-a-bitch hit me on the side of the head as hard as he could and threw me out into the hall! I hit the wall across from our door and fell to the floor. I was out cold. When I began to know what was happening again, my ears were ringing and something inside my head was pounding like a sledge hammer! When I began to rub my head, it was sticky. I couldn't figure it out right away. But then I looked at my hand and saw that it was full of blood.'

"I thought he was high when he had been screaming—you know, earlier on." Mr. Blake stopped and shook his head with amazement, and then continued, "But now he got even higher. With his hair clinging to his head, wet with sweat, his eyes fixed in a dead stare, he just moved up and up the scale shouting, 'That son-of-a-bitch might of killed her! That son-of-a-bitch might of killed her! That son-of-a-bitch might of killed her!' I thought the kid was going to blow up. He got even higher as he began to shout, 'That son-of-a-bitch, I'll get him if it's the last thing I do!'

"As he was shouting this, I didn't know what he might do next. Frankly, I was feeling scared as hell, feeling I was in too deep—much too deep."

"Well," Jack put in quietly, "what did you do?"

Mr. Blake gritted his teeth as he seemed to reenter the experience, and then he smiled. "I decided I'd have to wait him out," he replied. "So I just sat there watching him with as much cool as I could manage. He just kept raising hell and I just kept waiting him out. Finally, he began to shift. I felt like I was coming out of a storm as his angry shouting changed to more of a crying thing.

"All of a sudden Dick began to cry out, 'And I could hear her crying and pleading with him to stop beating her, but he kept right on beating her and called her a whore and all those names.' "

Looking exhausted, Mr. Blake stopped to take another deep breath. Jack commented, "Sounds to me like you were doing a first-rate job!"

"Let's just say I was working hard at it," Mr. Blake responded with a sigh of relief. "Let me wind up my story."

"Okay," Jack encouraged.

"Remember, the boy had been walking up and down that room for twenty to twenty-five minutes. He finally came back to his chair and dropped into it. He seemed to be down now—really down. He leaned on the table with both hands and closed his eyes. All of the previous expression had gone out of his face and I saw wrinkles on that kid's face that I had never seen there before, and an unhealthy color. It was a really strange, strange thing. That boy seemed to age visibly before my eyes.

"After a minute or so, he said real sad, 'I couldn't help her.' We must have gone on sitting there for five or ten minutes. Maybe it was fifteen or twenty. Anyway, I just let him take his time. When I saw he wasn't going to pick it up, you know, talk some more, I tried to draw him out of his sadness, real easy-like. I said, 'I think I understand your situation better now.' It sounded pretty weak to me, and probably did to him, too ... but maybe not ... maybe my feeling of caring got through to him, and that could help. But to get on with it, I said matter-of-factly, 'if you can tell me where your mother might be, we can try to locate her.' "

"Sounds like you did a nice job," Jack interrupted gently. "I'm curious; how are you going to handle the problem of locating the mother?"

For a moment Mr. Blake did not respond directly to Jack's question, but went on talking about his experience with Dick, ending with, "Boy, that was sure an eye-opener of an experience for me." Then he focused on Jack's question. "Oh, that. Well, I've already talked with Miss Smith who said she'll get in touch with the police and probation people in Dolan to check out what's happened to her. And then the police or probation people will let Miss Smith know. Either she or I will share what we learn with Dick. I think the main thing is to let the boy know that something definite is being done."

"I'm sorry I shifted your thought," Jack apologized. "How did you end your talk with Dick?"

"Jack, there's not much more to tell. Maybe one additional thing. I came back after all that business about his mother and asked him if there was anything he'd like to see changed—that is, here at Central State. He said he wanted to get going right away in his program. You know, Jack, the kid is right. We *are* taking too long in getting these kids into their schedules—much too long. We have too many people interviewing them, covering the same questions, and we don't have appropriate activities, especially in the cottages, to keep them really occupied for two whole weeks. They should be put into their regular program after one week at the most. Whatever personal problems Dick has have been aggravated, I think, by an overly long admission period."

"It's hard to admit," Jack acknowledged. "But I think you're right; our initial program is pretty skimpy."

"Well, I think we ought to push ahead to do something about it," Mr. Blake pressed.

"Okay," Jack agreed. "Let's take it up at our Thursday meeting of cottage supervisors. If we take a look at the problem together, I think we can come up with some strategies that will help us develop the program we need. Will you buy that?"

"Sure," Mr. Blake agreed.

"Now let's walk over to the dining room and see if there's any supper left. You know, we're an hour late." They rose together and walked through the door toward the dining room.

"That's good," Mr. Blake observed, "This will give us a chance to talk about Larry. You remember, he's the other boy I wanted to talk with you about . . ."

3

NOBODY LIKES ME
OR WANTS ME

Mr. Blake's and Jack's supper together had been interrupted on the previous day by an emergency in Venture Cottage, and they had not been able to talk about Larry, a boy Mr. Blake had indicated was puzzling him. They had resolved to talk about Larry at supper the following evening.

Mr. Blake came by Jack's office at 6:20 and they walked over to the dining room together. After going through the cafeteria line and rehashing the local baseball team's performance, Mr. Blake began, "You recall the other boy I wanted to talk with you about was Larry Higgins . . . I've had him over to see Doc Barth a couple of times this week. You know he's thin, his shoulders sag, and with that tall frame of his, he looks like a scarecrow. He keeps complaining about his stomach. Doc's given him all kinds of tests, but all he can find is a nervous stomach."

"Is it serious?" Jack asked with concern as they sat down to eat.

"No, not really. Not serious, you know, like having an ulcer; he's not sick by any technical standard. But he's sick just the same."

"What does Doc have to say about that?"

"Well, Doc said the medical name of what is wrong with Larry is a 'psychosomatic disorder.' He explained that Larry's stomach trouble isn't just his imagination and he's not trying to fake it, but it's real physical trouble that comes out of his personal or psychological difficulties. And it can cause him considerable trouble. To use Doc's language, 'It can incapacitate Larry.' And what he says makes sense because Larry can't seem to learn at school and he's not doing his work around the cottage . . . So, all in all, I guess he is sick."

"Did Doc say that this nervous stomach business might be worse when Larry is under some kind of pressure?" Jack asked.

"Right. And I've been looking for something in the unit that might be causing Larry pressure ever since the Doc mentioned it . . . but for the life of me, I can't see anything that might be doing it."

"How about Miss Smith—does she have any leads?" Jack inquired hopefully.

"No, she doesn't and I've also checked with Mr. Long, Larry's counselor at school. Both of them have details on his background—and it's pretty grim—but nothing new seems to be complicating the picture.

"What do you know about his background?"

"The thing that seems to run through like a theme, according to Doc, is that nobody has wanted Larry and nobody has cared about him. That all started way back. He's never had any real mothering, and of course his dad has never been interested in him, never even been in the picture," Mr. Blake explained.

"Did Doc have *anything* to suggest?"

"First, he's given the boy some medicine," Mr. Blake sighed. "But he was pretty strong in saying that the medicine itself won't be enough to get rid of Larry's troubles. The most important part of his treatment is to help him get over his emotional troubles."

"That sounds difficult," Jack said thoughtfully. "Did you get any coaching from Doc on what you might actually do?"

"Well, he said I should act as Larry's friend and show him some affection. He talked about Larry as though he was starved—or near to it—for affection. And he said I should encourage Larry to feel safe enough with me so the boy will tell me his troubles."

"Sounds sensible," Jack commented.

"Do you think these things will really help?" Mr. Blake asked with doubt in his voice.

"It's hard to know," Jack acknowledged. "As I said, they make good sense. But you seem doubtful."

"They do make sense," Mr. Blake agreed. "But I don't know if I can make them work. I really don't."

"Look," Jack pointed out with deliberate lightness, "don't sell yourself short. Larry needs all the people he can find to help him and you're in a key position to be useful."

Mr. Blake continued to look doubtful in spite of Jack's encouragement. "I probably shouldn't be saying this, but sometimes it's hard for me to let these kids say what they want to. Instead, I try to get them to say what *I* want to hear them say." He laughed with embarrassment. "I'm not really as bad as I make myself sound. But often, or at least sometimes, I find myself pushing the kids to talk about what they're *doing* about their gripes and problems and not just to go over and over the gripes themselves."

"Well, you may have to change that habit a bit with Larry," Jack chuckled to ease Mr. Blake's anxiety.

Sensing that Mr. Blake was feeling he somehow fell short, Jack said, "I know exactly what you're saying. The kids who are chronic complainers are hard to listen to, and your listening may feed into their complaining even more. On that other thing, about changing how you ordinarily handle what the kids talk about, well, I'd say that shutting the kids off may work pretty well in some situations, but you may want to add other techniques to your ways of handling their problems."

"Right, right," Mr. Blake agreed. "But I have a hard time—a really hard time—listening to and putting up with some of that crap, down-right crap, especially from the regular complainers and manipulators!"

"But the complainers and the manipulators are not the same types of kids," Jack commented.

"I know, I know," Mr. Blake responded with some desperation, "but they seem to have practically the same effect on me."

After a moment Jack shifted in his chair and nodded his head to indicate that he appreciated Mr. Blake's situation. He rubbed his forehead and continued, "I doubt that Larry will present you with that kind of a problem. He's not going to be giving you a lot of crap, though I'm sure he's going to be saying things you may not agree with or wish he wouldn't say—that is, if you really give him a chance to talk openly."

Responding to Jack's easy manner, Mr. Blake came down from his previous high pitch. "I agree Larry's not that type. Then, too, if I talk with him in private, I think that will cut out some of my problems."

"Right. You don't want a whole cottage of kids around, and neither would Larry."

"I'm getting the idea," Mr. Blake nodded.

"Sure," Jack said confidently. "The other thing to work on is what we talked about yesterday. You're going to have to get a hold on your own feelings about listening to the boys' troubles."

"Now that's a tougher thing for me," Mr. Blake pointed out with a half smile. "But I've been mulling it over . . . there are a couple of things I know of that tend to upset me. One is that I can't stand one kid bullying another one. So when that starts happening, I've got troubles with myself. . . . and . . . the other one is when a kid looks like he's about to cry. Somehow that really gets to me."

"Well, Larry doesn't fall in the first category," Jack observed.

"No, he doesn't," Mr. Blake agreed. "Unless somebody starts giving him a hard time. But I figure he's a sure bet for the crying. . . . He looks like a sure bet."

"The boy does look sad; at least he has when I've seen him. I get the feeling that when you give him a chance to talk, to unload some of his troubles, he will cry. I think you can count on that."

"Well, I guess I'll just have to brace myself and take it as it comes," Mr. Blake said with a tone of thoughtful determination. "That crying business really gets to me for some reason . . . I guess I must be a softy at heart."

They ate in silence for awhile.

"You know," Jack said, "you may not have to brace yourself as much as you think. You can share the feelings that Larry is having and still not get carried away by those feelings. In fact, your willingness to tune in to him may help the boy to sense you're really on his side."

"I get your point and it makes sense. I guess I'll just have to try it." Mr. Blake continued to reflect silently on the point for a minute, his eyes becoming misty. After what may have been some resolution of the problem in his mind, he nodded his head and in an appreciative tone said, "Jack, I think if I feel right along with the kid, it might help. It seems like a natural thing to do."

Mr. Blake's mood lightened as he shifted the conversation to general cottage problems. After they had finished their meal, he ended optimistically, "Thanks, Jack. I'll be in touch about Larry as soon as I have something to tell you."

Jack thought about Mr. Blake several times during the following week, wondering what made him so especially sensitive to the boys' crying. He reproached himself for neglecting to provide Mr. Blake with a chance to talk further about his response to the sad feelings expressed by his boys. However, as he mulled it over, Jack excused himself by reasoning that it was not his job or even his business to probe that deeply into Mr. Blake's feelings.

A week and a half after their discussion, Mr. Blake came in to talk about Larry. As he sat down, Jack observed that he appeared relaxed and in good humor.

After exchanging a few pleasantries, Mr. Blake began, "I thought you would be interested to know that Larry came to see me yesterday just before going to sick call and complained in his usual fashion about his stomach."

"Just what you were waiting for," Jack commented smiling.

"Right." Mr. Blake beamed. "I listened quietly, and after I felt he'd kind of said his thing, I asked him to drop back after seeing Doc Barth. I told him I wanted to know more about what kind of treatment he was getting.

"At any rate, after our earlier talk, I was determined to get to the bottom of Larry's complaining—to see what, in addition to his stomach trouble, was bugging him. When I saw Larry coming toward the cottage from the infirmary, I noticed that he was walking faster than usual, and when he came inside, I could see that his eyes were kind of bugged out. He really looked upset! Usually, you know, he shuffles along so slowly that he hardly moves, and his eyes seem sunk back into his head."

"That's quite a change."

"It sure was," Mr. Blake said emphatically. "He looked really uptight. I didn't know it right then, but two things were working for me. Otherwise, I suppose I would only have gotten more of his usual complaining. For one, the Doc had just come down on Larry pretty hard. Told him to 'get with it' and 'quit crying around.' I think Larry annoyed the Doc because he hasn't been taking his medicine, yet he goes on belly-aching about how bad he feels. The other thing that happened was a bunch of kids saw Larry leave the infirmary and called him some names—'the cop-out kid,' 'old sad-sac,' and a few vulgar ones that I won't mention. And all of that name calling was heaped on him right after Doc had shaken him up!"

"So, instead of everyone being full of sympathy, the world turned on Larry," Jack suggested.

Mr. Blake nodded and continued to talk, his voice rising with excitement. "Almost as soon as he came in the door, Larry began to wail, 'Mr. Blake, Mr. Blake, my stomach hurts.' I said something like, 'How can that be? You just saw the doctor.' Then he wailed some more, 'Doc Barth doesn't know anything. His medicine ain't any good.' Then his volume began to build up and he began to yell, '*Nobody* is any good!' '*Nobody* is any good! And those goddamn kids out there on the sidewalk called me a bunch of dirty names just because I'm sick!' "

Mr. Blake paused and chuckled as he recounted the experience. "I heard real anger in Larry's voice for the first time, so I figured I ought to let him get it out of his system. That 'goddamn' talk just hasn't been a part of his line."

"Great," Jack encouraged. "How did you do that?"

"I don't really know," Mr. Blake admitted. "I don't really know. All I said was, 'It sounds like this whole business made you mad.' "

Mr. Blake moved forward in his chair, intense. "But what I said sure broke it loose. I've never heard worse cussing from anybody. I mean it—from anybody! He s.o.b.'d and m.f.'d everybody and everything! And it wasn't just a few phrases. He raised holy hell with everybody for nearly ten minutes. Really raised hell!

"Well, I got to know another side of Larry and I felt some sympathy for him, at least a little. And Jack, let me say that I can stand cussing and that kind of stuff a lot easier than I can take the whining and crying. But as I took a hard look at what was going on, I decided I wasn't really getting anyplace with Larry, even though he was unloading a lot of his anger . . . I figured he wasn't really moving. So the first time he let up a little, I said, 'Larry, I think you expect too much from people and are not willing to meet them halfway.'

"I may have said the wrong thing," Mr. Blake observed, frowning. "It probably would have been better if I had given him more sympathy—support or whatever you call it—instead of telling him that I saw something wrong about him."

"Who knows," Jack shrugged. "It seems to me you were doing fine."

"I don't know, maybe not. Anyway, right or wrong, I surely got to him." As Mr. Blake talked, enthusiasm and anxiety combined to increase the pitch of his voice. "I tell you, Larry screamed and yelled, even louder than before. 'You're all alike, you sons-of-bitches; you're all alike. Nobody *likes* me or *wants* me. Nobody gives a damn what happens to me. *Nobody*!' "

Mr. Blake stopped and drew in a deep breath, relaxed a little, and then continued, "I didn't know what else to do, really, so I just let him yell. All of the kids had gone to school. So there wasn't any problem of his setting the whole cottage off or anything like that. The kid looked to me like he was beside himself. He seemed to be out of it. He was gone . . . I figured trying to restrain him would only make matters worse, so I let him alone."

"How do you mean he seemed to be out of it?" Jack probed.

"His eyes were wild looking and he kept swinging his head around in a funny way. The only place I've seen that kind of behavior before was on TV when some comedian would make a big gesture. Besides, he didn't do it just once or twice; he kept it up. Must have kept it up for several minutes! He seemed crazy.

"Let me tell you, all that yelling gave me a little time to think. You better believe I needed it! I figured I was in pretty deep and I'd just have to stay with him and see where it would take us. Well, like I said before, I just let him go on yelling and after he finally finished all his yelling, I could see that he had softened up a bit. As a matter of fact, as I looked him over, I could see that he was about to cry! Well, I just said to myself, 'Blake, you'd better get ahold of yourself on this one.'' Things were moving pretty fast, but I got control and made myself look at all of the stuff he had said—at least all that I could remember—and I tried to pick out the most important thing he'd been shouting so I could ask him about it."

"I'm interested to know what you picked," Jack said eagerly.

"Maybe it was because he had shouted it so often, maybe it was because of my past experience with him, or some combination—at any rate, I decided to get into 'nobody likes me or wants me.' "

"Sounds like you were right on target," Jack responded enthusiastically.

"But what part of that picture—that is, the 'nobody likes me or wants me' picture—did you decide to get into and how did you go about it?"

"I don't think I planned as carefully as all that," Mr. Blake said somewhat apologetically. "I just didn't go at it so orderly. Probably I should have. But Jack, I'm not that schooled in this counseling business. Now, with Larry, I did figure on two things, and Jack, you ought to be proud of me. One was that I would treat the boy with kid gloves—treat him nice. The other thing was that I would get to the bottom of that 'nobody likes me or wants me' thing."

"I understand." Jack reassured him. "And so what did you do?"

"Well . . . at some point when his yelling had slowed down a bit, I moved in and said kindly-like, "Larry, the feeling that *nobody likes you or wants you* is terribly important to you, isn't it?' I hardly had a chance to finish what I was saying when he came back at me shouting—and I mean really shouting—'It's true! It's true! Nobody *does* like me!'

"Well, the boy set me back a little, and without thinking, I tried to answer him with facts instead of trying to find out why he was feeling that way. I said, 'I can name a number of people right here in the cottage, both boys and staff, who like you.' He didn't shout back but instead said real discouraged-like, 'Yeah, but they're either kids in trouble like me or staff. Staff are *paid* to be nice to me. They all add up to nobody.'

"As it turned out, I think it was a useful thing to say," Mr. Blake added after a moment of thought, "because it started us down the path to his parents."

"How was that?"

"Well, it was kind of strange, but after he said that everybody who liked him added up to nobody, he looked over at the desk and asked me if the mail had come in yet. When he asked that, he looked the lowest I had ever seen him. I'm telling you Jack, he came across really, really sad."

Mr. Blake stopped talking and took a deep breath. The weight of Larry's sadness was apparent in his expression. "I've heard that question so often from other boys that I knew Larry was wondering whether his mother had written, and while I couldn't say for sure, I knew his mother hadn't written him for at least six weeks, maybe even for two months.

"So I said, kind of questioning, 'You haven't heard for quite awhile?' Well, that did it. The boy crumpled up and began crying again. I don't know exactly how long he cried but I'll bet you it was a good ten minutes solid. He couldn't talk while he was crying . . ."

"Did you ask him any questions or say anything while he was crying?" Jack asked gently.

"Yes, I tried to ask him about a couple of things," Mr. Blake said evenly, but there was an obvious tone of distress in his voice. "I said, 'It's okay to go ahead and cry' when he started because I thought it would be good for him to let it out, but let me tell you, Jack, I wasn't looking forward to it. That crying cracks me up . . . And I asked him a couple of times while he was crying whether he could try to tell me what was making him cry. He didn't answer any of my questions, so I tried to tie it together *for* him—at least those parts that I thought went together. I said, 'Your feeling that "nobody likes me or wants me" comes from home, doesn't it, Larry?' You know, I tried to tie the pieces together very loosely with a question, figuring if it made any sense he might say so, and if it didn't it might help him to get at what was really bothering him . . . but it only made him cry harder."

"It's hard to know," Jack commented, "but his crying harder might have meant that what you said was true."

"I don't know," Mr. Blake answered. "But he sure did cry."

"But he didn't say anything about the pieces you had put together?" Jack pursued.

"No, like I said, it only made him cry all the harder," Mr. Blake began, and then shifted. "Well, no, at one point, after a lot of wailing, he did sob out 'my mother' and then he went into another crying spell. After he wound down on the crying, I said, 'Can you tell me what's making you cry so?' He shook his head, wiped his eyes, and then got up from his chair there in the dayroom where we were talking and slowly walked out."

"You did try to pick up on that 'my mother' thing?" Jack observed.

"I tried, yes, I tried," Mr. Blake reported with a depressed tone. "But he just shook his head and dried his eyes. . . . In addition to what I've told you, I may have added something like 'Can you try to tell me about it?' But like I said, he shook his head, dried his eyes, and got up and walked out of the room."

"How did you end it then?" Jack inquired with a sense of uneasiness.

"Very frankly, I had to pull myself together a little. After that, I followed Larry out into the recreation room. Figuring he wanted to be left alone, I told him that I would be glad to talk with him further whenever he wanted to."

"Has he come back to you?"

"No," Mr. Blake answered softly.

"What's he been doing in the meantime?"

"He follows his schedule."

"What shape is he in?" Jack pressed, somewhat anxiously.

"He seems down," Mr. Blake replied with sadness in his voice. After an uneasy pause, Mr. Blake concluded, "He sure doesn't look good."

"Well," Jack said, trying to inject some buoyancy into the heavy conversation, "if you haven't gotten to the heart of Larry's problems, you've gotten very close . . . and there's no doubt that you have helped him move from his chronic pattern of complaining and demanding to expressing his more basic feelings. You probably have gotten the boy to look into himself."

Mr. Blake nodded, his expression brightening considerably, as Jack continued, "Be sure to make yourself available to him, be supportive, but at the same time, don't push yourself on him. Let's see what the boy does. I know you'll keep in close touch with what happens."

Mr. Blake nodded, smiling as when he came in, rose from his chair, and left.

But Jack was left with an image of the man's sadness.

4

WHERE THERE'S SMOKE

As Jack was going over a stack of papers on his desk, he came across a telephone message from Mr. Collins, the supervisor of Whittier Cottage. He recalled having seen it earlier in the afternoon, but other work had prevented him from returning the call. He felt little urgency over the delay, knowing Mr. Collins' capability in handling the boys at Whittier. Not the most explosive unit in the school, Whittier housed boys whose insecurity, absence of developed personal standards, and excessive dependence on the approval of others had led many of them into trouble. In some instances they had gone along with a gang in its delinquent activities, but only as fringe members. In other instances Whittier boys had been used as 'patsies' by a gang, given tasks to perform during a delinquent outing—such as stealing or destroying property— while the gang members stayed safely in the background.

But, the call had waited long enough.

"Well, I see you're still hard at it," Jack said cheerily when Mr. Collins answered the phone.

"I'm still here," Mr. Collins chuckled. "But I'm not sure about the rest of that."

"I am sorry I couldn't get back to you before now," Jack apologized. "The way you manage Whittier you may have answered your own question by now."

"I'm afraid not, Jack," Mr. Collins replied. "I've been keeping my eye on this thing for awhile, at least a week, and I think it's getting worse instead of better."

"You've got my curiosity up," Jack said. "What's happening?"

"I can't talk now because I'm in the dayroom," Mr. Collins explained. "If I could come by in about twenty minutes, I could describe the whole thing to you."

"Okay," Jack agreed.

Jack called his wife and told her not to wait dinner for him, then made several other brief phone calls, and was about to read some progress reports on the boys when Mr. Collins came in the door.

"I'm sure sorry to bother you about this," Mr. Collins said hastily, "but our kids are getting mixed up in smoking and pushing pot."

"No wonder you were serious on the phone," Jack said soberly. "Can you fill me in?"

"I think our kids are in on the tail end of this thing," Mr. Collins replied nervously. "From what my kids tell me, the ringleaders of the whole scene are from Venture and Anchor cottages. They're pretty tough, you know and they're putting the pressure on my top boys to buy and push it in Whittier."

Jack immediately noticed Mr. Collins' anxiety. A normally calm man, now his speech was rapid and his hands jerked nervously as he talked. Jack knew Mr. Collins as a conscientious person, one who preferred to handle matters entirely on his own and who felt personal failure in having to rely on another in resolving a problem.

But evidently this situation exceeded even Mr. Collins ability to control it. To put him more at ease, Jack said calmly, "We've had some marijuana smuggling and a bit of pushing before, so this problem isn't an entirely new one."

"I know," Mr. Collins agreed, "but the way this thing is organized and the extent to which my kids are involved is new. And I'd wager it's a bigger thing than this whole institution has ever experienced before!"

"How do you see this thing, Harold?" Jack asked, to rechannel Mr. Collins' anxiety.

"Jack, I know my boys are mixed up in this. "Beginning a couple days ago, more than the usual number of my kids began sneaking around the corner of the building to smoke. When I realized that the group's behavior was changing, I went after them. It was then that I got on to what they were up to."

"So you found out," Jack chuckled to ease Mr. Collins' tension. "Maybe regretfully."

"That's right. I had to find out what they were doing, but I was sorry to actually see it. About a dozen were gathered around Red Gibbons who was dragging on a reefer. Everybody was waiting his turn for a drag. By the smell of the stuff, I knew right away what I had on my hands, so I called them into the building and met with them. I included the other kids who were hanging around the cottage."

Jack nodded. "You had quite a subject to talk about. How did you get into it?"

"I told them what I had just seen and what I had seen going on for the past couple of days, and asked them where they were getting the stuff. That's about all. Then I pushed them a little."

"How's that?" Jack asked.

"Well, I told them that I couldn't afford to wait them out—to wait until somebody came forward to give me the full story—and that if they wouldn't tell me the story, I'd get it someplace else. I didn't ask them whether they were smoking pot. You know, they might very well have denied it, if I had taken that kind of approach. I just told them what I had seen, and then asked them where they had gotten the stuff. I didn't come on heavy by telling them they had broken the rules, or that they had let me down, or that it was bad for their health, or any stuff like that. I figured they already knew all that, and for me to lecture at them would only make them mad. Well, anyway, after that, they went through their usual line of keeping things vague—you know how they talk, Jack. One kid said something like, 'We got them from some of the guys at school,' and another said, 'Nobody special—just from the boys out on the grounds.'

"Well, after these dodges, the kids clammed up. As I was figuring out what to do next, I got a break. One of the boys, Ken Adams, who doesn't stand very high with the others, said, 'I think we ought to turn in all of the reefers to you and let you give them to Mr. Graves.' "

"That kid really put his head on the block," Jack said, shaking his own in amazement.

"Not really," Mr. Collins tempered. "He didn't actualy incriminate anybody, so it wasn't so bad. But some of the kids—especially the cottage tough guys—were mad as hell.

"Anyway, I let them jump on Ken's idea. Then I came back and said that I would not only have to have the reefers but I would also have to know where they came from."

"Sounds like you were beginning to apply the pressure."

"That's right," Mr. Collins agreed with a note of authority. "But it didn't carry the day. At least not right away because Larry Gravin, one of the kids who was bringing the stuff in, said something like, 'Why don't you let us flush the stuff down the toilets?' When I said that wouldn't do, somebody said, 'Make the guys who brought the stuff in take it back out.' As I looked around at the kids, I could see that they liked the suggestion. The traffic would be reversed and nobody would have to face up to the situation. But I obviously couldn't let it go at that."

"Then what happened?"

"Well, they went into a deep freeze and nobody would say a damned thing. I figured they felt caught between my pressure to talk and their own cottage code of keeping your mouth shut—especially after Ken had been jumped on. Determined as I was to get them to tell me where they had gotten the stuff and who had brought it in, I just couldn't get them to come through. So I told them I would leave the room for a half hour. I told them that when I came back in, I wanted the reefers to be on the desk—*all* of them. And I told them I wanted to know where they were getting them from, and to top it off, I wanted the pushers and whoever was bringing the stuff in to make themselves known to me. To make it easier on them, I said they could come and talk with me individually or as a group after our meeting broke up."

Jack grinned. "You were doing a lot of telling there . . . how did they perform?"

With a self-confident smile, Mr. Collins responded, "I never thought about it that way. I guess I felt pushed, so I was pushing them. Anyway, it worked pretty good. When I came back to the meeting room in a half hour or so, there were about three dozen reefers on the desk and a scribbled note saying that they had gotten the stuff from Bill Kurtz of Venture and Ed Marvin of Anchor, and that the boys who were responsible in Whittier would see me by themselves."

"And what were the kids doing?"

"Well, they were sitting around not saying a word and watching me very closely—you know, to see what I would do. After seeing the stuff and the note, I asked if they had anything else they wanted to tell me and when they said, 'No,' I sat there with them in dead silence for several minutes. Finally I said something like, 'I don't want any more of this business.' Then I let them go."

"That didn't end it?" Jack prompted after a pause.

"By no means. In a couple of hours, Chris Sargeant, Bernie Merriam, and Larry Gravin had been to see me and had owned up kind of indirectly that they were the go-betweens and pushers in our cottage."

"That was a nice development," Jack complimented. "Then what did you do?"

"You mean what did I *tell them* I was going to do about it?"

Jack nodded.

"Well, sir, I got the whole cottage together. That was about four or five hours after my first session. Anyway, it was early evening. I told the whole cottage that they were on restriction until we could get this cleared up. I also let them know that some individuals were going to catch some punishment on this deal. Of course, I said the whole thing would have to be run through the staff committee." Anger raised Mr. Collins' voice. "Personally I think Sargeant, Merriam, and Gravin should have their time lengthened. There's no sense in putting them out on the street. Not the way they're behaving.

"Anyway," he sighed, relaxing again, "they know that in a situation like this, the staff committee is going to get into it. And Jack, the specific punishments that come out of this are going to have to make sense from one cottage to the next. So the committee has its work cut out for it."

Jack frowned, thinking, then said, "Harold, I appreciate your work on this. From what you've told me, I'd better get over to see Len Hall at Anchor and Ed Snell at Venture tonight."

Mr. Collins nodded gravely.

"Oh, one other thing," he added after a deep breath. "I also found out that the headquarters for this operation are over at the school—I suppose because it's a place where they can all get together."

After Mr. Collins left, Jack rubbed his neck and paced awhile, planning a discussion with Ed Snell. His door opened to admit the director of the school.

"You're working a little late, aren't you?" Mr. Eagan greeted him in his usual hail-fellow-well-met approach.

Jack grinned and replied, "It's typical for me, but it's *your* behavior that surprises me."

"Personnel problems at the dining room. They really turn me on, bring out the best in me," Mr. Eagan answered, irritated. "I wish the hell some of these people would either report for work or quit. Having to get kids to fill in just doesn't work out!"

"Before you lose your good spirits altogether, Clarence," Jack interrupted with jovial sarcasm, "I'd like to ask you about your marijuana distribution department. I understand it's doing quite well."

"I usually do pretty well in whatever I undertake," Mr. Eagan responded with a chuckle, "but that's one business I haven't gotten into."

"Well, I don't know exactly what your situation is," Jack said, laughing. "It seems to me you're in it whether you know it or not. Besides, you ought to be getting a cut of the profits because at a minimum you're providing the building and office equipment to accommodate the business. One might say your schoolhouse is the distribution center."

"Wait a minute. Seriously now, Jack," Mr. Eagan said, nonplussed. "Can you fill me in on what the hell you're talking about? It's a little late in the day and things are getting by me, so you'll have to give it to me straight."

"Somebody is pushing marijuana in the cottages, Whittier for sure, and I have some evidence that pushers are operating in Venture and Anchor, too. I expect when we have a chance to look into this, we'll find it's in every cottage."

"So how does the school fit into this?" Mr. Eagan challenged, all humor gone from his tone.

"Several of Collins' boys said they had the stuff pushed onto them at school by a couple of fellows from Venture and Anchor."

"We try to provide a pretty full education, but we haven't included that in our curriculum," Mr. Eagan said frowning. "Actually, this is new to me, but I don't mean to say that it isn't happening. Many things go on there that I don't know about. How do you suggest I proceed?"

"Why don't you talk with your staff tomorrow morning—everybody, including your custodians. Informal. Don't call a meeting. Just see what you can learn by visiting around. Say as little as you can. We want to know what they know, not give them information."

"Sounds good," Mr. Eagan agreed. "I'll check with my people first thing tomorrow."

"Would you look into it before nine-thirty? I'd like to get a number of us together in my office at that time," Jack suggested. "I think we should move fast on this one."

"Of course. In fact, I want to make a few contacts on this tonight," Mr. Eagan said with determination.

After Mr. Eagan left, Jack checked the duty roster and learned that Ed Snell was on call. Rather than bother with a phone call, Jack decided to pay a visit to Venture.

As Jack entered the cottage, he saw a small group gathered around Mr. Snell. The boys were quick to greet him, conspicuously deferent, calling out, "Hi, Mr. Owens!"

After welcomes were exchanged, Mr. Snell suggested, "Fellows, I'd like to have you go ahead with cleaning up the storage closet."

"Okay, okay," one of the boys answered. "But we know you just want to get rid of us so you can talk with Mr. Owens."

The boys laughed good-naturedly and left. Mr. Snell, a friendly, confident man in his early fifties, watched them go with a smile on his face.

"Looks like the boys are right with you this evening," Jack observed.

"They are," Mr. Snell chuckled. "They caused some problems at school today, were kicked out, and restricted from the basket ball game tonight. But you didn't come over here to talk about school problems," he prompted. "So I ought to let you get to what's on your mind."

"I did come on another matter, as a matter of fact," Jack began. "Let me fill you in. Harold Collins was in my office earlier this evening and he told me that his kids have been getting marijuana from a couple of your boys and from a couple of boys in Anchor."

"Does Harold have any hard evidence?" Mr. Snell asked bluntly.

"He sure does," Jack said evenly. "The joints themselves."

"How about names? Did the Whittier kids say who's pushing the stuff to them?"

Jack nodded. "Bill Kurtz from your cottage and Ed Marvin from Anchor."

"What you're saying helps me make some sense out of what I've been seeing for about the past week," Mr. Snell said tensely. "Bill Kurtz and Des

Hite have been operating on the fringe of the group for about a week now. Once in awhile the other kids would gather around them and then they'd break apart again. I knew something important was going on, something that spelled trouble, but I couldn't get a handle on it."

"And you think what you were seeing was the distribution scene?" Jack asked.

"I'd bet on it," Mr. Snell said grimly. "I guess I'd better get busy running it down."

"Good, check into it," Jack agreed. "I still need to get over to see Len. Then let's plan on a meeting tomorrow at nine-thirty in my office. I'll get everyone together who might have boys involved."

Jack went immediately to Anchor. The staff assigned aggressive, antisocial boys to that cottage and worked to develop a program minimally designed to cope with them and maximally to help them establish new behavior patterns. Not only were Anchor boys tough, but they were quick to strike out and start a fight or provoke others into one. Impulsive and hostile, they blew up easily, reacting suddenly and violently to the slightest provocation. The boys in Anchor were highly selfish, shrewd, and self-centered. They looked to others—especially the supervisors, teachers, and social workers—to meet their demands; yet they felt no responsibility to contribute to anything. Ordinarily, they did poor or inadequate work in school or on a job assignment. Good production, when it did occur, was only sporadic; they either could not or would not sustain it. Most of these boys had a long history of getting into trouble with the law, or with social rules, or with both. They were generally unconcerned about their behavior, although in individual situations they appeared to feel some regret or anxiety. Jack believed such regret was feigned. Although the boys in Venture worked at conning one another, they were amateurs compared to the boys in Anchor.

Anchor's supervisor was Mr. Hall. Tall, athletic, friendly, and outspoken, he had an open and direct relationship with his boys. Like Mr. Collins at Whittier, Mr. Hall had organized a good cottage program and held regularly scheduled meetings with his boys; however, the Anchor meetings were much different from those at Whittier.

Mr. Hall was more direct, pushing the boys harder to stay on the track and discuss and reconsider their negative as well as their positive behavior, while he participated in the discussions actively. Yet, he was sensitive to their feelings. If he thought the tension associated with a discussion of fighting, running away, or homosexuality was beyond what the boys could handle at that point, he would immediately ease off the subject.

As Jack walked through the door into Anchor, he saw Mr. Hall at one end of the dayroom, which also served as a weight-lifting and exercise area.

"Say, you may be just the man we've been looking for to handle these weights," Mr. Hall called out in welcome. "Some of the boys need more help than I can give them, so we're looking for a new coach."

"I'm afraid you have the wrong man. Sorry about that," Jack laughed as he answered. "But it looks like you have some experts right around you."

Pleased at his compliment, the boys talked excitedly for a few minutes about their weight lifting and then turned to Mr. Hall for support and feedback. "Keep up the good work, fellows," he said, smiling, "while Mr. Owens and I talk for a few minutes."

When the room was empty, Jack commented, "I see a few of your boys weren't able to make it over to the ball game tonight."

"Yeah," Mr. Hall asserted. "These boys just aren't making it in the program right now. Got kicked out of school and work. So I thought I would keep them with me this evening. Basically, they're good kids but they just can't keep out of trouble when they're in a large group scene."

Jack nodded. "Len, I'm a little pushed for time, so I'll get to the point. Have you been having a problem with marijuana in your unit?"

"No, Jack, I haven't," Mr. Hall replied thoughtfully, "but I wouldn't be surprised to find it here."

"We haven't gotten into this thing very far, but it looks like at least one of your boys, together with at least one from Venture, has been pushing some stuff into Whittier. Harold Collins actually caught his kids smoking the stuff."

"Did his kids say who was pushing it?"

"Ed Marvin from your unit and Bill Kurtz from Venture," Jack reported.

"I'll get right on it," Mr. Hall volunteered.

"Good," Jack agreed, "I'd appreciate your getting on it fast. And I'd like to have you meet with Harold Collins, Ed Snell, Clarence Eagan, maybe a few others, and me tomorrow morning at nine-thirty in my office."

"I'll see you then."

Wild shouting and exuberance characterized the scene at the basketball game between Central State and a neighboring high school. However, five especially intent boys in the gym had little idea of what was happening on the gym floor. The tallest of the group, a wiry fellow with long, dark blond hair, was obviously in command—Bill Kurtz by name. Sitting next to him in a section of the bleachers furthest from the basketball court was his partner, a huge boy with brownish, crew-cut hair named Ed Marvin. Crowding around them were Des Hite, dumpy but otherwise nondescript, and two huskies, Alfred Signet and John Campbell.

"I'm telling you guys to forget about beatin' Sargeant's head in or anybody else's from Whittier," Bill Kurtz directed coldly. "If you figure a score has to be settled, we'll take care of it later. We've got enough trouble, so don't be so goddamn stupid."

"What the hell is the matter with you, Kurtz? Have you lost your guts?" Ed Marvin charged. "They've got it coming to them!"

"That's right!" John Campbell seconded.

"Look, you goons," Bill Kurtz shouted, in order to be heard above the noise of the crowd and maintain control of his lieutenants. "The boys at Whittier are the least of our worries right now, even if they did screw up the whole plan!"

"That's right," Des Hite echoed. "Our job right now is to hold on to as much of the stuff as we can and make sure that those school janitors—Sheppard and Cope—get all the blame."

"Right on!" Bill Kurtz hooted. "So let's just let the stuff in our lockers get picked up, pretend like that's all there is, and keep our mouths shut about what we got down in the machine shop."

Though still angry about the Whittier boys and being put down by Kurtz and Hite, the three from Anchor indicated by their silence that they would go along with the scheme.

The game ended, although it was unlikely that any of the five could have reported who had won. While anxiety showed on the faces of Kurtz and Hite, Marvin, Signet, and Campbell looked sullen. As they left the gymnasium, Bill Kurtz growled, "I don't want you guys to make any mistakes on this."

"I believe we're all here," Jack started. "You know the problem. Let's see if we can fill in some of the details."

Ed Snell opened the meeting with a tense comment. "Jack, we've got to take some time to work on the cottages. My kids are damned-near walking on the ceiling over this thing." His concern was reflected in the faces of Len Hall, Harold Collins, and Clarence Eagan.

"Yes, yes," Len Hall chimed in. "We've got to do some work on our units, or they—at least mine—will blow!"

"By walking on the ceiling," Jack asked, confused, "do you mean the kids are high on pot?"

"I'm afraid there *is* some of that," Ed Snell said anxiously. "But more important than that, my whole cottage is higher than hell on just plain excitement. They know that this is a big thing, and that they pulled something off—even though it didn't go the whole way. The way I figure it, they're hopped up about having been able to pull it off."

"My kids are riding high because they've put one over on me," Len Hall admitted sadly. "And they know we're going to close in on them."

Moving forward in his chair, Jack proposed, "Let me suggest that we hold the discussion on the condition of the boys until *after* we pool our information on where the boys have been getting the grass and how they're moving it through the institution."

Though the expressions around the table showed little enthusiasm about giving up the initial line of conversation, the men nevertheless nodded their heads in agreement. Jack added, "Mr. Graves wants to move ahead with whatever information we can give him, so after we finish hashing this out, perhaps Clarence can talk with Mr. Graves and we can go ahead to work on our cottage problems."

Expressions changed again. The group seemed satisfied. Len Hall began, "We've had a chance to compare notes before you came in, Jack. Both Ed and I have about four or five boys in on this thing. The picture we've put together is that the boys from Ed's group are calling the shots and my boys are giving them the back-up muscle. The kids in Whittier were the first to get their professional attention."

"That's right," Harold Collins confirmed. "And I wish they would have taken their business someplace else."

"Have you had a chance to find out where they're getting the joints?" Jack asked.

"My boys say they got them from Cope and Sheppard at the school. Len's boys say the same thing," Ed Snell said.

With some embarrassment, but well controlled, Mr. Eagan entered the conversation. "I've talked with several of the teachers and everything I've learned points to Cope and Sheppard. I haven't had a chance to talk with them yet."

"Clarence, I know that Mr. Siple from Industrial Arts tried to reach you this morning," Jack said. "When he couldn't get you, he came by to see Mr. Graves. He says that Cope and Sheppard had a couple of cases of the stuff down in their basement room at the school. They gave Siple some weak story as to why they had them."

"How did Siple get into this?" Mr. Eagan asked with a note of consternation.

"Well, he heard from somebody that you had been talking with some of the teachers last night—you know how fast news travels . . . well, when he went down to the janitor's room this morning to get some cleaning fluid to use in Industrial Arts, he saw a couple of strange-looking cases. He lifted the lid on one of them and even though he didn't clearly see what was in it, he said half seriously and half kidding to Cope and Sheppard, 'You know, Mr. Eagan and Mr. Graves have been looking for this grass, so you fellows better own up to it and turn it in.' Well, this was enough to panic Cope and Sheppard; at least this is what Siple said. He said, 'Cope just froze and looked scared as hell, and Sheppard began to laugh, kind of out of control, and tried to make a big joke out of it.' Well, you know Siple; he played it for real—tapped the cases a couple of times with his foot and said, 'Seriously, I really feel you fellows ought to turn this stuff in.' After a long, uncomfortable pause, he picked up his cleaning fluid and walked out."

Len Hall affirmed, "That sure lines up with what our kids have told us."

The group was silent, and it appeared that a consensus was building up to declare Cope and Sheppard guilty. But before anyone could say it, Harold

Collins interjected, "My kids were fuzzy but they didn't bring in Cope and Sheppard. They said they thought that Len and Ed's boys were getting the stuff from the people who run the Tasty Diner down the road—that would be the Johnsons. They didn't name the Johnsons; they just said the people who run the diner."

"Well, it looks like Cope and Sheppard are in on this thing—in some way. What, if anything, the Johnsons are doing in this, we'll have to see," Jack recapitulated. "I've been in a few situations here—and you've been in them too—when the boys have singled out a staff member because they don't like his discipline or for some other reason have tried to get him fired. This could even be the case with Cope and Sheppard. I admit it doesn't look that way but I think we have to reserve judgment."

He paused while the men digested his words, then added, "So, unless there's more information on this, maybe Clarence can go ahead and talk with Mr. Graves, fill him in, and leave us to our cottage problems."

Mr. Eagan nodded his head in agreement and, before leaving, commented, "This is one job I'd be glad to let somebody else handle."

After Mr. Eagan had left, Jack apologized to the cottage supervisors. "I'm sorry to have had to turn you off a little earlier on your problems with the kids, but Mr. Graves needs to move ahead on tracking this thing down."

The discussion that followed focused on staff concern that decisions be made rapidly concerning the punishments that should meted out. The supervisors emphasized the need for immediate backup of initial actions taken in their respective cottages so that staff control would be maintained. They stressed to Jack the need to avoid waiting for formal disciplinary channels in the institution to take action. They also made clear to him the importance of fitting specific punishments to the offenses committed by the boys.

After the discussion ran its course, Jack summarized: "We seem to be in agreement on using a three-month restriction for the pushers and two for the users. I think the staff committee will go along with us on that. But I don't think we should wait for the committee to meet. Not if I judge your situation right, especially Len's."

Len, Ed, and Harold nodded their heads vigorously in agreement.

"All right, let's do that," Jack concurred. "I'll talk with Doc Barth, Clarence, and some of the others before the staff committee meets so that they understand what we're doing." Jack then shifted in his chair. "Now let's take a frank look at our programs."

Mr. Collins led off. "Along with improving our cottage program, I think the boys need better supervision at school."

"Jack, he's right," Mr. Hall emphasized. "I was over there the other day and the kids were all over the damn place. I think they ought to either be in their classrooms or going to the next one. But they're all over the hallways, loafing and smoking in the rest rooms, messing with the tools and equipment in Industrial Arts . . . it's a bad scene."

"I guess it's a little unfair to talk about this without Mr. Eagan," Mr. Snell observed, "but it's a real problem. That loose a situation can only encourage the deal that's been cooked up between the boys and Cope and Sheppard."

"You may have something," Jack agreed, "but until Mr. Eagan comes back let's keep our talk focused on the cottages. If Mr. Eagan doesn't get back to our meeting, I'll take it up with him. Or we can invite him to talk with us sometime during the next few days."

After a lengthy pause, Mr. Hall chuckled to cover his seriousness and said, "I won't dodge it any more. There's just not enough going on during the evenings and weekends. Not enough things planned for the kids to do. They're left on their own too much. We've got to face it. At least—that's my situation . . . sad but true."

"I think that kind of says it for the rest of us," Ed Snell seconded.

"That's not quite the case at Whittier," Mr. Collins differed. "I don't mean to come across as bragging, but I think we're in somewhat better shape than that. We've been working on our evening program pretty hard and I think we're making progress. We still need to tackle our weekend situation, though."

"What's the secret?" Len Hall asked, curiosity and envy in his question.

"I don't know if it's a secret," Mr. Collins replied. "Our big step ahead was to see that we had a problem and commit ourselves to doing something about it. After that, we proceeded to do two things. First, we set up a study hall. That runs for an hour—seven-thirty to eight-thirty—four nights a week. Most of our kids are like yours; they just aren't real students. They can really use the study time."

Aware that he was under scrutiny, Mr. Collins qualified his last statement. "At least, the *Whittier* boys can use the study. For most of our kids, it's probably their last really concentrated chance for schooling. It wasn't easy, of course, to get the kids to buy it, but we've been both firm and supportive with them and they're going along with the idea. And the staff are really pitching in as informal tutors. The teachers are seeing some real improvements in the boys' skills and attitudes. The second thing that we've added— and this we do with the boys—is to have a group activity for forty-five minutes to an hour following the study hour."

"Well, that sounds fine for your kids," Mr. Hall said bluntly. "Our boys are a little older and they're anything but students. They just aren't going to go for the study hall bit."

"I know what you mean," Mr. Snell agreed. "My boys aren't as much for the rough stuff as yours, but they aren't students by any definition or stretch of the imagination. I just don't believe we could get our boys to tolerate or use a study hall program."

"You may be right," Jack asserted. "You may be right. But where do you go from here? If not some type of study hall, *what* then?"

"I think we have to start hiring a different kind of evening man," Mr. Snell suggested. "It seems to me that we have two kinds. One kind is able but since this is his second job, his energy is low—and besides, he doesn't have any deep commitment to our place. You know that most of these fellows aren't going to be around longer than a year, if that long. The other kind of a man is one who is really too old to handle a job out in the public eye, so he comes and takes a job here where it's sheltered."

"I think your description is accurate," Jack agreed, "but I think we can do something about improving our hiring practices. First, I think we're filling our jobs in too much of a hurry. When a vacancy comes up in one of these evening-shift positions, we fill it with almost the first person who applies because our day-time staff objects to working the additional shift. Another thing—we haven't tapped the community college. An evening shift might interest some of the more mature students there."

"In the meantime, we have our problem," Mr. Hall said impatiently.

"Yes, we keep coming back to it," Jack chuckled. "And I'm convinced that we can do more about it than we're doing now."

"Honestly, Jack, I don't know where to go with it," Mr. Snell confessed.

Jack thought a moment, then looked at each man.

"Do you fellows think that your evening men could carry out a structured schedule of recreational activities if it was laid out for them and if they were supervised and given some help?" he asked.

"I think they could," Mr. Snell said.

Mr. Hall nodded his head.

"We need that, especially on weekends," Mr. Collins agreed.

"I suggest that we get in touch with Mr. Alderman, the recreation man at the school, and have him meet with us and the other unit supervisors," Jack said with enthusiasm. "Together I'm sure we can hammer out an overall recreation program. After that, Mr. Alderman can sit down with you and your relief people and help you plan out structured recreation programs appropriate to the needs of each of your cottages."

"That's a pretty big order for Alderman," Mr. Snell observed. "Do you think he can pull it off?"

"Sure," Jack reasoned, "and we're going to help him do it! I think we all have to make a commitment, however, to be sure that this thing works. Remember, Alderman isn't going to be doing it all by himself. Mr. Eagan, myself, and especially you have a big part to play in this program."

"Here I thought we were getting out of some work, but it looks like we're getting ourselves into more," Mr. Hall laughed.

"You've sized it up exactly right," Jack reaffirmed and joined Mr. Hall in a good-natured laugh. "In order for this thing to work, you're going to have to give it your full support and backing in addition to whatever specific program Alderman comes up with."

Jack was pleased that the issue of supervisors' responsibilities had come into the conversation directly. He had developed a nagging worry that perhaps the supervisors tended to place blame and responsibility on other staff while ducking their own.

With this concern before the group, Jack continued, "Along with working out the specific activities and making sure they come off, you've got to talk up the program among the boys. While you don't want to oversell it, you'll have to build up some real eagerness on their part to get involved. You'll have to let the kids know that you think it's important—you know, that you value it. Besides, you'll want to get some ideas from them about what they want to do. There are a lot of nitty-gritty things that will have to be done, including your being on the scene when the relief men get into their expanded roles. You'll want to be around without actually running the program for them."

Jack felt a need to further stress the responsibility issue, but one or two of the supervisors seemed uneasy.

A brief silence was broken by Len Hall.

"I think this should help. I really think it will. When will you see Clarence about getting Alderman involved?"

"If not this afternoon, then tomorrow morning," Jack replied. "As soon as I can."

After another moment of silence, Mr. Snell said, "That sort of covers it, doesn't it?"

Jack looked around the group, read agreement on their faces, and said, "Okay, let's break up for today. I'll be back in touch with you tomorrow on this evening and weekend program plan. In the meantime, I'd like to have you give some additional thought to your group meetings with the boys. These have done a lot for the units and we ought to be capitalizing on them now."

Jack shifted in his chair, serious and intent. "I'd like to make one final point before we break up our meeting. Don't forget *yourselves* in this operation. There's no one," he stressed, "*no one* who can take charge and make things run but you fellows." The men's faces reflected their pride. After a few moments, Jack nodded his head to reinforce the group's sense of cohesion and said, "Okay. I'll see you tomorrow."

Later that afternoon Jack stopped in to see Mr. Graves, who laughingly asked him, "You haven't decided to go into detective work after this experience, have you?"

"I'm afraid not," Jack retorted, smiling. "As a matter of fact, I'll be mighty glad when it's over and settled. On the positive side, though, it's pushing us to improve our program—which I'll admit to you we probably wouldn't have done if it hadn't been for the marijuana jolt."

After describing in some detail the discussion he had had with the cottage supervisors particularly the plan to use Alderman, Jack asked, "How are things developing with Cope and Sheppard?"

"They're on their way over here now," Mr. Graves answered coldly. "I'm trying to keep an open mind. That's about all that's happened. Getting back to the cottage situation, I'm for the idea of using Alderman. You know, this will have to be handled carefully. Mr. Eagan and Mr. Alderman will both have to *want* this change to succeed or we may have real trouble making it work, even getting it off the ground. Mr. Eagan is going to have to juggle his school phys. ed. program around and . . ." Mr. Graves' expression changed slightly as he switched to another train of thought. "Since we've got two departments involved here—the cottages and the school—I feel this is one in which I should help. Understand, I'm not taking anything from you, but it might be a little easier if I got into the act. Candidly, what you're talking about is a full-time job. To transfer Alderman will take some doing."

Jack nodded. "I get your point."

Mr. Graves continued, "I don't want Clarence to hear about this from anybody but us. He could have some angry feelings about losing Alderman suddenly. Don't get me wrong, Clarence is cooperative and all that, but he's worked hard to build up that phys. ed. program. If the budget holds up, I can give Clarence a bit more money and he probably can come up with a replacement for Alderman. Anyhow, I'll need to sweeten the pot for both Clarence and Alderman."

"Right," Jack agreed. Mr. Graves had adopted a distracted expression. Sensing he wanted to be alone, Jack stood up to leave. "I need to make a few phone calls," he said. "I'll be back in an hour or so."

Mr. Graves gestured vaguely in farewell.

Two hours later Jack returned, sure that the meeting with Cope and Sheppard had ended. But he was surprised to see Mr. Eagan in the office conversing with Mr. Graves. As Jack entered the room, Mr. Eagan looked at him over his shoulder and said, "One thing about you fellows in the living unit business—you can spot a good man when you see one."

Accustomed to Mr. Eagan's humor, which often mixed sarcasm with friendly openness, Jack responded evenly, "No doubt about it. We have a big problem and I think Alderman can help us with it."

"Are you sure you're not staking too much on Alderman?" Mr. Eagan asked. "He's good, but I don't think he's got the background to do all that you're expecting him to accomplish."

"I don't think so," Jack said slowly. "We know that developing a useful rec program is a tough problem and that the basic job still has to be managed by the cottage supervisors. I pointed this out to Snell, Collins, Hall, and the others in our meeting earlier this afternoon. But Alderman can give us the leadership to mobilize on the recreation front and the momentum to get a program going that we need right now."

"What you say makes me feel a little better," Mr. Eagan replied. "But I sense some wishful thinking on your part."

Jack parried the comment with a slight shrug. "We'll have to keep a check on ourselves if that's the case."

Mr. Eagan turned back to the initial problem. "Assuming that Mr. Alderman wants this job, do you have a fair trade so I can keep the phys. ed. classes going?"

"I think Mr. Graves may be able to help us on the replacement problem—that is, if the budget can take it," Jack explained, turning to the superintendant.

"The budget will support a raise for Alderman and a replacement for him," Mr. Graves assured. "Clarence has okayed our recruiting Mr. Alderman. So, Jack, it will be your responsibility to work out the job description. I'd like to have it by lunchtime."

"That sounds fine to me," Jack added. "Before we leave, can you tell us how you came out with Cope and Sheppard?"

Mr. Graves frowned. "Well, I confronted them with what we know and asked them for information that would throw some more light on the situation, especially their part in it. They wouldn't talk—wouldn't say a thing. They just shrugged their shoulders from time to time. That went on for about ten or fifteen minutes. When I saw I wasn't going to get anywhere with that tactic, I changed my pitch and said that they had two choices: they could either go on administrative leave and come under investigation, or they could resign and we would let them go on their way without any investigation. Well, they jumped at the chance to resign! So I got them to sign the resignation forms and then asked them to leave the grounds immediately. They're gone."

"That was fast," Jack commented drily.

"There's another chapter in this story," Mr. Graves continued. "After the cottage supervisors began to bear down on the kids, it seems that they got in touch with Cope and Sheppard and told them that the heat was on. So when Cope and Sheppard came in to see me, they were scared but they had already worked out their strategy for keeping their mouths shut."

"How did you find out that the kids got to Cope and Sheppard?" Jack asked.

"Len Hall called and told me so," Mr. Graves said, then muttered half to himself, "Nobody planned that it would go quite this way but it did. I probably should have had them investigated, but I was so glad to get rid of them and get on with putting our program back together than I may have taken the easy way out."

"I think it's more important that we focus totally on shaping up our program," Jack asserted.

Mr. Graves nodded, then rose to indicate the meeting had ended. "Please keep this matter confidential. Of course, we don't know yet how this will come out, so I'd like to keep it as quiet as possible for obvious reasons. There's no advantage in getting people all excited."

Mr. Eagan and Jack nodded gravely and left.

After the two men left, Mr. Graves sat down at his cluttered desk and stared at it without seeing the books and papers piled before him. His anxiety over the marijuana situation had been substituted with reassuring thoughts. The programs and personnel, Mr. Graves reflected, had surely come a long, long way. The staff understood, or at least tried to understand the boys and worked with them in therapeutic ways. It was immensely satisfying to realize this major accomplishment had come about with his help and direction.

Mr. Graves was jolted from reflection by the ring of his telephone and by Thelma's scratchy voice. "Phil Trencher, Special Assistant to the Lieutenant Governor is calling about the dismissal of Sheppard and Cope."

A phone call from the Lieutenant Governor's office on such a matter struck Mr. Graves as highly unusual. He thought that a routine check might be made by the Civil Service Commission because of the suddenness of the mens' resignations. The forms were in order, showing the same date as their resignation, whereas for long-term employees these forms were filed in advance, along with requests for authority to fill the vacancies.

After taking a moment to compose himself, he answered the phone.

"Graves here!"

This brief salutation was interrupted by a gruff, aggressive voice. "This is Phil Trencher, Special Assistant to the Lieutenant Governor."

"Yes," Mr. Graves acknowledged. "What can we do for you?"

"We're pretty concerned up here about your handling of two long-term employees of the State, Mr. Sheppard and Mr. Cope."

"Let me assure you that I am concerned too," Mr. Graves said firmly, "but on a different basis than you—"

Phil Trencher interrupted abruptly. "With a combined service of twenty-seven years, your summary dismissal or forcing of their resignations is hardly the way to deal with hard-working men who, after all, have not only given a great, great deal of time to the State, but are family men and responsible persons in the community!"

As Mr. Trencher dictated his case, Mr. Graves' initial anxiety turned to anger and indignation. He hastened to control it. When Mr. Trencher climaxed his orders with, "So we would like to hear from you about this," Mr. Graves was able to respond coolly.

"It's strange that you should take this position," he said calmly. "There must be some error. We have clear and firm evidence that both men were peddling marijuana to the kids."

"That's not the information we have up here," Mr. Trencher snapped. "To the contrary, both Mr. Cope and Mr. Sheppard have stated that the charges were trumped up! That if the kids were getting marijuana, they were getting it from other sources."

Mr. Graves' retort was crisp. "Not only do the kids consistently say they got the stuff from those two fellows, but one of our teachers got a look at a box full of the stuff in the janitor's room at the school. What's more, Cope and Sheppard were right there when he called the box to their attention—and that's just a part of the evidence."

Mr. Trencher was quiet for several moments. When he began again, his words held a mildly concilliatory tone, and he stumbled a little at first. "Well . . . the story we've gotten here is quite different, and . . . we'll have to check into this." Seeming to recover somewhat, Mr. Trencher returned to his former abrasive tone, "But are you sure about your evidence?"

"Very sure," Mr. Graves responded confidently,"—even have it documented."

"God, Graves, these men have given years of good service! They are respected men in the community and you're simply turning them out!"

"I don't think I'm making the matter clear to you," Mr. Graves said concisely. "We cannot tolerate such behavior." Then he chuckled mildly. "You fellows up there wouldn't really want it any different. As a matter of fact, if I hadn't acted as I did, I would have expected a phone call from you or someone else up at the State House, a call on behalf of the boys."

Mr. Trencher seemed to have no other argument in favor of the custodians, and he reiterated, "These are responsible men in the community and they've served the State a long time—and have served it faithfully."

After a pause, Mr. Graves said carefully, yet with a note of finality, "That's simply not enough."

Mr. Trencher would not be moved. "Look, we've talked this thing over up here and we urge you to put Cope and Sheppard back on. Do it any way that you like, but get them back on!"

Mr. Graves replied, "Mr. Trencher, I can't do that and I think you know why. It's just out of the question."

"Look, Graves, you either find a way to put those men back on—and I mean *today*—or you'll have to answer to somebody else up here!"

Though Mr. Graves felt the tendons in his neck tighten and perspiration dampen on his forehead, he maintained his control. "And who will that be?"

"You keep taking that stance and you'll find out soon," Mr. Trencher threatened.

"I'm sorry," Mr. Graves said firmly, "but my position on Cope and Sheppard is firm. I will not risk the consequences of putting them back on the payroll. It would take a written directive from the Lieutenant Governor or the Governor to bring them back. Even then, you understand, I'd have to take it up with the Civil Service Commission because I'm not going to change my mind." Mr. Graves, calm now in his conviction, added quietly, "I'm filing a report with the Commission on my course of action. Would you like me to send you a carbon?"

"I told you son-of-a-bitch what you have to do! So don't give me all this crap. Either you decide to put those two men back on the payroll today or the finger will be on you."

Mr. Graves had no intention of responding, but he heard the receiver slam down with angry finality.

Wakened by the hall clock in his home as it struck five a.m., Mr. Graves, who had been sleeping only occasionally since he retired at eleven, got up and walked into the living room. An aura of an enveloping danger pervaded the house and Mr. Graves sensed that the danger pervaded all of Central State.

5

SEMINAR FOR LUNCH

"Every time a new kid comes onto the unit, especially if he looks a little scared, I have one devil of a time keeping the other kids from taking his measure," Len Hall complained. "I've been working on getting them to help new kids adjust, but I'm afraid I haven't gotten very far. In fact, I know I haven't."

"I have the same thing going on in my cottage," Harold Collins added, seeming relieved to find someone with whom he might share his concern. "I don't know what gets into these kids. You'd think they would remember how *they* felt when they came into this place. You'd think they'd try to make it a little easier for the next guy. But it seems to me they do just the opposite."

"Well, I *was* having a fairly light-hearted lunch," Jack joked, "until you fellows brought this problem up. But as long as we're talking about it, I don't know of a more interesting one. How about you, Dave, Al, Fred—how does this kind of thing run in your units?"

"I haven't been able to lick it," Dave Huberts admitted. "We always seem to have it going on, no matter what. It's the way the boys do things. They promote it. I had a bad, bad situation last week." He stopped, rubbed his chin, and continued, "Well, I'm not sure it was *all* bad. In fact, as I think it over, I'm beginning to wonder if maybe it wasn't such a bad situation." He chuckled.

"Anyway, it all started last week when Elton Green came into the cottage. I don't think you've had a chance to get to know this kid. He came onto the unit looking a little shook up. You know, like most kids when they first come in, bewildered. Well, I got him checked in, introduced around, and then we went to lunch.

" 'Course, the lunch period gave him exposure to the whole group. The boys crowded around him wanting to know where he was from, who he knew, and I suppose whether he had any cigarettes—the usual questions. After lunch the kids gathered outside the cottage. I went into the building for a few minutes—it couldn't have been longer than ten minutes—and when I came out I heard the damnedest yelling coming from a bunch of kids crowded around a couple of kids in the middle, who I soon found out were Green and Resnick. Resnick, as you probably know, is a real husky and a bullying type who only takes somebody on when he's absolutely sure he'll come out the winner."

"Green, being new and looking a little shaky, made him look like a real setup," Jack suggested.

Dave nodded. "I pushed through the crowd and found Resnick and Green squared off against each other. I didn't see anything wrong with Green, but Resnick had blood running out of his nose and down over his mouth, and one of his eyes was really puffed up!"

He chuckled, rubbing his face. "I hate to admit it, but it's true—I really enjoyed seeing what I saw, and though I knew I had to stop it, I really hated stepping in."

"Right on!" Len laughed, voicing the sentiments of the group, who followed Dave's story with a vicarious sense of enjoyment.

Laughing, Dave continued, "I did run in and break it up, and then I took the two boys into the washroom and told them to get cleaned up."

"I'd like to have a couple of Greens come onto my unit and beat the tar out of a few Resnick types that I've got," Len Hall broke in. "Dave, I'd say you've got a real winner in this Green kid!"

"Wait just a minute," Jack interjected with a raised hand and a smile. "What kind of talk is this—getting one kid to beat up another?"

"Now Jack, you know these kids put pressure on each other," Len said. "I think Green was putting on the right kind. He was an 'equalizer,' one might say."

"I know, I know." Jack agreed heartily. "But you know that when you encourage one kid to hit another kid, you're just perpetrating this cycle where the biggest bully becomes the leader. I tell you it's self-defeating!"

"Jack, you've pointed out again and again that when a new kid comes into a cottage, the others will test him," Len countered. "It's a part of what the kids and their peer groups push."

"Okay," Jack agreed, "the kids will test one another. But what I'm suggesting is that we focus on getting the kids to do their testing of one another in ways other than fighting."

Al Sears moved forward in his chair, eager to enter the conversation. Supervisor of Concord Cottage, he was an easy-going, intellectual man in spite of his limited education, who tended to be cynical. "Jack, even if we could get them to give up fighting and bullying, they'd just give more attention to bragging about how many broads they've laid. Would that be any better?"

"And don't forget their bragging about who has pulled the biggest or the fastest deal," Len reminded them. "You know, the con-man stuff and the outright stealing."

"Okay, okay, have your fun," Jack said amiably. "But after that, there are better ways for the kids to find their place in a cottage than fighting and bragging about their sexual or stealing exploits."

"Jack, if I'm reading you right," Len complained agreeably, "you're not quite putting us down but giving us a rough time."

"Well, I don't know about that," Jack said thoughtfully. "Let's take a look at the bigger picture: for example, the boys' own self-generated groups— you might even call some of them gangs—and how they promote the rough stuff in testing new boys. Roughing up newcomers is a part of their code—but you've got to find a way to work with these groups without giving over control to them."

"I think it's more a matter of individuals," Al interrupted. "You've got to approach them one at a time, especially on the sex thing. Besides, I figure they're just bragging."

"That's right," Len concurred. "I think their talk is really built up because they think it's manly. There's no way the other kids can know what the others *really* did back home. Remember all the stories that little Chester Hine was spreading about all the girls he'd made it with and then it turned out he hadn't even had any experience!"

Hearty laughter broke out, punctuated by shouts of "Let's keep it clean!" and "Here, Here!"

When the laughter died down, Len Hall said, "When I said 'that's right' a moment ago, I meant I agreed with Al on the bragging, but I don't agree with him that our approach to the kids' problems should be limited to working with individuals."

"Good point," Jack agreed. "Our approach has to be broader than that. Take Green, for example. I don't know what he's learned since he left the Intake Office in Administration, but from what you've told me he certainly has learned that when he's challenged, he'd better fight. We've got to work on our own programs so Green's life here will be better than that, and to do that we have to work with the boys' groups."

"I'll buy that," Al agreed. "But on very personal things you've got to go one-on-one."

Jack had no more than nodded his head when Len cut in. "My boys fight for position. I have more fighting going on than I think is good. Frankly, as I see it, much of it involves the boys' shifting around and jockeying for position and power when they come into the cottage or leave it. For example, when a boy comes in, room has to be made for him, and it's usually at the very bottom. The way I see it, those slots or rungs on the group's ladder are tied together. And when kids go on parole, that also opens up slots and encourages this jockeying for position. The boys on the scene have a vested interest in where a new guy is going to end up in relation to themselves. So they manipulate things with a push and a shove that can get pretty rough. But I don't mean to say that everybody in the group will be against the new kid. Maybe, for example, a certain clique of boys somewhere up the scale may see a new boy as being an asset to them. They may immediately include him in with them and no special pressure gets generated, at least no fighting."

"What you've said makes a lot of sense," Jack interrupted adroitly to pursue another point. "But I think you're leaving out an important part. Kids are more likely to be accepted as they come into the cottage when you and your staff *are really in touch with your kids*—when you're with them and they're with you."

"I agree with you one hundred percent," Len acknowledged. "But to be honest, Jack, you know we're not always in that kind of touch—and it gets awfully rough at times."

"We go through that rough stuff at intake, time and again. Right now, though, we're in pretty good shape." Fred Haynes moved into the conversation. "We go over our 'plays' for welcoming new kids just before each new boy comes in, just as routinely as a pro football team runs its special plays for the final two minutes of a game. But what I want to say is that we have real troubles at parole time and, as Len said, some of those troubles come as a result of the shifting that goes on with kids leaving positions in the cottage setup."

"You know, Doc Barth says the trouble at parole time comes from the boys who are going to stay being uptight because they can't return home," Len Hall explained. "What's more, he says they may be upset because they have to face up to the inadequacy of their homes, or they may feel shook up because they have to admit their lack of improvement here."

"I think those things do come into play in some cases," Jack said. "But in my opinion, they have been heavily overplayed. I'd suggest you check out the situation in your own cottage before you start blaming whatever may be brewing with the kids on their personal disturbances."

"Jack, you're making life hard today," Len joked. "Don't you know that with that kind of talk you're pulling the rug right out from under us—at least from under me?"

"How do you figure that?" Jack asked quickly.

"I've been using that emotional disturbance thing for a long time," Len jested. "Now what you're saying is I'll have to admit that how they react to new kids is related to the way they're organized or disorganized as a group. That means I've got to do some work with my boys. Otherwise, I could always plead sending them to their social worker!"

"Well, I don't know about your reasoning there, Len," Jack said lightly. "Seems to me there's work for the supervisors irrespective of how you figure a given kid's behavior."

"Yeah," Len acknowledged, serious now. "It's a funny thing though. When somebody, especially one of the psychologists or psychiatrists, says that a psychological problem is involved, just his putting that definition on the kid's behavior makes people think the kid's got a disease or something. And once a kid has a disease label on him, people see him as being less responsible, and what's more, they see the units as being less able to do anything to help him!"

"I know exactly what you mean," Fred Haynes added gravely.

Mr. Sears' mood mirrored Fred's seriousness. "There are real complications in putting a psychological tag on a kid. For example, after the initial easing of responsibility for the kid and you have to face up to managing him. Now, with the sick label on him—adolescent adjustment reaction, emotional disturbance, depression, acute schizophrenia, or whatever—you're expected to be exceptionally nice to him, expect less of him, and even excuse him from doing the most ordinary everyday chores."

"And then the crazy kid's behavior begins to spread through your cottage like an epidemic of measles because the other kids figure that what's working for him should word for them too," Fred added ironically.

"When we began talking about this, I thought I knew where I stood," Dave said candidly. "Now I'm not so sure. For example, I've been thinking that it's good to keep the expectations up across the board, that if you let them down you're not only going to have a harder time running your unit, but you aren't going to be doing the kids any good either. For the ones who are especially delinquent, it would only give them license to practice their skills. For those who are actually *psychologically* sick, it would encourage them to indulge themselves in their problems and probably cause them to slip further into their illness, firm up their symptoms, and what have you."

"I don't mean to cut Dave off, but let's get back to the problems concerning how the kids organize themselves in the cottages," Len suggested.

The group seemed to be in agreement, but looked to Jack for direction. "What's your pleasure? It's your lunch hour," he asked.

"I'd like to shift," Dave volunteered, following several moments of indecision in the group. His comment brought a nod of heads from the others.

"They sure are organized in my cottage," he continued. "I don't understand how they work it out, but I can usually tell you who the leader of the gang or clique is, who his lieutenants are, who's next in line, who's on the bottom of the stack, who's unattached to any part of the group. Sometimes they get themselves organized so tightly they're like the Mafia. Really. Sometimes I feel like I'm dealing with the underworld . . . at least a world very different from the one I live in. While we're interested in having them work toward real change, they are against it and resist it. While we want them to be honest, hard working, get a good education, respect other people's rights including their property, and so on, the boys' Mafia is just not interested in those things. While we push being clean, well groomed, and orderly, that runs against their grain. And then we want them to have good manners, at least reasonably good manners, but they're not about to buy that, except when they can use them to manipulate or fool somebody."

"Dave, you can't make Boy Scouts out of these guys!" Len interrupted.

"You can kid all you want to," Dave said vigorously, "but I'll bet fifty cents that you're struggling against a well-organized gang of kids whose interests are a long, long way from your aims or hopes for them!"

As Len was about to respond, John Waldo, a new night supervisor, broke in. "I've been listening to all this and I don't like what I'm hearing, not at all, especially this last stuff. Why, the way Dave and Len have been talking, it seems to me that they see these kids as something less than human beings, or if they see them as human beings, they don't respect them very much!"

Waldo's words drove a bolt of tension into the group, until Jack countered it with an easy chuckle. "John, I'm sure you feel strongly about the dignity of the boys, and I believe Len and Dave do too. We have to begin on that ground."

Although Len seemed on the verge of an argument, Jack pressed on. "If I may put words into Len's mouth, he sizes up the kids as delinquent, but he still likes and respects them as human beings."

"Right," Len cut in briskly. "If I were to improve your point, Jack, I'd say that because they've had their troubles and are delinquent, it makes me feel even more strongly about my responsibility to deal with them in a very human way, but not naively! The main thing I was trying to say was that the kids have their own philosophy about how to get along in the world and about what is important to them. They never talk about it that way—they don't use that kind of language—but that's what it is."

"How do you *know* the kids have their own philosophy?" Dave challenged.

"By sitting down and talking with the boys, and watching them," Len answered quickly and with force. "My God, man, if you're working in a cottage and look at what's going on around you, you can't miss it!"

"Yeah, I know," Dave responded. "But how do you get such a clear sense of their philosophy from what they say? That's what I want to know more about."

"I don't do anything different from what you do. I talk with the boys, listen to them, and watch them. It's just putting together all of the information I collect. So I guess the impressions that stick with me come out of my own sifting and sorting—nothing more, nothing less."

"Dave, you've seen what Len's talking about," Harold Collins entered the exchange. "You can't deny that. I see it in Whittier by watching who gathers around who. Who's passing the word around about what's happening. Who starts things—and that ranges from giving someone a bad time to saying when everybody should line up to go to supper."

"My boys behave about the same way," Dave added. "I get a lot out of the tone of voice they use with one another. It gives me a good idea as to who is talking up the ladder of command and who is talking down. But I was asking more about how you get at their philosophy than how they're organized."

"They're not unconnected," Len told him. "But I may have been talking beyond what I really know. By philosophy I meant how the boys look at things, how they spend their time, how they feel about different people, what they value. Now, as to how I really get there, I'm not sure."

Stimulated by the discussion, Fred encouraged Len to elaborate.

"Nothing like getting myself in too deep," Len said, slightly apprehensive but with a hint of professional pride. "Well, when a boy first comes in, he talks with the social worker and the psychiatrist, and the psychologist tests him. This usually loosens him up a little and gets him to thinking about his future, at least a little, because they are planning his schedule for him. So, as I have a chance—and I don't do it with every boy—I ask him what his plans are, you know, down the road maybe two or three years from now. I try to learn how he sees school and work, how he sees the future, what kind of a life he wants to lead."

"Len, you sound like you're giving another Doc Barth or social work talk," Harold chided good-naturedly.

"If I am, it's a lousy one," Len laughed, embarrassed. "I don't really interview the boys. I'm around them. So, besides my questions, they tell me a lot of things just naturally because I'm there and will listen. They'll show me letters. There's no use in me talking about this; you all go through the same thing."

Jack interrupted after glancing at his watch. "For the fifteen minutes or so before we go back to work, let's take another look at the boys' organization," he suggested. "For example, what gives a boy prestige or high status in his group? What do the groups value? I think we got into this before but it wasn't really clear."

"I think it's pretty much the same in all the cottages," Harold Collins said. "Now take my boys; they're the more shy, withdrawn, immature types. Yet I'll bet that on behavior that scores points for status and leadership, they're much like Len's boys—for pushing toughness, for being able to make whatever they say stick. So I'd say they really believe in being able to hold and wield power. That's really Doc's language, so I can't claim it. But it sounds right and I like it. And my boys are a lot like Ed Snell's boys—and I'm sorry he isn't here to say what he thinks—but my kids, like Ed's boys, put a premium on manipulating other people, on fooling them. And the third thing that my boys put a premium on is sex."

Everyone laughed.

"That's important to almost anybody," Len joked, "but not with your boys. They're hardly studs!"

"You'd be surprised," Harold countered mildly, "especially if you ever heard my boys talk about their one-night stands!"

"You can't believe that," Dave asserted with a grin.

"I don't," Harold assured him. "That's not the point. The point is that it's important to them."

Jack hurriedly summed up the issue. "Then it looks like toughness, the ability to be manipulative, and sexual experience are the main things that get a boy ahead here at Central State."

After a pause, Len Hall, seemingly speaking for the group, agreed. "It's not an ideal picture, but I think it's accurate, Jack."

Jack wearily rubbed his face. "We've got a lot of work to do."

Discouragement gripped the group—even Len, whose optimism usually persisted in difficult situations, vocalized it. "Add to that picture the fact that the boy's groups are pitted against the staff and you begin to see how grim it really is."

John Waldo, having listened unobtrusively for several minutes, regained a foothold in the discussion. "I can see your ideas better now. I think the reason we get discouraged about the boys is because we lack confidence in them—call it lack of respect for their dignity or whatever. The main point is that without that, we can't help but come to a sad end of the line, an end without very much hope of change."

The intensity of the group's concentration had made them oblivious to the fact that the dining room was empty now, as both boys and staff had completed the after-lunch cleanup chores and returned to their cottages and places of work.

In attempting to handle the group's mixture of discouragement and frustration and steer them back to the issue at hand, Jack observed, "There are also a number of *good* things in the picture we've been painting. But I'd like to stay with the particular problems that come out of the boys' self-made groups or gangs. They are real ones so let's not dodge them. Have the group meetings with the boys helped any with these problems? They're tough—the problems—but I don't think we have to go to the wailing wall."

A tone of reservation rang through Len's voice as he answered, "I'm finding that as I bring more things out into the open and talk with the boys, whether it's in group meetings or in some other way, it's cutting down on the tightness of the boys' organization and isn't really solving all of the problems.

But the talk, especially in our meetings, does bring the problems out in the open."

"That's true at Whittier, too," Harold seconded. "In addition to talking about problems openly, I try to feed the boys information about what's coming up in the program and what's going on in general as much as I can. This seems to break up some of their tightness and secrecy as a peer group. I'm having less trouble with rumors and gossip now. The group meetings are good as a means of letting them talk about things out in the open that they used to think they had to keep among themselves."

Al, intent on contributing, broke in with another point. "I agree that keeping in touch with the boys and letting them have more say in things helps the staff and boys to get closer to one another and helps each trust the other a little more. But I don't know how much it really influences the thing Len was calling their way of thinking about things and their way of doing things."

"There's a lot in what Al says," Dave supported, "and I think we're all in the same kettle of fish. Doc makes the point that we've opened up the channels of communication through these group meetings. Okay, so we've gotten together with our boys and some of the talk has been pretty useful. But I don't know that it has really *changed* anybody. I know it's improved the way I run my unit. I feel better about my work and the unit. I think the kids would say the meetings have been helpful, too. They've become a part of more things. They've been told a lot of things that they were never in on before. They've become involved in planning the program for the unit and all that. But when it gets right down to it, many of them still figure they haven't got a ghost of a chance in making it *when they leave here.* So they continue to figure on making it by stealing and they say so. Most of them talk about some hustle or racket, but by and large it's stealing."

"I think you're too pessimistic," Al challenged. "That is, if I'm reading you right, you're overlooking your own good work. It takes *time* to help these boys toward change. I don't know what all of this talking you're doing will actually come to. At least you have some problems—such as stealing, which is a very real one—right out on the table where you can get at it."

"That's what the Doc says," Harold said. "I don't agree with him. I think there's a real possibility that it'll turn out that what we're doing is conducting meetings on the philosophy of stealing and even how to do it!"

"If that's what you think, then you ought to be telling the Doc so," Jack suggested. "And the kids, too. There's nothing wrong with speaking directly."

"I have," Harold replied. "I've talked with Doc."

"And what does he say?"

"He says I shouldn't worry about it," Harold said with a shrug. "He thinks it's important that the kids are talking this way. And he pushes me to make it clear to the kids that my permission to let them talk about stealing doesn't mean that I *approve* of their stealing or that I encourage it in the future."

"Is that all he says?" Len asked.

"Not quite. What he recommends is that I give them a full chance to talk these things over. Then what's supposed to happen is that some of the kids in the group will challenge some of this slick talk. That hasn't happened yet, but Doc is optimistic that it will. In the meantime, though, I'm doing some questioning," Harold explained. "For instance I say, 'Let's think this through,' or 'I think there are some other parts to this stealing puzzle that you're leaving out,' or 'Is it really as easy as all that?' I watch myself closely because I don't want to get into an argument with the boys. Not that I mind arguing with them, but if we turn these sessions into arguments, there will be bad feelings and the meetings will have lost their purpose of giving the kids a chance to think through and hopefully consider alternatives to their delinquency. So this is where we are right now with them."

"What are you worrying about?" Len asked. "You know you had this kind of talking going on in the unit before, but you weren't in on it."

"I don't think there was as much of it going on," Harold objected. "I really don't."

"I'm a long way from your meetings, but I think you may be overly concerned," Len reassured him.

"Well, I've been holding out on you a little," Harold said, now with obvious anxiety. "Stealing has gone *up* in the cottage since we got involved in this whole thing."

Jack looked around the quiet group.

"What are the kids stealing?" Dave asked.

"One another's clothes," Harold said, hesitant with embarrassment. "Recently the parents of one of the kids left him a couple of model planes on visiting day. They've disappeared. Then a couple of the boys had nice sport shirts and they're missing. All of this bothers me." He rubbed his head and continued, "I've had one devil of a time trying to get the kids to talk about what's involved in their stealing—especially such things as gaps in our program, their earlier lives, how they see themselves, or whatever. The kids won't get into this because they won't or can't think that way. Oh, they'll blame people and make excuses, but they won't really think it through. And in the meantime, stealing is getting worse in the cottage."

"Could they be playing games with you?" Jack wondered. "What I mean is, are they testing to see if you'll be more tolerant about actual stealing around the unit because you're being tolerant and even pushing them to talk about stealing in the meetings?"

"I don't think so," Harold replied thoughtfully. "I don't tolerate stealing in the cottage. I punish them for it. I think all the talk is exciting them and making stealing one of their main activities. . . . I've set a deadline in my mind. I'll go along for another two or three weeks with this open-talk thing.

If I don't get things settled down in my unit by then, I'm going to shut down the group meeting talk on stealing."

"As long as your kids know where you stand on the stealing, and since you feel they aren't playing games with you in these two quite different situations, why stop the talk on stealing as long as it's serious talk?" Len asked. "It seems to me you're doing right. You tell them that they can't steal in real life, like in your cottage. Then you go on to say that since stealing has been a real problem for them in the past, and some of them at least are planning on stealing in the future, it needs to be talked about. It seems to me you're right on target!"

"It's pretty plain to me, but I guess I'm not making it plain for you," Harold said with annoyance. "It's because I don't think we're *solving* anything. Instead, I think we're *promoting* or at least stimulating stealing. So I'm for stopping it. As I said before, I'm going to shut down on talk about stealing soon unless I get some results."

Noticing Harold's growing irritation, Jack pursued his interest in Doc Barth's counsel to Mr. Collins. "Harold, I'm not asking you to repeat anything that you've already told us about the Doc's suggestions to you, but I would appreciate hearing anything else he may have said about this problem."

"He's always very much interested in what happens in these meetings. You know—he wants to learn what the kids are saying, how they're saying it, what I think it means, and stuff like that. He doesn't want to tell me what to do—Doc's not the bossy type. But you know he's committed to a talking approach—getting the important issues out in the open with the kids."

"It doesn't sound as though he's worried," Jack asserted to encourage Harold as well as to quell his own anxiety about the stealing. "But does he feel you're on course?"

"You're right," Harold responded thoughtfully. "The Doc's not worried. He thinks what I'm doing is useful. He figures the problem of kids stealing in my cottage is a part of what he calls their 'talking and working-through business.' When I asked him what he meant by that, he said, 'getting the kids to talk their problems through to solution.' When I push him harder to explain, he says that by 'working through,' he means we should expect some stealing from the kids while we're talking with them—that is, if stealing is really a big thing with them. Then he says we've got to work it out with them. Try to understand why they do it. Try to help *them* understand why they do it. Try to get them to stop it." Harold paused, then concluded, "All around, the Doc is a real practical man. But on this one, I'd say he's too hung up on theory."

Len asked skeptically, "Have you told *him* that?"

"Yes, I've told him." Harold said to everyone's surprise, because the staff generally deferred to Doc Barth. "We get along real fine. There's one thing about this business—you've got to be honest or you're sure going to get tripped up. The Doc is funny: when I tell him he's being too idealistic, he just chuckles and that's about all there is to it."

"Well, think it over," Jack suggested. "I'd like to see you continue to work with this stealing problem a while longer, doing just what you've been doing."

The conversation had reached another low point.

"This whole thing that Harold has been telling us is interesting," Len said, "but what's all of this got to do with the boys' organization?"

"Well, for one thing, their groups are likely calling the shots on the stealing that's going on now," Harold suggested. "Another thing is that the boys get together before the meetings to decide what should be talked about. In other words, the "in" group decides how the meeting should go and what should be brought up and by whom. So for awhile there wasn't what you might call much off-the-cuff, free discussion going on. In some ways it reminded me of the union-management negotiation sessions I used to sit in on back at the plant!"

Harold smiled weakly at the chuckles his analogy aroused. "But back to the boys. Early on, the leaders really controlled the meetings—by frowning, moving their eyes around, and other tips. They actually controlled who could talk. At the time it upset me; I didn't understand what was going on. I only figured it out later. But we've moved through most of that and things have loosened up a little."

"My impression," Jack interjected, "is that the meetings are really quite effective, and getting better. Besides loosening up the kids, I'd say you've probably loosened up the boys' tight organization. Then too, the kids are bringing their peer-group business into your sessions, so you can get at them there."

In Harold's next response Jack recognized the man's tendency to criticize his own work.

"Like I said earlier, though, I don't see how this is changing the kids' outlooks, their delinquent patterns. They still see themselves as getting the short end of the stick. They even figure that way about their winding up here, even though they admit that they've been in trouble over and over again. They figure that nobody will give them a chance and that the whole setup is rigged against them. So they say they've got to hang on to their lifestyle in order to beat the 'system.' I don't quite know what the system is, but it's the word they keep using. When I push them for what they mean, they name everybody: the judge, the court, probation officers, teachers, police—every part of the establishment that butts into their lives. But they never mention their parents."

"But you know Harold," Jack interrupted, "that if the boys feel they've gotten the short end of the stick and are planning to keep on with their stealing careers when they leave here, they're telling us 'where their heads are at.' It's the substance you've got to work with."

"It's a pretty sad picture," Harold said grimly and shifted in his chair uneasily. "It's a pretty sad picture."

"Obviously, the problem is quite grim," Jack acknowledged. "You don't want to forget, however, that you're right in the middle of trying to do something with these kids, *really* do something with them. I sure would like to see you keep going on it, in spite of the trouble and headaches. The easiest and safest thing in the world for us would be to call a halt to the effort, and we could find some good reasons to justify that action. But I would like to see us keep on trying to develop effective ways of helping these kids."

"Harold, my hat's off to you," Len said heartily. "I've had some of the same problems that you've had, and some I haven't. I'd like to tell you about some that I've had and especially those I still have, but I suppose that if we're going to make it back to set up for the boys coming back from school, we'd better break off for now."

"The time has really gotten away from us," Dave exclaimed. "This has been an incredible meeting, but I've got to cut loose."

"Okay," Jack affirmed. "With lunch as a natural time to get together, we'll have an opportunity to talk more about these things soon."

John Waldo took a deep breath and was about to say something when Len broke in and in good humor assured him, "You're right. Respecting the boys is important!"

The men, including John, broke into a hearty laugh and headed back to their cottages.

6

WHAT MAKES RICK RUN?

Jack had come back to the office to pick up some case records for review in the staff committee meeting the next morning, when the telephone rang. He picked up the receiver, wondering who would be calling at this time of the evening, but hadn't even finished saying hello when the caller said, "I saw the light in your office and hoped you'd be in." The voice, pitched high and intense, identified itself. "This is Bill Wellman over at Lexington Cottage."

"Hi, Bill," Jack said. "What can I do for you?"

"Do you have a minute? I want to talk with you about Rick Brown. I don't know if you know him, but he's the youngster who had a reputation for—well—acting kinda peculiar. His moods are different from day to day. One day he's up and the next day he's down."

"Yes, I know him."

"Well, he got all upset today about a fight and some school problems," Mr. Wellman continued excitedly. "He got a few other boys upset too. You know how it goes. Anyhow, Rick and three others took off about twenty minutes ago. I can't call the Blackburns because Andy's taken a few days off and isn't around. I'm covering the night shift until Andy gets back and we all pick up our regular schedules. Gene Butler is on with me."

"I understand," Jack said calmly. "Are you sure the boy's aren't around the grounds somewhere?"

"They could be," Mr. Wellman answered. "Jake, the night supervisor, and another fellow are checking on that now. We don't want anybody to call the

Highway Patrol until we're sure they're really gone." Mr. Wellman paused, then added anxiously, "I'm afraid the Patrol is getting tired of hearing from us."

"I expect they might be," Jack agreed soberly.

"Will you be around for a few minutes longer?" Mr. Wellman pressed. "I'd sure like to talk with you."

"Why don't I come over in a few minutes and we can talk there," Jack suggested.

Approaching the unit, he noticed that all of the yard lights were on, as were the lights in all of the unit's activity areas. Although Jack had not talked with Andy Blackburn about Mr. Wellman's work recently, the man seemed to be doing his job well. Though nervous during the job interview, Mr. Wellman impressed Jack as a stable person.

"Jack, is that you?" Mr. Wellman called anxiously as Jack stepped through the doorway.

"Right."

"That damn kid has done it again!" Mr. Wellman exploded when they were face to face. "If they've got room for him over at Anchor, I'll be glad to transfer him when we get him back. Or better yet, if he steals a car while he's out I'm for pressing charges against him in the adult court! There's no damned excuse for the kind of stuff he keeps pulling. We've knocked ourselves out with that kid and he just won't shape up. He won't hold up his end of the deal. I'm positive that's what Andy will want to do when he gets back."

"Wait a minute," Jack said slowly. "Let's not do anything until Jake comes back with a report on the search. How's it going?"

"He and Joe from the laundry are checking the campus for Rick and the others now. If they don't find them, Jake will notify the Highway Patrol. I forgot to tell you—the three others are Ralph Bolin, Roger Bolster, and Fred Medford. But I really want to talk with you about Rick."

"What's he done to upset you so much? Hasn't he responded to your efforts to help him?"

"Not only hasn't he responded to our efforts," Mr. Wellman exclaimed, "he's let us down! Like I said, the staff has poured so much into this kid. I really feel that we've been let down. Everybody thought a lot of Rick, figured he had gotten a bad deal at home. So they went out of their way to help him in any way they could."

"If you could fill me in from the start,—when this recent trouble started— it might be a way for us to get a handle on the situation," Jack suggested.

"Well, first of all, you know that Rick is a jumpy kid—always moving, never stops moving. He's friendly and smiles a lot, but I guess a lot of his smiling comes from his being so tense and doesn't necessarily mean he's all that happy. Rick's a funny kid. He doesn't seem to feel that he measures up. I don't know where he gets his super high standards. We've got quite a number like that here in Lexington, but I'd say he's the farthest out of the lot. He works hard around the cottage, hits the books at school—that is, when he's up. If he's down or upset, then it's another story!"

"What's the most recent thing that got Rick going?" Jack asked quietly.

"It started about a week ago," Mr. Wellman explained. Despite Jack's low-key questioning, Mr. Wellman continued to respond at a high emotional pitch. "He came back to the unit from school. I was on duty when he came in. He looked like the devil himself. I swear! His hair was sticking straight out from his head. His eyes were dark and blazing, and rimmed by red, irritated lids. The skin on his face was an awful white and looked as tight as the hide on the head of a drum."

"And then what happened?"

"Well, when I saw him come into the building in that mood, I figured I'd better stay out of his way. There's no use stirring up more trouble than you've already got. But I didn't dodge him. I stayed right in the dayroom here figuring to bide my time until he looked a little more like I could talk to him. I figured I'd ask him to help me take a count of some athletic equipment—you know, pull some of the new stuff out of boxes. He likes to do that so I figured it might be one way to set up a situation where he could talk if he wanted to. Well, when he finished putting his school stuff away in his locker, I said, 'Rick, we've gotten some new equipment in. Could you give me a hand?' Well, it acted like a shock to the boy. He stood there and shook his head. What I said seemed to bring him out of a kind of trance he was in. I don't mean to say that the mood he had been in just disappeared, but I broke through, and as he looked at me, I could see his expression begin to ease and brighten a little—not much, but a little. He looked like he might come out of it. I thought his working with the sports equipment would bring him out. Maybe that was too much to expect because, as it turned out, it didn't do much for him."

"Don't put down what you were doing," Jack said encouragingly.

"I'm not," Mr. Wellman replied, finally calming. "I was glad I had him working. But then I felt disappointed that I wasn't getting at what was upsetting him so. Maybe it was pie-in-the-sky thinking, but I was hoping he might open up and say something that would give me a lead on how to approach him. He didn't say a word. I said a couple of low-key things about the equipment, but he still didn't say anything, so I kept quiet and worked along with him, accepting his silence."

"What was your next move?" Jack asked.

"Knowing Rick, I realized that my aim—of having him tell me what was cooking with him—wasn't going to work out. About the time he finished pulling the new stuff out of the boxes and taking inventory of the old equipment, I got a phone call. Before I stepped away and took it, I asked Rick to go ahead and clear up the boxes and papers. Well, when I got back, two or three other boys who had come into the cottage were helping him. I figured that was good because the other kids would talk with him and maybe loosen him up, but it didn't work out that way."

"What did happen?"

"I don't really know," Mr. Wellman admitted with a shrug. "When I got back, Rick and the other kids were working, but nobody was talking. Funny thing, they had all taken on Rick's mood. Now, they may have been talking earlier and stopped when they saw me coming back. You know how those things go. But when I came in, they wouldn't look at me and acted like I wasn't even in the same room."

"Then what?"

"I worked with the boys on finishing the clean-up work. About that time the kids who were out on work assignments came into the unit to get ready for supper. I closed the equipment room and went to the washroom. The kids like to cut up in there so I try to keep my eye on them. Well, the next thing I know, I heard the damnedest fight going on out in the dayroom. First I heard the cursing and yelling and before I could get there, I heard the actual pounding. By the time I did get there, the fight was going full blast. I ran right into the middle of it—damned near got hit—and pulled them apart. Jesus, Rick's nose was bleeding and I could see where he had caught one on his right cheekbone. Calvin Walker, one of the boys who had come in from work detail, was fighting with Rick and he came off about as bad. His left eye was puffed up and his shirt was damned-near torn off his back."

"What started it?" Jack asked.

"I'm still not sure, but I know that some of the kids, including Calvin Walker, had begun teasing Rick about his trouble at school."

"What trouble?"

"One of the teachers' Mr. Cranston, told Rick that he had expected him to get a better grade on a test. Said it right in front of the class, evidently ridiculed the boy, and gave him a real put-down. Most of the boys in class could care less about what they might have gotten on that or any other test, but for Rick it made a big difference. He wants to do well and we've been pushing him to do a good job in school. You know he had real ability. And the teachers have been putting on the pressure too, especially Cranston."

"How did you find out about all this?" Jack inquired.

"From the other kids. I also talked with Cranston over at the school, so the story has hung together wherever I've checked it out!"

"So the kids who came off their jobs started it all up again when they got into the unit," Jack conjectured.

"I think so," Mr. Wellman agreed. "But you never quite know; the other kids who were already in the unit may have egged them on. Anyway, after I got them pulled apart, I told Rick and the boys who sided with him, and Calvin and the boys who were lined up with *him* that I wanted to see them all in the reading room right after supper. We finally got over to the dining room and supper came off without any problem. Or so I thought. Afterward, when I gathered the two factions together, they said that the fight was really nothing, nothing at all."

"Had they gotten together during supper and worked out their differences?"

"They had gotten together all right, but I don't think they worked out any real differences. They had just agreed not to disagree with one another during our meeting. We no sooner got into the meeting than they—both Rick and Calvin—had the nerve to say they were only fooling around! I was damned near knocked off my chair by that one and told 'em so!"

"That's really something," Jack remarked, surprised. "I've seen it before, but I never would have expected it here."

"Well, they finally admitted that they'd been serious at the time," Mr. Wellman said indignantly, "but then they played the whole thing down and said they had just lost their heads for a minute, that they didn't really mean anything by it. They were determined not to open up to staff. I pushed them pretty hard because I figured the basic problem was still with them and needed to be worked out, but I didn't get anywhere on it."

Jack nodded. "You did everything possible to draw him out," he said, then paused. "Could you check on how Jake has made out with his search? Then too, if he could join us, I think it would add to our thinking."

Five minutes later Mr. Wellman returned with a report. "Jake has already called the Patrol. Nobody could find a trace of Rick and the other kids. Jake's on his way over to Venture now. They have a problem over there, just a routine one, but one he has to follow up on. He said he'll check with you tomorrow afternoon, if he doesn't get a chance to see you tonight."

"Okay. Back to the specifics of Rick's case and your description of what happened. I'd like to ask you several things," Jack said casually. "First, could you describe to me how the staff here in the unit have gone about encouraging Rick with his school work?"

"Well, nothing fancy," Mr. Wellman answered. "Andy just passed the word to us that this kid is smart and can do well in school and that we ought to push him to use his ability. So that's what we've been doing. We've just told him that he's got a good mind and ought to make the most of it. We let him know that he's our best student in this unit and we expect him to come through in the classroom."

"How does Mr. Blackburn handle this kind of an approach?" Jack pursued. "For example, does he have one supervisor like yourself zeroing in on Rick and his school work, or are a couple of you involved?"

"Oh, there's no one certain way," Mr. Wellman explained. "The word just gets passed around and then we all try to do what we can when we get on our shift."

"Would you guess that the other supervisors have taken as much interest in Rick as you have?" Jack asked. "Encouraging him in his school work, seeing to it that he gets good grades, and that kind of thing?"

"I'd say that maybe I take the most interest, next to Andy," Mr. Wellman answered proudly. "Andy really wants Rick to do well and talks a lot with him about it."

Mr. Wellman frowned deeply. "You know, Andy's going to be mad as hell when he gets back. He's going to raise hell with somebody—and that somebody will be me. I sure wish this had happened when somebody else was on duty."

"Of course runaways are a serious problem," Jack said gravely, "but the person to be blamed is the one who isn't doing a good job. That certainly isn't *you*. So I don't want you wasting your energy worrying like this."

"I appreciate that," Mr. Wellman said gratefully, but not with total relief. "But Andy's going to be upset anyway. He was pretty proud of Rick's record in the school. You know, that kid kind of put us on the map in the school—as a matter of fact, in the whole institution. We were counting on a lot from Rick and he was producing. We had a lot riding on him. You know most of our kids are real losers. It's a bad thing to say, but our record is pretty poor . . . so when you have a winner like Rick, a guy who can really make it in school, it means a lot."

"I think you may be expecting *too* much of Rick," Jack said bluntly. "You may be pushing him too hard. Your encouragement may have come across like pressure to Rick."

Mr. Wellman countered, "If he's got ability he ought to use it. If God gave him this talent, then he ought to be developing it—and for something besides getting into trouble."

"Sure," Jack said easily. "But the technique of motivating him to use his God-given talent must be sensitive, and I believe you were pushing him too hard."

"I don't think so," Mr. Wellman persisted. "It's like Andy Blackburn says, 'You've got to push any talents these kids have so that they develop them—so that they'll learn how to do something besides steal. They've got to learn to make their way in the world and if we have to push them, we just have to push them!' "

"Perhaps it's partly a matter of degree," Jack countered amiably. "Encourage, not push. You know, you can encourage and support a youngster in his efforts without pressuring him. I think the boy was pushed too hard. It's something you may want to think over and discuss with Andy. From where I sit, it very much looks like it."

"Maybe you're right," Mr. Wellman conceded, though without much conviction. "But how about Mr. Cranston? I think he was wrong when he said in front of the whole class that Rick hadn't been working up to par, that he had gotten a lousy grade, and that he ought to get on the stick."

"It's a part of the same ball of wax. I don't know what your or Andy's discussions with Mr. Cranston and others at the school have been. As I said earlier, high hopes for Rick may have propelled Mr. Cranston and perhaps others into pushing him—pushing him more than he could take."

Mr. Wellman's spirits drooped as he digested this. Though the man was in obvious discomfort, Jack hoped it meant that Mr. Wellman had recognized the validity of his point.

After a few moments Jack said, "You and Andy will want to talk with Mr. Cranston. Understand, I don't want you to feel I'm putting the finger on you or Andy or Mr. Cranston, but I'd like to have you look the whole case over and see how you all can develop a plan to work with Rick after we get him back." Mr. Wellman's expression had brightened. "So stay right in there," Jack went on heartily. "It's all an ongoing operation of doing and evaluating, doing and evaluating. In that ball-game we've simply been doing a little evaluating tonight."

Finally, Mr. Wellman seemed reassured by Jack's attitude and the prospect of discussing Rick's behavior with Andy and Mr. Cranston.

"Look," Jack said, consulting his watch, "it's past eleven and I need to get on home."

"Oh, yeah," Mr. Wellman exclaimed, rising hurriedly. "I guess we've been talking quite awhile. I sure appreciate your coming over, Jack. You know, I don't think I would recommend sending Rick into the adult court or even over to Anchor. I think we can probably work it out right here."

"I have an idea you can too," Jack agreed with a smile. He said goodnight and left the building.

Stimulated by Rick's case, Jack stopped at the Administration Building on his way home and picked up the boy's folder, leaving behind the folders he had intended to review before the next morning's meeting. Once home, Jack sat down with Rick's material and a tablet on a clipboard on which to make notes. After reading the whole case, rereading some parts several times, he jotted down points he felt were most important in order to put the case in perspective. His notes ran as follows:

1. Mother died when boy was three. Four children, of whom Rick was the youngest. Taken care of for a year by homemaker-maid hired by father.
2. Father remarried when Rick was four to woman 10 years younger than self. Two children born during next three years.
3. Rick spent much time crying during year with homemaker. Seemed to

be happier with stepmother. Became very upset at birth of first child to stepmother. Broke into temper tantrums easily. Attacked stepmother and new sibling (male). After attacks ceased, behavior reappeared at birth of second step-sibling (male).

4. Father self-made man. Rose from laborer to section head in aircraft manufacturing. Fair but impatient, demanding, punitive.

5. Stepmother sympathetic to Rick but overwhelmed by family responsibilities from the beginning and never seemed to recover.

6. Circumstances immediately before commitment: (a) parental argument over discipline of "their" two children; (b) pressure by father on his (first group) children to excel and be examples; (c) Rick's excellent school achievement belittled by father who urged him to do better; (d) Rick's school performance deteriorated; (e) Rick irritated teachers, caused disturbances, was suspended from school; (f) Rick was severely scolded and beaten by father.

7. Information obtained at Central State:

A. Psychological and psychiatric impressions include:

1. Very bright adolescent with acting-out neurosis (when upset, usually handles his tension through some kind of physical activity including fighting, running away, stealing, and other delinquent behavior).

2. Drives himself to do well, especially in school. Yet is often dissatisfied and moody about his performance.

3. Cannot tolerate much competition or rivalry.

4. Needs adult relationships that support him.

5. Cannot take pressure.

B. Psychological and psychiatric recommendations include:

1. Arrange full program, including active recreation.

2. Place in appropriate grade level at school—encourage, support, and stimulate; however, *do not pressure.*

3. Cottage placement must include adult supervisors who are mature, steady, friendly, and who will not be threatened by Rick's acting out or by his challenging the supervisor's authority, which will undoubtedly occur as he tests the stability of the relationship.

4. Treatment should eventually work on the boy's conflict with his father; however, at first it should be limited to helping Rick make full use of the institution's overall program.

Jack wished that the staff's approach might have been different. As he sank back in his chair weary from the long day's work, he kept repeating to himself, "If we can just learn to use what we already know . . ."

7

SEX EDUCATION

"A good way to start this afternoon's session might be to observe that we spent the morning getting acquainted. While we did some serious talking about our work with the kids, it seems to me that we stayed with the problems that are perhaps easiest to talk about—homesickness, fighting, school, lack of programs. I think we might eventually have gotten to it, but since this workshop only runs one day, I suggest that we spend the afternoon talking about the kids' sexual behavior and problems. Would we agree that they're among our biggest hang-ups? I don't think we understand them very well, and for sure we don't know what to do about them."

Jack's comments brought mixed laughter—some strained, some almost boisterous—from the thirty supervisors of Central State Training School for boys and its counterpart for girls, Upper State Training School. The staffs were meeting for a one-day workshop to talk about their common problems in working with delinquents. Such a meeting had been talked about by the staff at Central State for several years and had finally materialized through the efforts of Superintendent Graves and Upper State's Superintendent Caldwell. Once the joint meeting was agreed upon Jack and Mrs. Oster were given the tasks of developing a program and making arrangements.

Their program had been condensed from a detailed draft which the inservice education committees of the two training schools (with whom Jack and Mrs. Oster worked at length) had rejected because they felt it was too much like an academic course outline that would stifle free-wheeling discussion by the supervisors. Therefore, the final schedule divided the topic "Identification and Discussion of Cottage Problems" into only four sections.

Morning Session

    I. Welcome and Challenge: Superintendents Caldwell and Graves
   II. Identification of Major Supervisory Problems and Discussion:
        Mrs. Jane Oster and Mr. Jack Owens, Discussion Leaders
        Dr. Harold Barth, Psychiatrist, Consultant

Afternoon Session

  III. Continuation of Morning's Discussion:
        Mrs. James Oster and Mr. Jack Owens, Discussion Leaders
        Dr. Harold Barth, Psychiatrist, Consultant
  IV. Concluding Remarks: Superintendents Caldwell and Graves

The boisterous guffaws that met Jack's encouragement to talk about sexual problems eventually gave way to an uncomfortable silence, which the group attempted to fill by shifting in their chairs and clearing their throats. Jack continued, "The problems are different for both schools." No response. He smiled. "Well, we can't do anything about them if we don't *talk* about them."

Again, mixed laughter broke from the staff, less strained this time, although again followed by silence. It seemed that each supervisor was hoping someone else would open the discussion.

Finally, Doc Barth piped up, "Since some people say psychiatrists are interested in sex, it might be all right for me to break the ice on this topic." He scanned the group, watching them relax, then continued. "I think we may have many problems in common . . . though I don't want to oversimplify our situation. There's much to what Jack has said: there *is* a difference. Maybe a good way to open this up would be to ask the staff from Upper to report the reasons the courts give for committing girls there. Then someone from Central could describe *our* commitments." He turned to Mrs. Oster. "Might you or one of your staff members start by describing your situation?"

Mrs. Oster, accepting the role of spokesman for Upper State, cleared her throat. "I suppose that about sixty to seventy percent of the girls are committed to us because their sexual behavior was upsetting somebody in the community, upsetting them enough to commit them. Perhaps the percentage is even higher. They get picked up for street walking because they're too inexperienced to be able to handle themselves. Out on the street they're pretty open to being picked up by the police. I'm not promoting sexual activity or protection, but you know that if some of these kids were just a bit more experienced, we wouldn't even get them."

She paused, thought a moment, and then continued, "It's hard to classify them. Some stay on the streets—that is, as long as they last—others migrate to bars or shady clubs. Then there are the girls who have run away from home and have been sleeping with somebody, maybe a pick-up or maybe even their steady boy friend who has run away too.

"There are three other groups of girls that we get. They may be mixed up with the kind of problems I've already spoken of—I'll try to make that clear in a minute. First, there are the pregnant girls that the courts send us because they don't have any other place to put them. We fight taking these cases . . . I should say fight against *keeping* these cases, because we don't have anything to say about the cases that are sent to us. Next, there are the shoplifters and the girls who have gotten involved in other types of stealing. Third—and we don't know what to do with these—are the drug users. We just aren't set up for them. In fact," Mrs. Oster concluded, "I'd like to stop at this point by saying that I think we get a lot of girls we shouldn't get."

During Mrs. Oster's comments, Jack could see interest replace the supervisors' self-consciousness. However, when she stopped talking, they still seemed hesitant to continue. Jack interjected, "Thank you, Mrs. Oster, for getting us off the ground with that excellent picture of your commitments at Upper. Would one of the supervisors from Upper like to pick up on what Mrs. Oster talked about and develop it further?"

The group was restless, on the verge of contributing, when Len Hall picked up the conversation. "I hope I'm not out of line here, and there's a lot in what you've told us, but aren't most of the girls pretty run-down at the heels when they come in? I mean, many times the police haven't just rushed in and picked them off the streets."

"That's just my point," Mrs. Oster countered. "That's just it! I'm saying that sexual misbehavior should *not* be seen as delinquent behavior. Right now the police and the courts are defining it that way, especially if the girl doesn't have parental support and is out on the street. I personally don't think it should be this way. The girl's behavior may be immoral—depending on your standards—but I don't think that sexual misbehavior—even if the girl is run-down and her parents don't care about her—should be adjudicated as being delinquent. And as long as I have the floor, I want to make two other points. First, we are discriminating against kids. You know that *adult* females are much less likely to be picked up for such behavior, and when they are, they're not packed off to some institution. My second point is that the police and the courts hit a particular type of kid—the one who's poor, can't operate or handle herself very well, and doesn't have any influence to help her out."

"So what's the community or the cop on the beat supposed to do?" Mr. Hall challenged. "Something has to be done. I don't really know what else you can expect the cops and the courts to do. If they don't move in on the problem, the newspapers will be putting the heat on them."

Mrs. Oster replied, coolly, "If they really think the behavior is serious enough to warrant some action, there are a number of things they can do rather than send the girls to us. But I'm afraid none of the alternatives is as convenient as Upper State. They could push the social agencies to work with the youngsters and their families. Or they could set up a residential center of some kind for short-term care, if they haven't already, and could expand it and its services."

She fixed Len Hall with a steady stare. "Mr. Hall, you know that what we've neglected in this whole conversation is the question of how many boys you have at Central who are committed for some kind of sexual misconduct!" She grinned and added, "Since it takes two to tango, I suppose you have a percentage of admissions for sexual misbehavior similar to ours."

Smiling sheepishly, Mr. Hall responded, "I guess you've got something there."

"In answer to Mrs. Oster's question," Jack cut in, "you know we've never had a kid committed to us for getting a girl pregnant who ended up at Upper, or who stayed in the community and handled the pregnancy some other way. That's unusual, especially in comparison to what's done with pregnant girls without means, but it's the truth!"

"Jack, I'm not attacking you. It's the court's fault," Mrs. Oster said with restraint. "But that's really, really unfair."

Jack nodded, embarrassed.

"How about rape?" she asked.

"You're not going to like what I'm about to report, but you might as well know—we get even fewer of that kind of commitment."

"Like how many?" Mrs. Oster pursued.

"I think we may get one every two or three years," Jack answered. "Doc, does that sound right?"

"No oftener," Doc Barth confirmed. "And then some special community furor has to pressure the court to commit the few they do."

"Crass, crass unfairness," Mrs. Oster lamented.

"You're too kind," Len Hall commented. "It's unfair as *hell*!"

"You can't blame the court for all of this," Jack echoed Mrs. Oster's earlier statement. "You know that the informal rules on sex in any community usually give the advantage to the boy. So what *we* might agree is rape is not apt to be interpreted as such by John Q. Public or the police."

"Yeah, I know the point of view," Len Hall said sarcastically. " 'She got what she had coming to her.' "

"Or 'she got what she asked for' " Mrs. Oster added, then, with a tone of futility, suggested, "Why don't we get back to our line of conversation before we got onto this horribly unfair topic!"

"Do you mean the failure of the police and courts to pursue the sexual irregularities of the boys as vigorously as they do the girls?" Jack asked.

"No," Mrs. Oster objected. "I'm not for giving the boys any more *grief* than they've already got. What I want is for the community, especially the police and the courts, to *get off the backs* of our girls! Unless, of course, you want to have the police, along with the courts, serve as keepers of public morals. I'm saying that's *not their job*. I'm also saying that sexual behavior that is voluntarily entered into is a moral matter—not a legal matter."

"That's true only for adults," Mr. Hall corrected. "Sexual intercourse between juveniles and adults or between juveniles gets to be a legal matter."

"It's hardly as clear as that," Mrs. Oster countered. "And if it is, where are the male commitments that ought to follow from it? Jack and Doctor Barth claim you get only a fraction of them." She paused to take a breath. "What some of you may not realize is that most of the girls sent to Upper by the courts are hardly children. They're experienced much beyond what we expect of their age—whether they're fourteen, fifteen, sixteen, or seventeen years old. They're street-wise and have a sexual code very different from what our police and courts expect and approve of. Besides that, I would plead tolerance for them.

"If the community really wants the police and the courts to help it with its morals—especially the morals concerning kids' sexual behavior—then I think the community needs some way other than using the juvenile court and the state training school! To me the church and the family are much more appropriate and useful means."

"You've described some knotty problems very well," Doc interjected quietly. "Now, where do you take them from here? From what you've said, I get the impression that there's little likelihood of change."

"In my pessimistic comments, I may not have been entirely fair to the police and judges," Mrs. Oster tempered. "My talks with them have paid off, at least in some small ways. In recent months they've been more tolerant and they've pushed the social service agencies to get some help on these cases. Then we've also been moving on a different front. We're trying to get some consideration of this problem through the State Social Welfare Conference and the State Bar Association. Hopefully we will jointly go to the legislature to work for a revision of the Juvenile Code."

With a mixture of hope and resignation, Mrs. Oster concluded, "We know it's going to take more than what we've been doing so far, but it's a good start."

The discussion had reached another plateau. Even Mr. Hall seemed satisfied that his points had been considered seriously. After a pause of several moments, Jack asked, "Perhaps you could tell us a bit about your program problems at Upper—that is, the problems you have after the girls are admitted. Then after that, I think we should take a look at Central."

Mrs. Oster scanned her staff. "We do have problems, but rather than my doing all the talking, perhaps someone else would describe some of them."

Mrs. Oster turned to a middle-aged woman whose face and manner suggested confidence. "Isabel, you've worked in several of the cottages during the past five years. Would you describe some of the girls' problems?" To the group she added, "This is Mrs. Isabel Script."

Mrs. Script, temporarily ruffled but nonetheless pleased, nodded a greeting to the group.

"I'd say that many of our girls have fairly serious personal problems, even some of the street-wise ones. I suppose, though, that as a group the street-wise girls have fewer personal problems than the others. When I say street-wise I'm thinking of the ones who have gotten used to their way of life—prostitution, shoplifting, drug pushing—and more or less like it. I believe most of them are terribly lonely and terribly in need of somebody to want them, to think well of them, to think they're pretty, to love them. A lot of them—well, nobody has wanted them, and that includes their parents. They have just, to put it plainly, been 'kicked around.' Nobody has ever shown them real affection, you know, for very long. And in the meantime they have grown up, at least physically, and have come into their own.

"With their deprived and mixed-up backgrounds, the girls are real set-ups or suckers for anything—especially sex. They're picked off by the kids or older men who size them up and play them for all they can get. Sometimes the boys are in about the same shape as the girls themselves. To be fair, I guess I'd better add that they aren't always that preyed on because—let's face it—some of our girls are pretty aggressive and help promote whatever gets put together. . . . But anyway, whatever it is that gets these kids together, the togetherness may only be a one-night stand or something for a little longer, like with a runaway. Or if the girl is already out on the street and on her own, besides the one-night stands she picks up, she may move into a guy's room. Maybe he's a drifter of some kind, and she may be in his room for a week, a couple of weeks, or even several months. On the other hand, he may move into hers."

Mrs. Anderson, another Upper staff member, interjected, "And that's when things *really* get messed up."

Incorporating Mrs. Anderson's comment as if it were her own, Mrs. Script continued, "That's right. That's right. Because the honeymoon is over in a hurry. Besides their immaturity and their not being able to get along all that well with anybody for a very long time, neither partner is likely to have any money. She may want him to work—you know, be somewhat straight. But chances are he can't hold a job even if he gets one. The guy may force her to prostitute for him, or if she is already prostituting, he may force her to prostitute more. He may get her involved in drugs, taking and pushing them. It isn't long before they can't stand each other any more. An irritation will grow into an argument and an argument will grow into a fight, and the girl will end up getting a beating and being thrown out on the street."

"It's a funny thing," Mrs. Anderson, who seemed to function as Mrs. Script's second, added. "Even though some of these pairs fight each other like cats and dogs and do bad things to each other, they actually believe they love each other. I just don't understand it. It's a sad, sad mess."

Mrs. Script shook her head bleakly. "I don't understand it either."

Doc, who, like the whole group had followed Mrs. Script and Mrs. Anderson closely, asked, "How do the girls see these affairs and what do they say about them? How do they explain them?"

"Well, from the ones I've talked with, they just want somebody to love them so badly, or someone to care for them so badly, that they'll take almost anything. You have to remember, too, that they get themselves in with a certain crowd of people where this kind of thing, which we think is pretty *bad*, goes on all the time—and they think it's pretty *good*! So, what they have to go by as a standard isn't much different—if it's different at all—from what they're mixed up in themselves."

Al Sears, Central's genial Concord Cottage supervisor, commented, "I've been able to follow most all of this and it sure has been an eye opener for me, but you'll have to go over that part again where you said that one of your girls and whoever she may be shacked up with think they love each other, but they really don't. It seems to me that if they think they do, chances are they probably do. And from what I've been able to make out of their sexual get-togethers, they sure do."

Though Mr. Sears' comment brought considerable laughter, Mrs. Script merely smiled and nodded. "I don't know what you want to call it. It doesn't last and it's mostly physical. They aren't able to settle down and make plans for their future. They just keep shifting from one person to another."

"I think Mrs. Script is making an excellent distinction between love and lust," Doc said. "Her point that many of the girls have very limited chances of catching someone who can offer himself as a steady partner is a very important one. Remember that they're going to be circulating mainly where the drop-outs, runaways, pimps, drifters, and exploiters hang out. Remember, too, that the girl herself may not be able to sustain a relationship over a long period."

"I'd like to hear somebody say something more about the girls' opinions of themselves," Mr. Terman of Lake Cottage said. "with the boys, a lot of them have pretty poor estimates of themselves. Some of them, I think, get into stealing or some other kind of trouble to prove themselves. They want to be *somebody*, and they feel they aren't. I don't mean to say they don't have a great time enjoying the car they've stolen, and I think it helps them feel like big shots, like they're making it. Overall, though, I'd say their opinion of themselves is very poor and they're forever trying to overcome it."

Mr. Hall reentered the discussion. "Well, I think this 'trying to improve their estimate of themselves' thing is often tied in with their trying to be men.

We have to keep in mind that they're coming of age—trying hard to be men. And of course they don't know how. Not really."

"Don't you think they may know how, at least what they are supposed to do," Mrs. Script queried, "but that it's not a real part of their system?"

Seeming to recognize in Mr. Hall a debater, she continued, "For instance, if you were to ask them, any one of them, 'How do you make it in your town?' they could tell you. But they can't pull it off because they can't stick it out in school, they won't take or keep the small-time jobs they can get, they won't take orders from a job supervisor, and so on. I'd say they 'know it,' but 'don't have it.' "

"You're absolutely right," Mr. Hall agreed. "They may know what to do, but they still don't know how to do it. That is, as you said—how to 'pull it off.' Besides that, their style of living and ways of feeling and thinking are not going to help them develop along the lines of becoming 'men' according to our definition. Their notion of a man means being a tough guy, an operator, one who makes women. Their idea of what it takes to be a man is the worst kind—the kind that you can see on television any night of the week. I don't know if that's where they get it, but that's their image of masculinity."

The newest contributor was Mr. Talford, a supervisor in Friendship Cottage. "And with their poor opinion of themselves and having to keep proving themselves, they're set up for one to follow the other because they're afraid of being chicken. So, whatever background a kid has for getting out of line, his fear of not measuring up with his buddies gets to be an even bigger thing."

"Before this discussion goes any further," Doc interrupted, "It's become pretty apparent that we have a double standard going on right here on this sexual thing. Let me point out that when we talk about the girls, we are interested in talking about their sexual lives, sexual intercourse . . . the real thing. But when we talk about the boys, we talk about their wanting to function as 'men,' 'making it,' and so on, and then we skip over to their social behavior—speculating that their sexual inadequacies may push them into stealing, following the gang, fighting, and so on. So, fellows, I think we need to review what we know about the boys' sexual behavior. It may turn out that we don't know very much because we're not really pursuing it as we should be."

"I think you're right, Doc," Mr. Hall acknowledged. "Let me give you an extreme—Pete McDone. He's just sixteen, and I'll be dam—darned if he didn't have four girls, fourteen and fifteen year olds, prostituting for him. And he was taking about fifty dollars off of each one per day, and on weekends he was doing better than that! Then besides, he had a couple of kids—boys in this case—pushing drugs for him. But to get back to Doc's point. Pete was sleeping regularly with one of the neighborhood girls. He had kind of a club-office arrangement in one of the vacant buildings left from urban renewal."

Al Sears laughed and said, "The next thing you'll be telling us is that he was sent here for income tax evasion!"

After hearty laughter from the group, Mr. Hall said, "Jack, you may have to check me on this, but I seem to remember that Pete was sent here for being incorrigible and out of parental control." This comment brought on another wave of laughter from the workshop people.

Jack shook his head. "Not Pete. Remember, he was picked up for a traffic violation, and then the police found it was a stolen vehicle. So he came in on auto theft. But back to what Mr. Hall was telling us—none of that was in his record. We found out about it from Lieutenant Harper over at Culver City, after the boy was here."

Jack paused to let the group quiet down, then continued. "So the boys do have sexual contact, and some, like in the case of Pete, promote it. But pimping with the kind of organization and stability Pete had built up is not a typical pattern. Most of our kids have had some sexual contact, at least from what I've been able to gather. This is not a statistic. It's just an opinion from what we've put together from talking with the kids. And on that, we don't know how much they're holding back from talking about sex because they're bashful or concerned about how we may react. Then there are those who like to brag about their sexual experiences. So, our estimates are awfully tentative.

"Their talk is confusing in other ways, too," Jack explained. "For example, some of the kids who have really opened up about their sex lives have described behavior that runs the whole gammut of sex—heterosexual, homosexual, with its various forms. Furthermore, we've got some unwed fathers here who know it, and we probably have some here who are but don't know it because they and the girl have moved around among other partners. We've got some here who have been sexually active since nine or ten and are thoroughly experienced, and we have some who have thought a lot about sex, have had a lot of day and night dreams, but have never gotten involved—maybe because they were too shy."

"I'm glad to hear you confirm the fact that your boys have had sexual experiences," Mrs. Script interposed.

Jack laughed. "I guess this is one of the points that Mrs. Oster was making earlier: since the boys' sexual behavior is not defined as delinquent, not only is it unlikely they'll be sent here as a result of it, but it's unlikely that the courts and agencies—and we, too—even collect any systematic information on it."

"A point I'd like to get in here," Doc Barth said as he moved forward in his chair, "is that what we're reporting about the sexual activity of our boys seems to indicate that we are pretty casual—even careless—about gathering such information about our kids. We listen, occasionally we ask, and then we do quite a bit of guessing about what our boys know and don't know and do and don't do. Seems to me we need to be as thorough in tuning in on sexual matters and activities as we are in getting to know about school behavior, work patterns, family life, and the like."

"I agree one hundred percent," Jack said. "So let's talk with Mr. Wilton in Social Services next week, get our heads together, and see how we might get started on this. In the meantime, so the folks from Upper don't think too badly of us, we ought to tell them about our sex education class. I'm sorry Mr. Eagan, the superintendent of our school, or Mrs. Hogelin, who actually conducts the class, isn't here. I can give you the general picture and others can help out. Briefly, Mrs. Hogelin came to us with two advantages: she had had some training and as an outsider she could see the need more clearly than we could."

"That's right," Len Hall interjected. "But that doesn't mean we saw the need as she saw it. At least not at first. Figuring it was a little frivolous and school-teacherish, we fought her and Mr. Eagan on it. However, after hearing them out, the cottage supervisors went along with it."

"Yet you weren't fully convinced?" Mrs. Script challenged.

"Not at all convinced," Mr. Hall agreed. "We could see the need, at least in part, but we wanted to avoid dealing with the whole subject of sex. When they said they would run a regular class on it or make it a part of a hygiene or biology course, I've forgotten which, we went along. We figured a regular class was all right to explain about sex, but we objected to a woman, Mrs. Hogelin, handling the delicate questions."

"So, after some discussion and a bit of argument throughout the institution, Mrs. Hogelin got underway," Jack came back, "and by and large we think it's been a success."

"Sounds too good," Mrs. Oster observed. "What were your problems?"

"Well," Jack began uneasily. "The straight classroom instruction went very well. You know, like learning the physiology of the male and female including their sexual organs, and the reproductive process. That went great. The boys learned things they didn't know. Their ignorance was tremendous in spite of all their smart and vulgar talk."

"And the number of mistaken notions that Mrs. Hogelin corrected would fill a book!" Len Hall added.

"And then what happened?" Mrs. Oster persisted.

"Uh, well," Jack mumbled, "there were problems in the cottages."

"I'll take Jack off the hot seat because I was responsible for putting him there when we were having the trouble," Len Hall volunteered. "We had trouble with the boys in the cottages. They talked and talked the sex thing . . . you know they got to doing some private things . . ."

Len Hall's candor came to an embarrassed halt.

"I guess it's my turn," Jack commented easily. "Frankly, the cottage supervisors, Len and the others, noticed that the boys' masturbation increased and the boys began to masturbate in the showers with each other. It got kind of wild. At least for us."

"Then what did you do?"

"After we quit wringing our hands about the kids' behavior and blaming Mrs. Hogelin, we told the kids to stop their masturbating, stepped up the shower room supervision, and talked with the boys—casually—about sexual feelings—their naturalness and handling them in ways other than masturbation or intercourse. We weren't sure how well that went over . . . probably less great than we would have liked, but it seemed to help."

"I'm curious about what you told them," Mrs. Script said.

"Well, we talked with them about the importance of sports, activities in general, developing good friendships, and things like that," Jack explained.

"Doesn't sound very convincing," Mrs. Oster commented with a challenging smile.

"We weren't convinced either, but it was the best we could do," Jack responded with some distress.

"While we're leveling about our problems, we might as well share one that rocked the campus, at least until it got worked out," Mr. Hall interrupted with his earlier candor. "I'm sorry Mrs. Hogelin isn't here because her presence would show her strength of character better than our talk. Anyhow, when her class got going and the kids loosened up and developed confidence in her, they began to reveal more and more about themselves, and they began to ask more and more about Mrs. Hogelin. As she and the kids got used to one another and began talking more and more openly, some boy asked her how often she and her husband have intercourse, and without thinking, she answered him. Well, the way the class was going, it wouldn't have amounted to much. But then a couple of other things happened. First, some kid who was caught up in the emotion and all of what was going on asked Mrs. Hogelin how she felt at the time of the penetration. And then word of his question got out on the campus and we had one big furor about that!"

"How in the world did she ever get herself in such a situation?" Mrs. Oster asked with amazement.

"The question of penetration she handled well by telling the boy it was a private matter. He accepted her answer and they went on talking about other things. But as I said, when word hit the campus, there was a *ruckus*! Everything from accusations against Mrs. Hogelin for teaching the kids to be immoral, to being immoral herself. And of course, everybody, or almost everybody, was for getting her fired. It took Mr. Graves, Mr. Eagan, and Jack to get the institution back into shape and convince us to be a little rational on this sex thing."

Expressions on the faces of the staff from Upper as well as Central reflected respect for the dedication and capability of those who saw the boys and the school through a potentially catastrophic incident.

After a long pause, a youthful woman from Upper, who introduced herself as Mrs. Elms, entered the discussion. "I wanted to bring this up earlier, but our discussion took a different turn. Anyhow, what I think we should recognize is that wanting to be loved and being lonely without a suitable outlet can result in a number of sad situations besides the kind we've been talking about. Some of the girls get very depressed and withdrawn, and I mean really withdrawn. We've even had a number who have tried to commit suicide because of that very fact. They gave up hope, and felt so unwanted that they tried to end their lives."

Responding to her comment, another woman, Mrs. Frank, added, "We've had suicide attempts of a different kind—when the girl's guilt feelings about previous sexual behavior and her loneliness lead her to want to kill herself. The guilt is a strong, strong pressure."

"I guess you have to take each case by itself in trying to figure out what's going on," Mrs. Elms commented. "On the suicide thing, we're very careful if we have a girl such as we've been talking about—and then you add the problem of her delivering an illigitimate baby, who is then taken away from her. . . . When you have all of those problems wrapped up in one girl, you've got a serious situation on your hands. And we've got more than a few of them."

Mrs. Oster interjected at this point to explain. "We get pregnant girls sent to us, and some even deliver when they are with us. The welfare department of their home county takes the lead on what's to be done with the child if it's illegitimate. Now, we don't think it's right for the court to send pregnant girls to us, especially when their delinquency is minor. It would be a rare case—and we haven't seen one yet where the pregnant girl is so delinquent, indeed so criminal—in which she couldn't be cared for in the community. The courts and the welfare department really use us as a welfare home for unwed mothers. But the training school is no place for them! I talked about this situation earlier and I don't want to make a 'soap box' speech on it, but it's a serious problem."

Mrs. Script moved the point further. "So what rehabilitation are we supposed to give the girl? Should we teach her better methods of contraception? Should we tell her where she might have gotten an abortion? Should we teach her how to be more discreet in her life? Should we teach her how to choose more considerate boyfriends?"

Her voice, moving to an increasingly higher pitch, reflected indignation. "Well, we do some of this, but we don't have a formal program to do it. Our nurse does a little, our social workers do a little, we in the cottages do a little. So, all in all, we don't do much, and what there is of it is hit or miss.

"Usually, I think, we don't do anything unless the girl's problem or the girl herself pushes for this kind of help. I'm getting into pretty deep water on this, but since I'm in, I might as well keep going, and say that I'm only talking for myself. I think some of our problems—at least *my* problem—is that I don't know what to do, and that's because the courts and others in the community—including the good citizens—don't really know what to do! Oh, there are some who would like to have us teach the girls morals, and of course there are those who wouldn't want us to touch the subject. Some want us to offer good education—you know, academics and homemaking—and others push the treatment thing. But it's always very *general* program talk, and while nobody says so, even the most sophisticated of the spokesmen seem to think that somehow or another these good things will help carry the girl over until she gets married, and then the whole thing will be mysteriously taken care of. The only other thing I can figure from listening to all the talk about what ought to be done to have a good program is that if we do other good things for the girl, the sex thing will take care of itself, or maybe it will go away!"

Mrs. Caldwell had not spoken since her introductory remarks that morning, but now interjected, evidently feeling the discussion had reached too emotional a level. She spoke with calm deliberation. "Mrs. Script and Mrs. Oster described earlier our problems with the girls who shouldn't be sent to us, and I think theirs was a clear description of the problem. I think it has still other aspects which I won't take your time to talk about now. If you like, we can come back to them later. What I would like to say a little about, and then remove myself from the discussion, concerns what we do about the sex and morality matter. We do not encourage premarital or extramarital sexual intercourse, and I suppose that someone listening to us at work would decide that as a staff we are middle-class conservatives. And I suppose we are. At any rate, we do work to make the girls assume responsibility for themselves, and in doing so, I suspect we get a little moralistic at times.

"We tell the girls that sexual intercourse may result in pregnancies. We have gone slow on providing them with information on contraceptives, but beginning in the fall we will be providing full information on them in our health curriculum.

"Frankly," Mrs. Caldwell continued in her even tone, "we've been afraid of the communities' reactions, at least the reactions of certain church groups, and we've struggled with our own morals too—that is, we've been thinking that by providing the girls with information on contraceptives, we might be encouraging promiscuous sexual behavior, but I believe we've been wrong on that. Besides, I think the question is not whether knowledge of the use of contraceptives encourages promiscuous sexual behavior, but is how we can help our girls in their sexual experiences, since most of them are going to continue with some type of involvement."

Relaxing somewhat, Mrs. Caldwell concluded, "I believe this is all I have to say . . . except to encourage you to continue your good discussion."

"And I thought *we* had problems," Mr. Hall commented. "I think we should be a little more sympathetic with the people at Upper. Not that I mean to give the impression that we don't have some tough problems—we have plenty of them, especially fights, bickering, bullying, stealing, and running away. You name it and we have it. But overall I think my main problem is the fights, the actual no-holds-barred rights that break out—and they can be dangerous."

On this subject nearly all the boys' cottage supervisors could contribute. Mr. Wellman, who had not spoken before, broke into the conversation. "If you think fights are bad, you ought to try working with kids who are constantly worried, up-tight, and wringing their hands over something—over anything. It's nerve-racking. A fight is a fight. It's a good clean activity. It's out in the open and it's direct, straightforward. It has a cleansing effect; it lets the boys get some things out of their systems, it lets them get things settled among themselves. And when it's over with, and the dust settles, chances are it's over for good. But with my kids, their agonizing and worrying just goes on and on. If they aren't worried about one thing, it's another."

"If we are playing the game of who has it the hardest, then let me put in a plug for us over at Venture," Mr. Snell said with a note of challenge. "If there's any group that's tough to handle, it's the boys who in frank language are the con men—and we've got them. They're always out to manipulate or exploit somebody."

"Before this competing for who has it the hardest goes any further," Jack interrupted with a chuckle, "I get the feeling we are ducking our sexual problems."

"I was wondering when somebody was going to say that," Doc Barth observed drily. "Unless my memory serves me badly, it seems that sex problems of one kind or another come up every day. Let's talk about *that.*"

"I guess we better own up to them," Mr. Jeff volunteered from the rear of the room. "that we were interested in the sexual problems at Upper but shy about talking about our own." Ignoring the laughter this brought on, he continued. "I'll just talk about our problems at Hardy. If anybody else wants to talk about his own cottage's I'll leave it up to him. First, I've got a kind of mixed group of kids. They're all twelve and thirteen years old—I guess you could say that's the main thing that binds them together. Doc Barth here calls it their 'common characteristic: But after that, we have tough guys, manipulators, scared and shy kids, depressed ones. But they're all immature.

"Now what happens, unless I'm on my toes—and even if I'm on my toes, it happens sometimes—is that some of the tough guys turn into bullies and force some of the weak kids to take it in their rear, jerk them off, and what have you!"

The group was caught off-guard by Mr. Jeff's blunt description. It was undoubtedly the frankest report anyone had made during the meeting; almost vulgar in its directness. Embarrassment and shock ran through the group.

However, with striking ease, Mr. Jeff talked on. "And while I'm telling all, I have to say it has happened right in the cottage when I've been on duty. So I can't make excuses—like it only happens during somebody else's supervision, or when the kids are out on work detail."

As Jack watched the group, he could see that their initial reaction of shock had changed to concern. Obviously, Mr. Jeff's candor in the face of their repulsion had enabled them to regain their rational attitudes.

"Occasionally," Mr. Jeff continued, "if no one can prevent it, we have real troubles when we get a feminine-type boy in the cottage. It's been an eye-opener to me. Still is. That is, how a feminine type coming into the cottage throws the whole cottage into a tizzy. Even some of the most square types get all interested in the effeminate kid. It bugs me. It really does."

"Maybe it's how your cottage is made up that makes your unit such a hotbed for sex," Ed Snell observed. "From what you say, I figure it's more of a problem than we've got over at Venture. I think that when you put weak kids who are a bit on the effeminate side in with more aggressive types, it generates the sex stuff. Of course, not always, but I think there is something to the idea.

"I've got the manipulators, and some of them are interested all right, and they may work at each other—that is, try to seduce one another, but usually that's about where it stops. It's left at the point of foul or lewd talk, a few foul remarks, maybe some unsuccessful pressuring, but that's about it. Now, I admit I work awfully hard to prevent all the homosexual stuff, horse play, or the hard stuff Mr. Jeff was honest enough to mention. I'm a great believer, as I know Len is, in sports and activities to keep the kids busy. It gets their minds on something else. It drains off their sexual steam. So I think recreation—and don't forget work—are great to combat this kind of thing. And, I don't mean to pat myself on the back, because others are doing it better, but you just *have to* acknowledge it and work on it."

"Where I see the roots of this problem—at least one of them," Jack said, "is right when the kids come into the institution. The toughs who are looking for some victim to exploit keep an eye open for the new kids who are scared and vulnerable. Those kids are natural prey for the boys who want to make them. The new kid is scared, friendless, and shaky—and maybe he hasn't worked out his sexual identity yet. And along comes the bullying, manipulative and he scares, cons, may even beat the hell out of the new kid in order to wrench some kind of a perverse sexual deal out of him. For the sexual 'favors' he gives the kid protection from the others and generally takes care of him. Cigarettes, extra issues of clean clothing, extra helpings of food, and whatever the bully has or promotes from the local rackets become a part of the deal with his boy. So, unfortunately, sometimes the cottage situation encourages homosexual behavior that in another environment might never have occurred.

I'm convinced we should do more in our *intake* program to try to prevent this."

"Jack, you recall we've got a committee working on that very thing," Mr. Jeff said.

"Right, right," Jack enthused, "and we're looking for more good ideas to come from that group. For those of you from Upper, I should point out that we've gone over this a number of times and have just recently decided to provide the newcomers with a genuine reception program. Also, we're sharpening our supervision, and with these changes are trying to cut down on this problem. And, as you heard Mr. Jeff say, we also have a committee working on it."

All tension over the issue of homosexuality had cleared. Mrs. Oster cleared her throat. "Well, our girls are together on this kind of sex thing, too. I don't like it, but in talking with other institutional people I find that it is very common. But our girls operate quite differently from your boys. First, I sense they just aren't as violent. There is plenty of urging by our 'studs,' but they go after the 'chicks' more like a courtship. They try to win them, rather than beat them down. I don't mean to say the studs won't put on pressure and bully a bit, but it's just not violent.

"I'm afraid our whole school is tied in with this sexual thing, or whatever we want to call it. Most of our girls develop 'families.' There is a mother and a father and children. Then to accommodate other 'adults' who are married and have some kind of a sexual thing going, there are assorted relatives, aunts, uncles, and others. There will usually be at least one family in each cottage, sometimes more than one. These families are pretty close, but they aren't set up against the staff—at least *I* don't feel threatened by them. Not the way I understand the boys do, where they get so organized and uptight that they're a physical threat to the staff. That's not our scene. It probably could develop into that, but not so far."

"There *is* a threat here, at least to some of us, by the boys," Len Hall said. "By design, I have the toughest kids assigned to my cottage. Given the chance, they would take over the unit and run it by kangaroo court. Like I said, that's if anyone would let them. They're a physical threat to staff. Not that they constantly lie in ambush to get you, but if they feel they can knock you off your perch by a fight, they may try calling you out or trapping you into one. Whether they threaten you physically or not, they are always a threat to your authority. If they can't remove you, they like to avoid your authority and do what they want to do. If that happens—and it can if you're not careful—the first thing you know, you've lost your unit and your job."

To bring the discussion back into focus, Jack summarized. "Recalling what has been said, it looks like the girls organize themselves into families for sex and family purposes. Our kids organize for power, status, and, if given a chance, for bossiness. Sex seems to come into the picture only incidentally. By this I mean our boys don't seem to organize themselves into cliques for sex."

"We had a professor from Hallmark University come over and talk at one of our staff meetings a couple of months ago," Mrs. Marshal, a new speaker, said eagerly. "He said that these families the girls set up come about as a result of their copying how people organize themselves on the outside—in their homes. He said they do this on the inside because they are deprived of their families—so they set up their own. For myself, I can't get used to them and I've been at Upper for three years. They seem very peculiar to me."

Mrs. Elms interrupted, "Professor Johnson did say that the kids get most of their ideas from the outside, but he also said they generate new ideas in living with one another at Upper. You know, like any other group does. Then he was pretty hard on us and said that a lot of what our kids do is set in motion by our limited program. He said it's probably so short on what the kids actually need that they 'fill in' to cope with what he called a 'deprived situation' with strange friendships, homosexuality, stealing, and you name it."

Mrs. Oster picked up immediately on the tail of Mrs. Elms' sentence. "He was pushing us a little, and I don't blame him, because that's what we asked him to do. Anyway, what I think Mrs. Marshal was referring to is that Dr. Johnson said that the girls have their marriages with one another and tie other girls to them as their make-believe families because the institution closes them off from normal relationships. You know, they have very little contact with men—and their own families for that matter. Then he said that when our program doesn't have enough education, recreation, and general activities in it, the girls will fill in the gaps. We didn't like what he said, but he's probably right!"

"What about those marriages you mentioned a while ago?" Doc asked. "I don't quite understand them."

"To the outsider, I'm sure they do sound peculiar," Mrs. Oster began. "Even to the insider, if she steps back from the situation and gets a little distance from her work, it's peculiar. It's like Mrs. Marshal described earlier. Anyway, the girls team up. The more masculine ones will manage to get their hair cut a little shorter and comb it straight back. This is only one of the ways the stud or butch makes up. She is also very sure to wear slacks and open-necked blouses. She generally acts quite aggressive. It's amazing how the studs can turn up a bit of male clothing—a cap here, a belt there, a shirt, and so on. The chicks are the real females in the setting, and the designation of fem or chick gets attached to them by the other girls. They have the potential of becoming sweethearts of the studs and, if a courtship goes the whole way and is followed by a formal marriage, they can even become 'wives.' Because courtships and especially marriages are kept quiet, even highly secret, it's hard to know exactly what the situation is with some couples. For example, when you see two girls walking with their arms around each other, it's hard to tell whether they're good friends, involved in a courtship, or a 'married couple.' "

"How do you mean 'involved in a courtship'?" Jack asked.

"They are just involved," Mrs. Oster answered simply. "The courtships take place like many others on the outside, except that on the inside I'd say there's a lot more pressure on the feminine girls to submit or get tied up with somebody. Also, it gets to be the thing to do: any new inmate is sized up for her potential." She paused. "No, that may sound a little strong, but it goes on to a great extent.

"Besides being sized up, there is another side of it that you have to remember. The girls are cut off from their previous contacts. They're scared, insecure, and lonely. They're looking for somebody to look out for them, care for them."

"But how does the courtship go on?" Jack persisted.

"Okay," she said, taking a breath. "Here's what happens. The stud will let 'his' interest in a certain chick be known. Most likely it will be in a direct way, like anybody striking up a relationship. Maybe 'he' will pass the word through a friend. Or maybe 'he' will write her a note. And these notes can really be something! They compare in some ways with your most passionate love letter. They aren't all that way, but there are some that are pretty racy! This is followed by the stud paying more and more attention to the chick, especially if she gives 'him' some encouragement. The stud usually has gifts to offer and sometimes 'he' will try to make 'his' big impression this way. So the studs who work in the kitchen, dining room, commissary, infirmary, or any place where they can get something for gifts have an advantage. Food, aspirin, and clothing all put the stud in a bargaining position for a chick. Besides, with these things to offer, it puts the stud in the role of being a provider—a role that's like what the man is supposed to do for his woman on the outside. These courtships I suppose are trial periods. A lot of them break down and never amount to anything. But we don't really know because we're not likely to know the difference between a couple of girls just striking up a more normal relationship and a relationship that is developing into a serious romance."

Up to this point, Mrs. Oster's role as teacher had lent her tone firm matter-of-factness. However, as she ended this last sentence, Jack noticed a subtle change in her expression; she had become more reflective.

"This is fascinating," Doc observed.

Mrs. Oster responded more slowly, "Some of the friendships turn into courtships, and some of them turn into marriages." She stopped abruptly.

"If a couple decides to marry, how do they proceed," Jack asked. "How is a marriage actually handled?"

"Well . . . they carry out a whole wedding ceremony . . . given the opportunity," Mrs. Oster explained, now uneasy. "But we don't witness them. We, or at least I, don't even know when they're carried out. I haven't studied it all that carefully. It gets mixed into the whole stream of things at the school and so I only know bits and pieces of it. Besides, it took us a long time before we could really face it and talk about it among ourselves. Maybe some of the others could answer that."

None of the women from Upper filled in the silence she had created.

Remembering Mrs. Caldwell's comment about the middle-class conservative views of her staff, Jack suddenly realized that Mrs. Oster and the other women were probably disturbed by the girls' mockery of the marriage ceremony. Before he could interject a comment, Mrs. Oster deftly asked, "Mrs. Marshal, what has been the experience in your cottage?"

Mrs. Marshal responded with ease. "There's a lot going on that we're not in on, Mrs. Oster. Yet there's a lot we do see. In answer to Jack's question, 'How do they proceed?' it depends on a number of things. For example, the amount of their idle, unsupervised time, the extent of their ingenuity, and so on. Now, given a lot of unsupervised time, they may put on a real ceremony— with preacher, veils, attendants, and music—and follow it up with a reception party. If, on the other hand, their free time is very limited and closely supervised, such a ceremony is much less likely. Instead, a quickie commitment or vow will be exchanged. These quickies can be pretty intense, however, such as scratching each other's wrist until they draw blood and then rubbing the two wounds together: an 'exchange of blood.' Now, not all marriages have ceremonies. There are some that develop through 'an understanding'—something like a common-law relationship. As I said before, given the opportunity, the girls will build these ceremonies up. And if the couple has a big following, a ceremony is more likely to take place. I believe a couple's preference plays a part. If they don't want a ceremony, it's not likely they'll be pushed into one—that is, unless they have a big following."

"I agree with Mrs. Marshal's report," Mrs. Script declared. "From what I've seen, I'd say whether or not these marriages take place depends a lot on how well we supervise the girls. If they have a lot of time that's not covered by a supervisor, this whole sticky relationship thing gets out of hand, including full marriage ceremonies. If there's supervision, I think that cuts down on the number of marriage ceremonies, but increases the number of understandings—and of course the supervision cuts down on the sexual acts themselves. And *those* really bother me.

"When you have two girls assigned to a room, it's a set-up that promotes an affair whether it's covered by a ceremony or not. And of course such a situation can't be completely supervised," Mrs. Marshal added with a discouraged tone. "So it seems like a losing battle to me."

Mrs. Elms elaborated. "Now, if you put three girls in a room, if there *is* room for three, you're really promoting trouble because you invariably set up a triangle, not only for all kinds of arguments, but sexually. Sometimes it looks like you get two chicks and one stud. Of course 'he' is really having a ball in that situation. Other times you have the opposite combination, and there's trouble for sure, with two studs after one chick. Still other times there seem to be all of one kind and then they have their contacts outside the room."

"So, if you had dormitories, like most of our units, what would happen?" Jack asked.

"We have some dormitories," Mrs. Oster answered. "They are easier to supervise—that is if we can keep our night supervisors awake until the kids are asleep. We insist that they do but it doesn't always work." She stopped abruptly. "Uh oh, that was a bad slip," she said with a grin, surveying the angry scowls on the faces of several night supervisors. After the group had had a hearty laugh, Mrs. Oster recovered by joking, "Now, girls, we'll have to admit that sometimes we beat the kids to bed!"

Jack broke in here to remind them of their main issue. "From what was said earlier, you know we have our sexual problems at Central too. I think we have them fairly well in hand right now. Everybody has been working very hard, and Doc Barth has been of special help. Doc, could you say something about our situation?"

"Why pick on me? You're doing fine," Doc said laughing. "On the other hand, now that I have the floor, I'd like to say a few things. Perhaps you and the others will want to add to what I've got to say. We need to point our discussion toward how to work with these problems. I agree with Jack; we have the situation pretty well in control at the moment. By that I mean, I don't think anybody is crawling into anybody else's bed at night. I don't think anybody is making anybody in the shops, and our toilet rooms and showers are under control. But that's talking only about our situation during the past couple of weeks. In view of how things go around here, I expect that this will change, so that in a week or two, we may have some kid or two or three in somebody else's bed and our situation in the shops may change."

"Frankly, I'm not ready to buy all of that," Mrs. Oster interrupted in a tone of friendly doubt. "If what you say is even near what goes on in the units, that's great, but I'd like to ask how you got it that way."

Doc responded in an even tone, "I think a lot of things have helped. Mr. Jeff got us started. He really shook us up. He brought us out of our complacency. He got us going."

Mr. Jeff, though pleased with Doc Barth's statement, smiled modestly.

Doc went on, "Mr. Jeff didn't pull his punches—even as a new man—in staff meetings. He described behavior he was seeing late in the evenings, in the shops, even in the showers. What we had been trying not to see, he made us take a look at and decide what we were going to do.

"I don't really understand the psychology of it. Maybe it's an accommodation to the setting one is in. Maybe it's a change in one's values, perceptions, and motivations as one works in an institution. Maybe it's complacency—or just plain laziness—that sets in. At any rate, people who are around these institutions year in and year out, myself included, overlook many matters they ought to pick up on, like this sexual thing, or stealing, and all kinds of abuse that one individual or group inflicts on another. What is even more perplexing is that these same year-in and year-out people, myself included, become defenders of the abuse and find every reason in the book not to do anything about it."

He paused to smile at the group. "Well, after getting that off my chest, I'd better return to Mrs. Oster's very good question of how we got it this way. Now we're really working to program the kids. They're very active and we have tighter night supervision. A couple of other things have helped. Stepped-up home visits is one—we've liberalized those a lot. The other is our group counseling program . . . the home visits give a boy a chance to maintain healthy relationships with his family and friends. These visits can't be over-rated. The group counseling keeps the staff close to the kids, and that prevents a lot of things. The meetings have raised a lot of important points. Homosexual threats or invitations haven't gotten into our discussions, but they'll come up as everybody becomes more at ease with the meetings and sex becomes a topic that the kids and the staff feel comfortable talking about. So far, I suspect the sexual problem has lurked behind the kids' talk about other kids picking on them or threatening them. Some of that talk has had a strong sexual undertone. You know, the kids are bullying for a purpose and the purpose hasn't been just to get a better position in the group or to express raw hostility. So in some cases that's what I believe they were really trying to tell us—that they were being bullied for sex. We have to remember that sexual problems are always going to be with us. Right now we've got our whole program working to deal with them.

"I don't think we want to overly psychologize the youngsters' sexual interests. Yet at the same time, I think we must watch what the kids do and say and be ready, if the circumstance presents itself, to sit down with them in an easy, common-sense way, and let them talk. And if they won't talk, gently ask what is preoccupying them. If you feel pretty sure it's a sexual matter, you might ask about it, without pressing, accusing, moralizing, or pushing a problem onto them that they may not have. Here one needs to be cautious. That's why I said earlier that we shouldn't overly psychologize by making big personal problems out of small or nonexistent ones. However, I don't want to obscure my main point and that is that sex and sexual problems are part and parcel of life, especially so in adolescents. So, be sensitive, be confident, be understanding, give the youngsters time, and keep what you permit and say within the do's and don'ts of the community outside the institution."

Doc's comments brought an appreciative reaction from the group; many nodded their heads in agreement and sat for several moments absorbing his words and counsel.

"Doc might have mentioned, but didn't, that to help our situation we put effeminate boys into the infirmary when they are admitted, or later on if a boy starts showing feminine behavior after he's been here for a while," Len Hall explained.

"And what do you do with them there?" Mrs. Oster asked.

Jack explained.

"The infirmary gives them protection beyond what can be offered in a living unit, and it also removes the stimulation from would-be aggressors. That's not enough, but it helps a great deal. The population in the infirmary is small, so people have a little more time to work with the boys and we try to add some planned program. They're under supervision and they're kept busy.

"How long do you keep them in the infirmary?" Mrs. Oster pursued.

"We have kept boys in there for as long as six or seven months," Doc answered, "but our aim is to move them out as fast as we can because our infirmary just doesn't have a program to carry the kids over the long haul of their stay. We try to work most of them into a regular living unit after maybe four to six weeks. That's after they've settled down and gotten over the initial shock of being admitted here. So, when they're new and going through periods when they're shaky and looking for protection and support, we have pretty good luck with them. Some, especially if they aren't very delinquent, we return to the court and ask that something be worked out for them in the community."

"How many judges tell you about a youngster's homosexuality when they send him to you?" Mrs. Oster challenged. "And if they tell you, how many will give you an honest evaluation about the part that the homosexuality played in their deciding to commit the boy?"

"Not many," Doc answered honestly. "It happens. We try to describe what our environment can do to this kind of kid. But that doesn't always work because the judges envision more facilities and staff than we really have. So we have to make those facts real to them. We don't usually get into whether or not a youngster's homosexual behavior in the community is delinquency. I don't believe it is. But to tell a judge this is probably not the most effective way of talking with him because it puts his judgment and decision-making in question. They, like anyone else (maybe even more so), don't want their judgment questioned, especially since theirs is a public decision. You know, it's out there for everyone to see—at least for those who want to look."

"What do *you* think?" Mrs. Oster asked directly.

"As I said," Doc continued, "my opinion is that it's *not* delinquency. It may be immoral behavior, but that's a moral question. . . . It may even be a psychiatric or psychological problem. In neither instance is it a problem of delinquency, and surely it's not one that a training school is prepared to do much about. Instead, a training school—even Central State—is apt to be harmful to such a kid."

"I've had a couple of good talks with Judge Linton and Judge Roe during the past year," Jack said. "I've known them for several years and had a chance to talk with them at a training session at the Hallmark's Extension Center. What they said is that in their work they're always having to choose the least among several evils in trying to figure out what to do with a boy. They rarely have a good choice available to them. Instead, they usually have a whole range of bad choices."

Mrs. Caldwell's strong interest brought her back into the conversation. "Just how do you approach the boys if you have a strong suspicion that they've been together? Or for that matter, if you have real evidence of it?"

"It's easier said than done," Doc Barth responded. "Generally, we try to do it in as low-key a way as we can. That is, we don't rant, rave, and moralize. We're direct about it. The reason for the low-key approach is that we assume the kids are going to be sensitive about it. That's not always the case. But you would be surprised—even the hardened ones have some shame, at least about being faced up. Besides respect for their feelings, it seems to be the best way to make some progress with the problem."

"That makes sense," Mrs. Caldwell assented. "But what do you actually say? How do you talk with the boys to let them know you won't permit it, that you want to help them in a way that doesn't embarrass them, and still sound positive?"

"Everybody does it his own way. There's really no one way to go about it," Doc said vaguely.

"Okay," Mrs. Caldwell responded promptly. "Could you pick a case and describe what you actually said? That would give me a better idea. Actually," she laughed, "I'd like to see if we at Upper really do moralize too much."

"Now you really have me on the spot," Doc admitted, but smiled and continued. "First, the kids see me as a middle-aged man and a doctor working here in the clinic—somebody who deals with personal problems, including sexual problems. Because of that my job may be a little easier than for other staff members. . . . Yet, I'm not sure whether it's really easier for me—it may actually be easier for a cottage supervisor. . . . At any rate, I'm quite direct and I try to take a fatherly approach in these matters, because I think it's consistent with the way the kids see me. Now, to get at your question about what I actually say to the boys, let me give you a couple of examples. One of our social workers had sound information that one of the kids the court was sending us had a homosexual problem. She asked me if I would see the boy immediately after he was admitted to the school. I saw the boy—had a good talk with him. After a few pleasant opening comments, I asked him to explain why he was committed to Central. He talked quite openly about his delinquency, though he didn't brag about it. Then I told him that I routinely ask new boys whether they have any personal problems, and so I wanted to ask him the same thing. Before I could go further, he shook his head 'no.' But since he looked awfully uncomfortable while he was shaking his head, I got the impression that more was involved. So, I very calmly said, 'Maybe I should have told you at the start that we had a phone call from the people at the detention center and they told us you were involved sexually with some of the boys there. My interest in talking with you about it is to see if we can avoid that kind of thing happening here.'

"I won't go into the details now, except to say that he maneuvered around some, and I gave him plenty of opportunity to do that . . . but I faced him with the fact of the phone call each time he finished his little denial. I wasn't hard on him, but at the same time I wasn't about to let him off. Well, finally he said, sad-like, 'I was bothered by the other boys.' And then he began to talk. A lot of anxiety poured out, and after he got more comfortable, I asked him if he might not want to start out in the infirmary instead of one of the units. He looked relieved and agreed.

"Now that's one illustration. Let me give you another one," Doc continued. "Two kids jumped another kid and raped him in the dormitory. They took turns using his rear. First one would do the screwing while the other helped hold the victim down, and then they would trade places. The cottage supervisor, Len Hall, had really dressed down these two boys and a social worker was seeing the boy who had been attacked. Jack or Len Hall asked me to talk to the two wolves. As I said, they had been given some type of restriction as punishments. Furthermore, in the way we staff usually do things, the wolves had gotten our hostility and the victim our sympathy. So at first I couldn't really figure out what I might add. The only lead I had was that Len said he really had 'shaken them' about what a low-down, dirty thing they had done. I had similar feelings, but I figured if they were really shaken up, they might be ready to talk. So I decided to see them together. They came into my office looking sheepish and I was low key and matter-of-fact in my manner. After asking them to sit down, I said without anger but seriously and directly, 'Len Hall was by and asked me if I could see you fellows—talk with you—to understand the sexual goings-on in the dormitory.' My aim was to loosen them up and give them a chance to talk. They put on expressions of not knowing what I was talking about, and then one of them said, 'What do you mean?' Continuing to be low key, I encouraged them, 'Pick it up any place you like. I'm referring to your sexual relations with Blaine.' They didn't say anything, and of course I sat waiting. I followed with something like, 'How did you fellows get involved in this?' They shrugged their shoulders. I asked again, 'What led up to the whole thing?' Again they shrugged their shoulders. Then I waited for several minutes, after which I said, in the interest of pushing them a little, 'I sense you're kind of upset by what you did or by what might happen to you as the result of what you did.' Not a word out of them. I tried a combination question-suggestion comment: 'You do have some feelings about this? Is there anything you fellows want to talk over with me. Is there anything you think I can help you with? Especially your feelings, whatever they might be.' I kept pushing the feelings thing because I thought that would motivate them to talk. But when they didn't say anything, I said matter-of-factly, 'If you fellows want to talk this problem over some time, I'll be glad to see you.' I telephoned Mr. Hall and asked him to send somebody over to the office to pick them up."

Doc concluded, "No great psychiatric insights and no great changes in either situation. In the first case, I felt satisfied with the interviewing and the temporary disposition of the boy. In the second situation, the interviewing never got off the ground. The best that can be said is that I tried to get the boys to talk, and when they didn't, I left the door open for them to come back. The only other thing I might add is that I was careful not to undermine Len Hall's management of the cottage."

Jack intervened after a moment. "Thanks, Doc. We've been hard at this for quite awhile, and now I think it's about time we took a short break."

Mrs. Marshal was the first to open the conversation fifteen minutes later. She began eagerly, "I was glad to hear Doctor Barth say that he tried to help the boys but was careful not to undermine Len Hall's discipline. That discipline must come first. I think we are all too liberal about these expressions of homosexuality. In fact, we are downright negligent! I know there are supposed to be all kinds of explanations for it, but none of them make it *right*. I've talked with a lot of girls who are involved, and they tell me they are lonely and that everybody else is doing it. So they get involved and then excuse themselves. Some even tell me that it's the new thing out in the community. That it's overlooked out there. Of course, then they complain that we don't look the other way at Upper. But I say it's downright abnormal. What's more, when we take this overly tolerant attitude I think we are actually encouraging and reinforcing their homosexuality."

Mrs. Caldwell asked, rather gently, "Don't you think we have a problem here that goes perhaps beyond the moral consideration?"

"Sure," Mrs. Marshal agreed. "There are many things that go into the making of this problem—the whole history of the girls and the fact that our institution closes them off from the outside, especially from normal contacts with men. Nevertheless, I believe this behavior is not only immoral but is *abnormal*—and it ought to be stopped! When we look around for all its causes, we really seem to be using all those causes for excuses for not putting a stop to it! And then we end up being tolerant of behavior that's hurting the girls! My plea is that we recognize our part in contributing to and even encouraging their sexual activities!"

Mrs. Marshal stopped only long enough to catch her breath. "I've asked many a girl, 'What about your boyfriend? What will you tell him when you get out? What will you tell your husband when you get married?' "

"I think for most of them the institutional involvement passes, Catherine," Mrs. Caldwell said in an effort to decrease the growing sense of drama. "I think the girls get involved with other girls at Upper because they are lonely and want to be loved. Once they leave the institution, their involvements here end."

Though perceptibly uncomfortable with Mrs. Marshal's angry display and implicit accusation that Upper State was not effective in halting homosexuality, Mrs. Caldwell did not interrupt her again. Mrs. Marshal maintained the initiative.

"I personally doubt that the girls will be able to trade their inside roles for outside roles that easily. It just isn't a mechanical trade-off of one role for another, especially if the girl is really involved at Upper—and most of them are. It seems that each is going to need a good male on the outside, one who can really turn the girl around and turn her on. And I'm not sure how many of those are around! As a matter of speculation, I'd say there probably are very few such types available to our 'graduates.' But we've been assuming that our girls even *want* a man after they leave here. I can see where the studs, especially those who have been quite successful and have enjoyed playing a male role, may not even be interested in finding men once they get out. They not only would have to involve themselves with a man instead of a woman, but they also would have to reverse their part in the sexual relationship, unless of course they got tied up with a man who wanted to play the role of a woman."

The group was electrified—not only by what Mrs. Marshal was saying, but also by her courage to say it. Jack was amazed, as was his staff, at the vehemence of her words, which implied that her feelings had never been expressed in regular staff meetings at Upper State. Mrs. Caldwell's silence seemed to confirm this.

Upper's staff exchanged looks with each other, looking finally to their administrator for a response to Mrs. Marshall's heated speech.

Mrs. Caldwell broke the long silence. "As I was about to explain earlier," she said, smiling at Mrs. Marshall, "the after-effects of institutionalization, including effects of institutional sexual experience, are probably worse than we would like them to be."

Tension eased among the women from Upper State. Jack interposed, "Doc Barth only had time to hit the highlights of our struggle at Central State with this problem. Let me report that we're *still* struggling. Now if the Central staff will permit me to talk quite openly . . ." heads nodded to indicate permission, "it became obvious to us all that our situation concerning sexual behavior was bad. But as time went on, that realization didn't really mean much. To put it bluntly, some supervisors were taking advantage of the fact that some kids would be easier to manage if they were allowed to form steady, satisfying, homosexual relationships. A sort of trade-off system developed. These permissions were quite well understood by the supervisors and the boys even though the supervisors never put them into words. The trade-offs amounted to the supervisors' turning their backs to the wolves' sexual exploitation of the lambs, and in return, the wolves helped the supervisors keep order in the cottages."

Mrs. Marshal challenged, "What do you mean by 'keep order'? It seems to me that they were getting *out* of order!"

"You're right in the larger sense," Jack answered with forced ease. "No doubt about it. Yet, in a smaller sense, the supervisors were getting day-to-day help from the wolves in keeping down the number of fights in the units, keeping down the number of runaways, keeping down the amount of stealing—generally in helping to enforce whatever the supervisors wanted.

"Now, it took us quite a while to approach this problem. I think you would all agree, especially in light of today's stories, that getting at such reasons for allowing homosexual behavior is a very, very sensitive thing. Nobody, or hardly anybody, would want to admit to such a thing, and while I'm not trying to play psychiatrist, I really believe that some of those supervisors were involved in this trade-off business without even being fully aware of it . . . not even conscious of it."

"One detail," Mrs. Oster pressed. "I'd like to have Doctor Barth go back to his comments about interviewing those couple of cases—you know, the ones who had sexual problems. Well, I was expecting more of a treatment thing. Instead, it seems like you simply imposed or supported a kind of management or control over the kids . . . the kind of thing I could do. But you didn't do anything about their underlying problems."

Doc replied directly to her. "Let me answer it this way. We work on improving the total program. You know, the institutional environment. That involves control—and control helps us create a reasonably good environment for boys. It also involves treating the boys well."

"But how about individual therapy?" Mrs. Oster asked.

"We do some of that and we like to think it helps," Doc replied. "But remember that most of the sexual problems our boys have are created by the closed institutional setting. So it's really the setting we have to work on the most."

Seeing that Mrs. Oster looked somewhat disappointed in his answer, Doc continued, "I don't mean to say that some kids don't have individual problems with sex—and individual treatment can help them—but even for them, a good overall environment is necessary. We're working to create a setting where homosexuality is not the prescribed way of life."

After the emotional rigors of the afternoon, the session seemed to have reached a stopping point. A sense of closure pervaded the group, reflected in calm faces.

Jack looked down at his watch and observed, "This may be the right time to point out that we've run past the time when we agreed we would stop. It's now a quarter of five. Before we close, however, I would say—and I think I may say it for everyone here—that it's been a good day. We've learned a great deal about each other's programs and problems.

"We'll have a summary of our meeting typed up and sent to you within a couple of weeks, but just to give the meeting an orderly conclusion, I'd like to note several issues of major concern we've identified. Since we had a summary of this morning's session before we broke for lunch, I'll only touch on this afternoon's meeting." He consulted his note pad.

"First, there was concern about who the courts judge to be delinquent enough to send to a training school. The staff from Upper felt that the courts send many girls because they don't know what else to do with them, but that in sending them, the courts are doing a number of inappropriate things. They felt that girls are sent to an institution as a result of sexual and other behavior that adults would never be institutionalized for—or boys. In this discussion, the staff from Upper talked with great concern about the special problems of the pregnant girl who gets committed. In short, we have bias in the courts and very probably in the police and other agencies in the community, too. On that point, Mrs. Oster talked about Upper's work with the courts to improve this situation.

"Second, there was mutual agreement that more than a few of our problems are generated by the poor quality of our programs, and since we're responsible for the kids in the cottages, we took a hard look at those programs and talked about ways we can improve them.

"Third, after ducking the subject for some time, we took up the problems of homosexuality in our institutions. In this connection, we shared a number of different ideas and attitudes about sexually different behavior and how we ought to respond to it. Differing ideas were expressed with courage and I think we all learned from that discussion.

"Somewhere along the line, we talked about the boys' aggressive behavior, so I'll make that the fourth major point. Fifth, we shared some thoughts about how the kids organize themselves into tightly knit cliques and how those cliques affect our programs. We at Central surely learned some things from the staff at Upper about the make-believe families the girls form. I know it was all new to me. And Doc Barth talked about facing the kids up to their abusing others sexually, so maybe I could list that as point number six."

Jack looked around the room. "I think these several points give some coordination and structure to our discussion this afternoon. Before closing, I would like to ask Mrs. Caldwell and Mr. Graves to make any final comments they feel are fitting."

With a gesture from Mr. Graves that she should proceed first, Mrs. Caldwell commented, "Jack, I think you have expressed many of our feelings about this meeting. I do want to thank you here at Central for having us over. It's been an excellent day for all of us. We've had a useful chance to talk with one another. We've had a chance to think together. Now I believe we've got some homework to do—at least at Upper." She turned to Mr. Graves and said, "Mr. Graves, I don't believe you have said a word since you welcomed us this morning. If I were asked to second guess your silence, I'd say that you wanted the staff to have a full opportunity to talk, to discuss, and therefore you left the floor to them. Why don't you give us a few final remarks . . . a few words of parting wisdom before we break up?"

Mr. Graves rose at the back of the room. Though it was a poor place from which to address the group formally, his tall figure was conspicuous to all. "It's been a good day; it's been an honest day," he began slowly. "Let me join in your candor by saying that from an administrative point of view, it's a headache to take youngsters who don't belong with us, especially if their commitments are for some type of sexual misbehavior which, if not quite common in the community, surely happens more than occasionally. And, of course, as you have been pointing up so clearly, it's an even bigger headache to develop a program for these youngsters.

"As you have already discussed with great thoroughness, we as institutions have to guard against becoming the kids' greatest enemies by permitting, indeed even encouraging by our neglect the development of a homosexual community." Mr. Graves' tone had mounted as he talked, but he lowered it again to stress the gravity of his words. "It's at the point of institutional daily living, and in cottage life, that we can be of real help to the youngsters who are sent to us. And it's *you* who have their charge longer than any other staff during the youngster's daily life . . . *longer than any other staff.*"

"Ask any institutional worker, ranging from the custodian to the psychiatrist, and he'll tell you that the cottage supervisors have the greatest opportunities to influence the kids. Indeed, they'll tell you that the cottage supervisors have the most important job! And if we really believe that, we'll take the time and make the effort to continue these meetings and talk together about *how* we can make our influence even more effective.

"It's late in the day, but never too late to think creatively about kids, so I would like to say one more thing. Mull over today's discussion, sift and sort out the ideas, and then *try* some of them. If there is any fun in this business, it's the opportunity to work with different ideas."

He smiled into every face turned his way. "We welcomed you this morning; however, now I am afraid it's time to part. This has been such a good meeting that I can assure you there will be more. We have a committee to whom we are appreciative for this meeting and upon whom we'll be calling to plan the next one. In the meantime, face your work with new inspiration, perseverance and insight."

8

IS THERE MORE THAN
ONE WAY TO GET OUT?

"From reading your reports, I get the impression that Sam Walker has come a long way since he was admitted," Doc Barth began, concluding a staff meeting that had been considering the progress of several boys and their readiness for parole. "He looks very good in contrast to the other boys we've discussed this morning. Now, in order for us to finish early enough to catch some lunch, I'd like to have a brief statement from each of you so that the final summary can be prepared. Let's start with social service. Miss Smith, can you give us a statement?"

"Okay. I'll be as brief as I can. I've seen steady progress during Sam's interviews with me. At first he was so seclusive, so reticent, so withdrawn. It was readily apparent that he was disturbed. Things were bothering him, but he wouldn't open up and talk about them—and wouldn't for a long time. When he finally did, he talked about his impossible home situation. He had a hard time coming to the subject, but he was finally able to face how bad his father's desertion and his mother's constant nagging had made him feel. Once he was able to face those facts and talk about them, he began to improve. I should say, too, that he expressed great sadness and anger about his father's desertion and real annoyance with his mother. . . . So it was pretty rough going for awhile. I didn't know whether we were going to make it or not." She stopped here. "I guess I'm beginning to repeat myself. Anyway, since I've written all of this out for the record, why don't I end by saying that Sam has definitely improved, enough to be sent to the home of an uncle in Lamar. All of the arrangements have been made."

Doc turned to Mr. Eagan. "Clarence, you reported earlier that Sam has improved in his school work."

"Yes," Mr. Eagan commented. "In two semesters of work, his achievements in math and English have increased so that he is now about where he should be in these basic areas for a boy of his age with his abilities. His behavior is reported to be all right, though a couple of the teachers have mentioned that he's sneaky—they feel they can't always trust him. However, it seems to me they may be expecting too much. After all, I'm not sure that *anyone* can be trusted *all* of the time." After a hearty chuckle from the group, Mr. Eagan concluded, "From the standpoint of the school, Sam's achievement is almost equal to his grade level and his potential for learning. His behavior has been a bit marginal, but overall it's been satisfactory. I'd leave my statement at that."

"Can you tell us anything about his performance in the recreational program? And has he had a work assignment?"

"Sure, let me add several things," Mr. Eagan said. "Mr. Dermer of the intramural program reports that Sam isn't much of a participant in any of the sports they offer: volleyball, basketball, dodgeball, ping pong, pool, and so on. It's taken a lot of encouragement, in fact a lot of push, to get him to participate in anything. In the area of work, Mr. Joseph, who has him on the yard force, says the same thing about his work performance. He'd show up, but that's about it. In Sam's behalf," and Mr. Eagan paused to laughed, "I guess it might be difficult to get inspired about cutting grass, raking leaves, and doing clean-up work. On the other hand, many of the boys have responded well on the yard force because of the good supervision there. Mr. Joseph has done a very fine job with the tougher kids. In fact, I'd say that some of the boys have actually learned to like working on that detail. But getting back to Sam, both Mr. Dermer and Mr. Joseph report a recent 'spurt,' which I guess you could call improvement. Sam has involved himself in some of the recreation and has put forth some effort at work. But overall, I would say that his performance in these areas has been marginal, at best."

"Thank you," Doc commented and then turned to Jack. "What can you say about Sam's group living, Jack?"

"Sam's record in Ranger cottage is somewhat like Mr. Eagan's description of his work and recreational performance. The picture is mixed. His behavior and attitude currently are okay. Both have improved significantly compared with what they were at first. He's more cooperative now. He also gets involved in activities more easily. Earlier, he was uncooperative, moody, and sometimes downright surly.

"There is a characteristic about him that we really haven't been able to do much about. It's the sneakiness that Mr. Eagan mentioned. Sam continues to operate by manipulating. He's pulled fewer stunts lately, at least there have been only one or two that we've been aware of during the past month or two. So I guess we shouldn't be too hard on him in that category. Earlier he was selling protection to the new boys coming into the cottage. After we stopped that, he was caught selling protection to the kids from other cottages—to protect them on the way to school. During the past month or two we've not seen as much manipulative behavior, so I believe he has improved in this area as well as overall." Jack paused. "But he's no star."

"I sense that you're recommending him for parole even though you don't see him as a prospective model citizen," Doc said, amused.

Jack smiled as he nodded.

"Okay," Doc said, "I guess it's my turn next. I saw Sam for two diagnostic interviews when he was admitted, now almost nine months ago, and I interviewed him again last week. My diagnostic impression is that he is much less tense now than when I first met with him, and perhaps more important is that he appears much less hostile and calculating. For example, he's much more relaxed now. He seemed genuinely friendly and talked quite openly about himself. His candor especially impressed me. He told me about his treatment interviews with Miss Smith, which," Doc shifted his attention to Miss Smith, "I believe were first rate.

"Sam has picked up some striking insights about himself, especially the causal connection between his delinquency—whether it be stealing, strong-arming, cheating, or conning—and his disappointment and anger with adults. Furthermore, he knows that his disappointment and anger stem basically from his exceptionally bad relationships with his parents. What's important about all of this is that Sam is beginning to use these insights about himself to control his delinquency.

"For summary purposes, from a psychiatric point of view there are three things worth repeating—and then a note of caution. First, Sam now seems substantially less hostile and calculating than when he came in. Second, he has demonstrated a capacity to benefit from treatment. And third, as a result of his insights into the causes of his delinquency, I would predict that he is a substantially better risk for prosocial behavior than he was when he came to us. I would agree with each of you that we ought to parole him. But I must conclude that he is only a *marginally* good case for parole. Despite his improvement, he still is a pretty angry, aggressive, and shrewd boy with well-established behavior patterns. We have to remember that he had a long, long way to go when he came in."

The staff sat in momentary silence until Jack commented, "I think that we're in general agreement on Sam, though each of us has described different aspects about him. But our separate pieces of information have led us to pretty similar conclusions."

"I think that's right," Doc acknowledged. "Though I sense that Miss Smith may feel a bit more positive about Sam than some of the rest of us." Turning to her he said "I may have overstated your position."

"No, you haven't," Miss Smith replied thoughtfully. "I think your estimate of my position is accurate. I *am* more optimistic about Sam's future, but I'm very much aware of the problems that you, Clarence, and Jack have pointed out."

Looking around at the staff, Dr. Barth concluded, "Very good. I think that winds up our morning's work. Miss Smith, if you would prepare to implement the arrangements to place Sam, we'll consider this meeting over."

"Is Sam being staffed today?"

Jim Watson and Bill Wilson, Ranger Cottage's two supervisors, were talking in the cottage staff room where they crossed paths during their overlap in shifts.

"Yeah," Bill said between sips of coffee.

"I hope he makes it. Sam has shown some nice progress."

Bill frowned and challenged mildly, "How do you figure that?"

"He's been a pretty good kid lately, at least on my shift," Jim replied. "Besides, he's really improved across the board during the time we've had him."

"Well, that kid has conned about everybody into believing he's going straight." Bill said sharply. "I can see that he's taken *you* in along with all the others."

"But just look at how much he's improved," Jim insisted. "Now, whether or not I've been taken in is another matter."

"What makes you think he's improved?" Bill asked wryly.

"He behaves better," Jim began. "He does what you tell him to do and he does what you expect of him. I know he hasn't always done that, but during the past month or two, or maybe even three, he's toed the line pretty darned good!"

"What exactly does he do better than he used to?" Bill persisted.

"You're really convinced he's the same, aren't you? I can name a few things. First, he agitates less than he used to. You know, there was a time when he was always griping and getting the kids stirred up about one thing or another—the food wasn't any good, the passes home didn't come often enough and were given out unfairly, and on and on. Then, his manipulating the other kids was worse. Remember how he used to push some of them into stealing and running away and fighting? You name it and he was involved: pressuring, manipulating, and strong-arming the other kids. Well, there isn't any strong-arming anymore that I know of and the pressuring and threatening are way down. You hardly ever see him behave that way."

"How about his conning? You forgot to mention that."

"Well, he's cut it way back."

"But it's still there," Bill countered.

Irritated now, Jim returned, "What do you expect him to become before you give him another chance on the outside?"

"Jim," Bill said, quiet and serious, "we've been working together for a long time now. So maybe I can be direct with you. It looks to me like Sam is conning you. In fact, I sense he already has."

Jim flushed, then responded with measured control. "I won't bite on that. I'd still say Sam's conning is way down. But let me turn this conversation around," Jim said sourly. "If he *is* conning me, then maybe he's getting to you because you can't manage him."

"I can handle him," Bill returned. "Don't worry about that. But that doesn't mean that he wouldn't like to run the cottage or that he wouldn't like to have me running errands for him."

"Oh, I doubt that," Jim said coolly. "He hasn't given me that kind of trouble. Not even when he first came in . . . sure, he was hot-headed then and was for a long time afterward, but I never fed into that behavior and he always went right along with what I asked."

"You mean to say he never gave you any trouble?" Bill challenged.

"I didn't say that," Jim answered in the same tone. "What I did say is that I never let him get to me or set me up."

"You make it sound awfully convincing, Jim," Bill interrupted. "But what about his attitude?"

While plenty of sparks were generated between Bill and Jim, their argument had for a time maintained the quality of a dialogue in a case conference or seminar—erratic and undisciplined, but nevertheless incisive and thought-provoking. However, the argument was becoming overheated.

"I don't know what you mean by 'attitude'; that crappy word throws me," Jim said sharply. "Anything that somebody doesn't like about a kid gets called a 'bad attitude'—the way a kid looks and acts and how he talks to supervisors and teachers all gets referred to as 'attitude.' "

"All right, all right, I get you," Bill replied. "But after you've said all that, you have to ask yourself what you think is really cooking with the guy. You have to ask yourself what his basic attitude is."

Maintaining the heat of the argument, Jim continued. "What's cooking with the guy for me is what I see him do—actually do. It's not what I may think his reasons are for doing something. You would say his reason for behaving well, if you would ever admit he behaves well, is to fool us. If I looked at him the way you do, I'd think he wasn't capable of improving, too!"

"Well, it just goes to show you," Bill observed with an air of triumph, "he's got you fooled."

"No, hasn't got me fooled," Jim insisted hotly.

"Look, you need to really *look* at what Sam is pulling," Bill said, warming to the argument. "Haven't you seen him talking to the kids on the sly? Haven't you noticed him being super polite with staff? Haven't you seen him work at being the first one in the chow line? Haven't you heard him call staff's attention to the fact that he was the first one into bed at night or the first one out in the morning?"

"Sure, and he's brought his papers home from school and shown me the grades he's been getting. And he's shown me his weekly rating for his work at the laundry," Jim responded. "And what's wrong with that? Basically Sam has been doing good work and he wants us to know it. Now, if you want to play the crystal-ball game, you could say that he not only is doing better, but that he also wants to relate better to other people—even you! So he's using the fact that he's doing better work to talk with us, to be friendly, and that kind of thing."

"You sure go a long way to try to make a point," Bill said with a sigh. "What you seem to be forgetting is the kind of a guy we're talking about."

"I haven't forgotten," Jim asserted.

"Let me remind you anyway," Bill said impatiently. "Remember the social worker telling us about how he was beating up on drunks and rolling them before he came here? And when he was first here, how he was catching pigeons down at the barn and the using them like kites? First he would tie one end of a long string around one of the pigeon's legs and then let it fly, only to pull the bird back to the ground once it had taken off. He'd keep this up until the leg was torn off the poor darn pigeon by his yanking it back to the ground. Then there was that whole series of problems with him when he was selling protection."

After a brief pause, Jim responded in a discouraged tone, "Yes, I remember, but you can't keep judging the kid forever for what he's done in the past."

"Accchh!" Bill said with disgust. "And how about his drowning those guinea pigs . . . after stealing them from the Department of Health's animal building back of the gym?"

"None of that history is good," Jim admitted. "I agree. But you can't keep pinning the kid to it. If you keep pinning the kid to his past, Bill, he'll never escape from it."

"Well, he was involved in too much of that kind of stuff to ignore," Bill charged. "You just can't say that the boy is ready for parole because he's behaved himself for a couple of months."

"I still say that you're pinning him to his past. You're not giving him any credit for changing his behavior. You've got your mind set against him," Jim maintained.

"Well, I guess all we can do is agree to disagree, Jim," Bill concluded.

"Man, you sure have got them eating out of your hand with all that brown nosing you've been doing," Cal said with a laugh. "If you get out of here with that record of yours, it'll be one for the books. Man, I swear I've never seen a better con job since I've been in here."

Sitting across a game table from Cal in the recreation room of Ranger Cottage, Sam answered with a slow smile, "Cal, you're laying compliments on me I can't handle. I like to hear good words about me, but I don't like to hear things that aren't true. You're a goddamn liar and what you're giving me is a lot of shit!"

"Man, what do you mean 'shit' when I'm telling it like it is?" Cal protested amiably. "Besides speaking the truth, I'm trying to treat you fine and pay you a compliment—to give credit, man, where credit is due."

"How can you sit there and lay one lie on top of another, one piece of shit on another, and call them the truth, and then go ahead and insult me by saying you're paying me a compliment?" Sam chortled, and then continued, "If I weren't such a good guy, I'd say you're not only insulting me but you're trying to put me down, too. If I weren't such a nice guy, I'd beat the hell out of you!"

"I'm just telling you what I know," Cal persisted with a grin on his face. "Now, if you know something more, you'll have to help me because all I know is what I been seeing."

"Look Cal, quit doing a number on me," Sam chided. "We're old buddies so I ought to be able to count on you for a little trust."

"You're right in calling me a 'buddy,'" Cal affirmed with pride, then broke into a scoffing laugh and added, "And on the trust thing, I'm the only guy who will give it to you straight, whether you like it or not. So I'm saying it to you straight: You sure are giving them a nice shag. Yeah! You sure done a good job, now let me tell you."

Cal listed Sam's achievements one by one until his voice crescendoed with a loud shout. "Whoooeee! You done good! No doubt about it Sam, you done very good! You made 'em all feel great about helping you. I'll bet they really feel good about getting you to change . . . to go straight, to go along with the program, and all those nice things."

Suddenly, he lowered his voice confidentially. "Now that what's happening is out in the open, at least between you and me, you know and I know that they're up there right now in the Administration Building saying their piece for you! Planning how to get you out of here all legal! Now, why shouldn't your buddy give you credit for that?"

Cal tipped his chair back on two legs and looked at Sam through squinting eyes. He shook his head. "Knowing you, I'd say you going to get mad at me, even though I'm your friend, for telling you the truth—the kind of truth I'm laying on you. Besides the truth, friend, I just can't help giving you credit for doing such a *fantastic* job."

Sam listened carefully and in spite of his protesting seemed to be enjoying Cal's babbling.

"I can just hear 'em up there in the office building saying how good you done here," Cal droned on. "And I bet old Doc Barth and that little sweety pie Miss Smith are leadin' the song. You know, I sure give you credit how you went up there and paid those people some time when you figured it was getting close to paroling. Yes sir, you sure have it coming to you, Sam. Now tell me, old buddy, did you really have to let it all hang out for those people up there to get them to work on getting you out of this hole?"

Sam's tolerant expression changed to sour disdain. "Cal, I know you're trying to treat me good, but that kind of goodness I don't need," he said mildly. "You're running me down by saying I've been using them people, and you're running them down too because you're making them look stupid."

"You got it figured almost right," Cal replied, "But not quite. I'm saying you was smart enough to outfigure them. I'm running you up, not down. And I'm not running them down. It's just that you outsmarted them."

"Yeah, yeah, I get you," Sam said impatiently, then winked at Cal, shrugged, and walked out of the rec room.

9

TIMMY'S HUNG HIMSELF

"If that's it, then let's adjourn," Jack said pleasantly.

Pete Robb shoved his chair back, causing a break in the prevailing atmosphere of good will. A frown cut furrows in his forehead as he opened his mouth to speak. His voice contained a mixture of trust and anxiety. "We made some progress, but not very much. Not really."

He walked out of the conference room and out of the Administration Building.

Starting down the walk toward Outpost Cottage, he saw its door burst open. Four or five boys sprang out of it, almost as if they had been shot from the barrel of a cannon, and began running wildly toward him. Before they had covered the thirty yards or so between the cottage and Mr. Robb, the boys began shouting, "Timmy's hung himself! Timmy's hung himself! He's hanging in the showers!"

He broke into a run. In moments he was in the shower room.

It was packed with boys. Some were crying. Others were just standing in shock. Several were cursing quietly. Mr. Robb elbowed his way to the shower stall at the far end of the room and pushed aside several boys who were blocking the entrance to the stall. He looked inside. Timmy was hanging, slowly turning from a rope that was attached to a water pipe near the ceiling.

Mr. Robb forced himself to turn his eyes to the floor. A toppled-over Coke crate beneath the boy's feet indicated that after tightening the noose around his neck, Timmy had kicked the box out from under himself.

While Timmy had undeniably done an effective job in the final sense, he had not done an expert hangman's job. His face, now blue and almost bursting from compressed blood, showed that he had died a slow and agonizing death, a choking death. His was no sudden death brought about by a broken neck; the distance he had fallen after he kicked away the crate was too small to produce a sudden or severe jerk of his neck. Instead, the fall had probably produced only a mild jerk, followed by a continuous tightening of the noose.

Mr. Robb's surveillance had taken but a few seconds. Almost immediately after peering into the shower stall he shouted, "Get me a knife! Give me a hand!"

He scrambled to right the crate and mounted it. As some of the boys held the box firm, he gently raised Timmy's limp body. A boy passed him a knife, and, holding Timmy in one arm, he cut him loose with the other. Timmy's body immediately slumped over Mr. Robb's shoulder. Dropping the knife to the floor, he cradled Timmy and brought him down to the floor. A new wave of panic swept through him as he realized Timmy was indeed dead. Irrevocably dead.

Rational thinking left him then. Fastening his mouth on Timmy's, he began desperately to apply artifical respiration. So strong was Mr. Robb's need to believe he could bring the boy back to life that several times he was sure Timmy had started to breathe on his own, find only to that he hadn't. His irrational self was demanding that Timmy come back.

In the meantime, although the boys were milling around the shower room and the day rooms, the cottage was deadly quiet. A few had run up to the Administration Building to notify the people there, and several minutes later Doc Barth broke into the room with a stethoscope draped around his neck. He nodded affirmingly when Mr. Robb looked up from his efforts, and with a slight motion of his hand, suggested that Mr. Robb move his body to permit him to examine Timmy. As Mr. Robb continued his efforts, Doc Barth carefully moved his stethoscope over Timmy's chest, and his expression of grave concern turned to sadness. Tears welled up in his eyes and dropped onto the boy's chest. He shook his head several times, then stopped his examination. However, he encouraged Mr. Robb to continue.

Mr. Robb continued to apply artificial respiration for the next thirty minutes. Finally, he knew it was hopeless. He motioned for Doc to reexamine Timmy and then began to cry, at first softly, then in great sobs. Mixed with deep gasps for air, the sobs shook his body in violent writhing motions. Two boys responded to Mr. Robb's agony by moving close to him and putting their arms over his shoulder and crying with him, while several other boys nearby started to cry. Having completed his examination, Doc moved to Mr.

Robb's side, put his hand on his shoulder and quietly said, "Pete—I am sorry—Timmy is dead."

As Mr. Robb's crying subsided, he looked up at the people around him. He became aware of the staff who had come into the room and were interspersed among the boys: Jack, Miss Leaf, Mr. Wilton, and Mr. Eagan.

As he stared at them, his glassy eyes filled with contempt.

He rose and wiped the tears from his eyes. He took a deep breath and with it took full measure of the staff. He began to shout violently, "It's murder! Murder! Nothing less! I warned you, I pleaded with you, and Jack tried to tell you. You wanted a good placement! You wanted clearances! You wanted agency cooperation! You wanted more time! Well, by Jesus, you have it now—a real placement. Every one of you better face up to this. Every one of you, and the agencies you keep talking about, better find a procedure that will keep this from ever happening again. You better find a way other than just talking, talking all around the problem! Well, *now* you have a real problem!"

The group stood in shock. Before anyone could respond, Mr. Robb stalked out of the cottage, across the school grounds, and out the front gate of Central State.

A week prior to this episode, Mr. Robb had stopped Jack as he was coming out of the dining room and had said with much concern, "I'd like to talk with you about a situation that I've got in my unit."

"Sure," Jack replied. "Why don't we head for the office and talk about it now."

Walking toward the building, Pete began in measured and thoughtful tones, "You know the kids in my cottage have fewer problems than those in most of the units. As a matter of fact, if there were just someplace for most of them to go, and if the courts and the police were just a little more liberal about trying them back in their communities, I believe we would clear out quite a number of them."

"You're right," Jack admitted. "Most of your kids are here mainly because their homes are in a mess and the judges don't know where else to send them. Sure, they've pulled some delinquent stunts, maybe shoplifting at worst. More likely they were truant from school, stay out late at night, running away, and that kind of thing."

As they entered the Administration Building and walked to Jack's office, he observed in a friendly tone, "Well, I expect you've got something more specific in mind."

"My problem is with four or five boys who have been here—I believe too long. They're discouraged and seem to have given up hope. Take Timmy

Stover; he's in the worst shape of the lot. He's written home a half-dozen times during the past couple of months, but he doesn't get any answer. We have information—grapevine information—from his parole officer that the mother is still at the same address. The father—who really drinks it up—has pulled out again. Now the mother is shacked up with someone she picked up at a local bar. The P.O. as much as said that Timmy can't go home under these conditions."

"I don't quite understand this grapevine," Jack said.

"I've known Ed Catton for years—he's the officer. I happened to see him over at a friend's house on a weekend, and he told me," Mr. Robb explained.

"Does Timmy's social worker know this?" Jack asked.

"Well, yes," Mr. Robb responded, mildly frustrated. "I told her what I'd learned and asked her to check it out—to see if it's true or not. And if the home is really so messed up that the boy can't go back, we ought to be working on another place where he *can* go. And we ought to be talking to Timmy about it."

"Has she checked it out?"

"I don't know," Mr. Robb answered, "I'd better ask her."

"Does the boy know this story?" Jack asked.

"I doubt it. Nobody is going to give him rumor. At least I'm not," Mr. Robb countered. "I'm sure he has the bigger picture—that his mother doesn't really want him. I'm pretty sure Miss Leaf hasn't told him a thing."

"What makes you think that?" Jack inquired.

"Well, when he doesn't get any mail," Mr. Robb related, "he comes to me and without my saying a word, he raises the issue by making lame excuses for his not getting a letter—excuses I feel he doesn't really believe himself, such as, 'She's too busy working,' or 'The mail delivery is bad.' "

"I think I'm getting a clearer picture of Timmy's situation," Jack said thoughtfully. "But you say you've got a number of boys who are in the same shape?"

"That's right," Mr. Robb said. "Three others. It's not that they're doing anything bad—you know, like running away, stealing, lying, or strong-arming. These boys are sad. They mope around. They don't talk much. They look depressed, like they're about to cry."

"Earlier you said you might have as many as five," Jack recalled. "That means you have four in addition to Tim?"

"Hell, Jack, there might even be six or seven, but on hard judgment, I'd say there are four we *must* take action on now! And of these four, Timmy's in the poorest shape. I'm no psychiatrist, but some of the stuff that he's been doing lately doesn't make sense. I keep passing along what I notice to Miss Leaf and Doc. Everyone seems concerned, but everybody is 'terribly busy.' "

"Like what stuff?" Jack pursued.

"The other day the kid gave away some of his favorite clothes to his close buddies," Mr. Robb answered, wringing his hands. "And he needs those clothes. When I told him so, he just looked at me, and without batting an eye, he said, 'No I won't.' It may be like what the Doc calls 'being out of contact with reality.' Well anyway, when I asked him something like 'what do you mean?' he just shrugged his shoulders and walked off."

Jack's frown had deepened. Timmy's indifference was dangerous news. "Well, what's being done about Tim? And about the others?"

"Many things—but really nothing," Mr. Robb reported glumly.

"What do you mean?"

"First, let me try and describe what I'm doing with them," Mr. Robb began. "I'm trying to keep them busy. I don't let them hole up in a corner,—I just don't think that would be good for them. I personally spend time around them, talk with them, and try to get them into things with the other kids." With a grimace Mr. Robb concluded, "And that's really about it."

"Good enough," Jack said encouragingly. "But you started by saying 'first.' What else?"

"Oh yeah," Mr. Robb said, recovering. "Second is what the other staff members are doing. I guess the school people are also trying to encourage the boys. The social workers try to see them once a week, and the Doc consults with them and us—kind of 'stays in touch.' I think the social workers have got out some letters to the courts and maybe they've made some contacts with social work agencies, too, to see if they might not turn up some place where these kids can go."

"But what about the other half of what you said before—that you're not really doing anything?"

"That's right," Mr. Robb reaffirmed, "even though it may sound crazy. People, including myself, are making all these motions, but they don't amount to anything. The motions should be producing placements, but they aren't."

"Let's face it," Jack countered, "there's no place for them to go. And that's only part of it, because when a place is turned up, it's quite a job to get these kids to consider it. They want their own home regardless of what shape that home's in."

Mr. Robb moved forward on his chair and said, "My point is that we have to move off the dime. I say if a kid's home is no good and you won't let him go to it, then find him another one. If he won't buy the idea, then work with him until you get some solution, but for God's sake, do something!"

"Look," Jack bargained, "would you go for a meeting on Timmy's case tomorrow afternoon?"

"*Yes,*" he said emphatically.

"If we can include Doc Barth, Miss Leaf, and Mr. Wilton, we should have a useful meeting," Jack assured him.

"Why include Wilton?" Mr. Robb objected. "He's not going to be any help!"

"If you plan to bring up the placement of kids as an issue, then I think he's got to be included. After all, he's in charge of social services," Jack explained. He was curious. "Why wouldn't you include him?"

"From past experiences, I predict he won't be of any real help. He's first and always a bureaucrat, and very frankly Jack, I don't like him!"

"Well, he's in the picture whether you like it personally or not," Jack said bluntly. "So count on his being there."

"Okay," Mr. Robb reasoned, "if he's going to be there, I'd like to make the most of a bad scene and bring in the other three cases I mentioned earlier."

"Be prepared to talk about all of them," Jack suggested, "but don't count on having them all considered tomorrow. At most, we'll probably cover only one or two."

"I want three considered." Mr. Robb said firmly. "In addition to Timmy, Sam Harris and John Mann need immediate consideration."

"I'll go along with what you ask."

The following afternoon, Miss Leaf, Mr. Wilton, and Jack met in the Administration Building. After exchanging pleasantries, they entered the staff conference room. Miss Leaf and Mr. Wilton took seats on one side of a large, highly polished table while Jack sat on the other. Doc Barth and Mr. Robb had not yet arrived.

After a moment, Mr. Wilton asked sharply, "Who are we waiting for?"

"Mr. Robb," Jack answered evenly. "Doc won't be able to make it."

"Mr. Robb, eh," Mr. Wilton commented. "I don't understand why he's late. He's such a bundle of efficiency that I can't believe he'd allow himself to be late for a scheduled meeting."

"Pete works hard," Jack responded, ignoring Mr. Wilton's sarcasm.

"Listen, Jack, I don't know how Robb strikes you, but from where I sit it seems he's been so busy since he arrived here that he must feel that all of the Outpost operation depends on him alone."

"As I said," Jack said calmly, "Pete's a hard worker. He'll be here shortly. Count on it."

"And what about Doc? Didn't you say he would be joining us?" Mr. Wilton asked with measured politeness.

"Regrettably not," Jack answered in a neutral voice. "As you probably will be hearing officially very soon, Doc has decided to give more time to his private practice. So he'll only be with us one day a week."

"Oh, yes, I heard that was in the wind. It's a sad story. You can talk all you want about psychiatrists' humanitarianism, but you always come out with the same profile: they are most humanitarian to those who pay them the most money. I have a wicked sense of humor," Mr. Wilton confessed merrily. "But truly, Jack, that's where regulars like you and me have to carry the work in the public sector."

When Jack did not respond, Mr. Wilton returned to Mr. Robb's absence. "I don't mean to distress you with my sense of humor, but Pete might still be over at Outpost solving all of its problems."

"Oh, come off it," Jack implored in good spirit. Mr. Wilton replied with a hands-out, palms-upward gesture.

Jack copied the gesture with a bland smile.

Mr. Robb burst into the room ten minutes late. "I'm sorry, everybody," he said without preliminaries, "but I got tied up with a cottage problem."

"You'll have to learn how to manage a demanding schedule—that is, if you're going to last," Mr. Wilton instructed.

Mr. Robb responded sharply, "I've learned that you have to act on a youngster's problem *when he has it* if you're going to do any good."

Mr. Wilton's tone changed to condescension. "Well, now that we are all finally assembled, what can we do to help?"

"It's pretty much as I explained when I talked with you yesterday, Wilt." Jack began informally. "There are a number of kids in Outpost who have done well, and if they had better homes to go to they would have already been placed. But they had to remain here and now are peaking out, if they haven't peaked out already. We want to see if some of these kids can be placed, particularly Timmy Stover, John Mann, and Sam Harris. There are several others, but let's concentrate today on these three."

"Surely an important enough problem," Mr. Wilton affirmed pompously. "But to place these boys as fast as I sense you want is out of the question." Acknowledging Miss Leaf by a nod of his head and indicating their agreement on this matter, Mr. Wilton continued. "We work on these problems all the time. So, while we can't place these boys immediately, please be assured that we are doing all we can."

"All right," Jack said. "Let's move to the case of Timmy Stover."

However, before Jack could summarize the case, Mr. Robb, who sat facing Mr. Wilton, interrupted, "These cases must get some extra push in order to get them out of here fast. I'm sure the court, the probation officers, and others back in these kids' communities will argue with you, but I think they get too comfortable about these cases being here. You know, out of sight, out of mind."

Jack waited uncomfortably for Mr. Wilton's response to the outburst.

Mr. Wilton grimaced and then said with deliberate calm, "Mr. Robb, while we know we have some real problems here that have to be dealt with, I don't think it's fair to say that the people out in the community aren't aware of what we want for these boys. You have to remember that they have all kinds of problems facing them."

"And don't forget," Miss Leaf, who had been passive up to this point, put in, "these cases are hard to move. With most of them, when it's all said and done, there isn't anyplace for them to go."

Again Mr. Robb seized the initiative. "If their own homes can't pass muster, then I think we ought to level with the kids and tell them so and then go ahead and work out some practical alternative for them. And," he continued with increased intensity, "I don't think these things have really been done for the boys we're going to concentrate on this afternoon."

Clearly annoyed by Mr. Robb's challenge, Mr. Wilton folded his arms abruptly and sat back with an intent scowl. Then he leaned forward to rest his elbows on the arms of his chair and glared at Mr. Robb. "I would like to think I am in the presence of a colleague rather than an unthinking critic. If it's the latter, then these cases have a rather poor future."

As he paused, there was an audible intake of breath around the room. But Mr. Wilton appeared not to notice and resumed in an angry voice, "Look, we came here to talk about three kids and getting them placed. If you don't want to talk about them, then I think we ought to call off this meeting."

Mr. Robb shot back, "We don't need talking—we need action."

"All right, all right," Jack broke in sharply, then lowered his voice. "The pace we're setting is a bit fast; I can't keep up with it. What I'd suggest is that we take a look at each case, beginning with Timmy, and see what we can do. We're all here, and we've all got work to do. Now what about Timmy?"

Mr. Wilton complained, "I didn't get a chance to finish what I was saying." With obvious restraint he went on, "But no matter. Let's get on with it."

Mr. Robb began, "We all know about Timmy Stover's history. What I want to do is tell you about how he is *now*. He's been going downhill steadily since the staff felt he was improved enough to recommend him for parole three months ago. But he wasn't placed because of his bad home situation. Right now he's moody, doing poorly in school, and loafs on his work assignment. Besides, in the past week he's begun to do crazy things. He's given some of his clothes away—and after he did that, he seemed happier than I've seen him in a long time. Then yesterday he told me that he wants to quit school because he won't need any more education. Coming from someone who used to be a first-rate student, that just doesn't make sense."

Mr. Robb took a deep breath and pressed his point. "I personally think he ought to be placed right away, if not at home, then with relatives."

"Let me tell you how I think this shapes up," Miss Leaf interjected blandly. "Timmy can't go back to that home, at least not as it is now. An uncle who lives in Dalton is a possibility. There's just him and his wife, no children in the home. They are a bit old. He's on retirement from the railroad. It's not the best placement, but it might work out."

"It's good to hear he has some prospects," Jack commented optimistically. "Have contacts been made?"

"The staff is working with the child welfare people of Washington County to see if it can be arranged. Remember now," she explained, "he still hasn't fully accepted not being able to return to his own home. I've suggested it to him, but I haven't told him bluntly that he cannot go back home. This is something that has to be worked out over time."

"Probably so," Mr. Robb acknowledged, "yet you *have* to be direct at some point. I don't think you can keep these kids dangling, hoping they'll get some subtle, indirect message you want to get across. Besides," Mr. Robb bulldozed on, "when the word finally gets across, like in the case of Timmy, and you don't talk it over with him, he's left saddled with the message and no way to find his way through the problem it creates for him!"

Mr. Wilton's frown deepened as he listened to Mr. Robb and finally he shook his head angrily. He turned on Jack. "I cannot tolerate further talk of this type—talk that is loose and by one who is not qualified to judge! Since Mr. Robb lacks the knowledge and the skill to make determinations about case-work issues, I would ask that he stop his nonsense!"

Mr. Robb flushed deeply, but before he could retort or Mr. Wilton could continue, Jack interceded in order to keep the meeting from blowing up. He said firmly, "Some things are being said here that ought not be said. Let's give up that kind of talk. Let's get back to concentrating on solving our problem. Can we return again to Timmy? After all, it's in his interest that we're gathered here."

Jack turned to Miss Leaf who, despite the optimistic information she had provided earlier, seemed to have sided with Mr. Wilton. The heated exchange between Mr. Wilton and Mr. Robb had made her nervous. Jack asked her quietly, "Now, where are we with Timmy's uncle? And what you have heard from the child welfare people?"

Miss Leaf moved a case folder around the table in front of her. "We haven't heard yet," she said in a monotone.

"Do you have any idea as to when we might expect to hear?" Jack asked, his voice even and polite.

Miss Leaf fidgeted in her chair. "I would suppose in a couple of weeks, but it's hard to tell."

"How long has it been since the letter was sent to the probation office or to the welfare people—or whoever it was supposed to go to for the contact work?" Jack persisted.

"It's only been about a month," Mr. Wilton broke into the conversation. "Of course you know that we have to work through the probation office of the court. They either make the necessary contacts themselves or farm them out to the child welfare people or to some other agency."

Mr. Robb said wryly, "A month may not seem long to us or the probation people, but that's a long, long time for a kid. This I know."

Jack broke in quickly to ask Miss Leaf, "Might you telephone whoever is handling Timmy's case to learn what progress is being made? I think Timmy needs fast handling, at least faster than usual," Jack emphasized. "The merits of the cases are strong."

There was no response. "Well, where are we?" he prodded.

Miss Leaf turned to Mr. Wilton. After pondering a moment, he said "I think that's about all on this case. Of course, there are many important points that have to be considered. First we must see if the uncle's place is really the one for him, and second, we need to see if Timmy will accept the placement."

"All right," Jack acknowledged.

"As I said earlier," Miss Leaf explained softly, "when you switch youngsters' homes, you have to work with them."

"Along that line," Mr. Robb interjected, "perhaps it would be best during this business for us in the unit to refer Timmy to Miss Leaf when he wants to talk about what's happening on planning for his future home and how he feels about it."

Jack looked at his watch. "Can we leave it, then, that you'll call the parole and welfare people to push the case, and in the meantime we'll refer Timmy to Miss Leaf for all discussion about placement?"

"Time has gotten away from us," Mr. Wilton agreed. "We'll go along with that, Jack. I'm going to suggest we consider just one more case today. I can only stay for a half-hour longer this afternoon. The other case can be put on the calendar for next week's staff conference."

"Okay," Jack said, "if that's all the time you have." Then he turned to Mr. Robb. "Who would you like to consider in the time that remains?"

"Let's take John Mann," Mr. Robb suggested.

"His is a different kind of case," Miss Leaf commented. "In his situation it is clear that he doesn't have a home to go back to. In fact, that was clear when he came in. So we've had considerable time to work on his problem."

"Then he's about ready to go," Mr. Robb said hopefully.

"Not exactly," Miss Leaf corrected. "The Southerlands, where John has been spending some of his weekends, have recently decided that they would like to adopt the boy. That has complicated the situation. At first they talked about having John come and live with them in a boarding-home type of arrangement. He was to have lived with the Southerlands, doing some late-afternoon and weekend chores for his keep and spending money, and riding the bus to and from a school in Starkville.

"The Southerlands live on a farm," Miss Leaf added neutrally. "Now, with the possibility of adoption in the picture, it wouldn't be wise to set up a boarding-home arrangement for John. All the details of an adoption proceeding will have to be followed, and they take time."

"Sounds great," Mr. Robb exclaimed. "That kid needs a break, and this could be it."

"Well," Miss Leaf said doubtfully, "we aren't so sure that it's that great a break."

"How do you mean?" Mr. Robb challenged. "The Southerlands have stopped by the cottage a number of times, and I find them to be good, everyday folks."

"Well, you may or may not know that we've questioned the amount of work they make John do when he's out there. You know, I visited them one afternoon last summer when John was there." She paused and then emphasized, "And let me tell you he was *working,* and he was bushed."

"Has the boy complained?" Jack asked.

"No, but you really wouldn't expect him to, Jack," Miss Leaf said, frowning. "After all, he *is* a very conscientious kid and I think he appreciates going to the Southerlands." She stopped again. "But he was so dirty and so sweaty—so very dirty that I hardly recognized him. And those barns smelled so awful. The whole set-up just went against my grain!"

"What's wrong with a little honest sweat? Or a little dirt? Or a little smell?" Mr. Robb teased.

"Nothing," Miss Leaf defended. "Nothing. It was just that he looked so unkempt, and so awfully tired, too. I know he was working too hard. I talked with him and learned that they had been grinding feed for the cattle since six that morning. It just seemed too much. . . . I came away feeling that the Southerland's dominant reason for wanting to adopt John was to work him!"

"Farm work has never been easy," Mr. Robb asserted.

"I know that," Miss Leaf snapped back. "But that boy was exhausted!"

"So you are questioning the home on that basis?" Jack asked.

"Yes," Miss Leaf answered more soberly. "That placement smacks of work exploitation."

"It's too late in the day to take you fellows to task again," Mr. Wilton said sarcastically, though he was not as angry as he had been before. "I must tell you bluntly, nevertheless, that you're just not qualified to second-guess a clinical judgment. It's very clear that Miss Leaf had an exceptional opportunity to make some critically important observations and she used that opportunity. Her observations and their implications are crystal clear."

Jack took the floor. "Let's just say the Southerlands are stable, honest, hard-working farm people who have, I understand, raised a normal daughter. They aren't likely to ask more of John than what they do themselves—probably less. Let's place the boy there on a boarding-home arrangement until we can get an evaluation of the home for adoption.... I respect Miss Leaf's reaction to the farm scene, but we haven't a shred of evidence that shows the Southerlands to be exploitative."

After a long silence Miss Leaf agreed. "Okay, we'll go ahead with a temporary placement. If the Southerland's home is satisfactory and if John makes a final decision that he wants to go through with the adoption, we'll make every effort to make it work."

"Could we make all of this a little less complicated?" Mr. Robb pleaded. "If we could get several things going at once, it would cut down the time that's needed to run this thing through."

"Several of these 'things' are already in motion," Mr. Wilton commented. "You would realize that if you thought back over the case."

"I can't top that one," Mr. Robb answered with resignation.

Mr. Wilton rose and announced, "I'm going to leave you and get on to my next appointment. Miss Leaf can work this one out with you and fill me in later. Whatever you come out with on John, I believe we should review it at next week's staff conference."

As Mr. Wilton walked toward the door, he placed a hand on Mr. Robb's shoulder and said jokingly, "It isn't every day that I have a meeting with such a congenial group."

After Mr. Wilton left, Jack said, "I take it the Southerlands want the boy and the court will look into the adoption prospects."

"Yes," Miss Leaf replied. "Also, the Southerlands have gotten themselves an attorney to look into adoption laws and procedures."

"Where does John stand on this?" Jack asked. "We've been assuming that he *wants* to be adopted."

"That's right," Miss Leaf answered, "though I think he has some deep, underlying, perhaps even unconscious hesitancies. I believe, though, that he can work through his uncertainties."

"Now, what do I tell him when he comes and asks me what he should do?" Mr. Robb asked.

"How will he approach you?" Miss Leaf asked.

"Well, he'll mope around—like he's trying to tell me something or wants me to ask him what's wrong. If I don't ask him, he'll probably come by and after a lot of hedging he'll come out and ask me, 'Do you think I should go live at the Southerlands?' "

Now that a decision had been made, Miss Leaf responded with enthusiasm. "Could you just let him talk and help him review what he is considering? But please don't tell him what to do. I'm giving him a chance to think this through—as much on his own as he can. It's kind of painful to watch him go through some soul searching, but we have to let him work this out for himself. I don't mean by this that we just let him drift, or make him feel we aren't interested. Just the opposite: we are very much interested, but we should not decide for him."

"Okay, I'm with you. So what do I say? *Specifically* what do I say?" Mr. Robb pressed.

"Let him talk for awhile, and then say something like, 'These are things you'll want to think through and decide about,' or 'I think you're right in thinking these things over,' or 'I'd be glad to hear how you see the situation, but what you decide is really up to you.' You see, the worst thing in the world would be to urge him to take this home or not take it. First, he's old enough to make up his own mind, and second, he must learn to be responsible. If you or I or Jack tell him what to do, he won't really feel that it's his choice and he probably won't work very hard to make it go."

Mr. Robb listened attentively as Miss Leaf continued to coach him. "Now if he pushes you for an answer or tries to wheedle one out of you, you'll just have to hold yourself in check and tell him that you're sorry, but it's a decision he'll have to make, and encourage him to make it. Tell him you have confidence in his being able to do that, and I take it you do have confidence in him. That kind of an approach should help him in making a decision."

"I think I can use that kind of talk with him," Mr. Robb replied appreciatively. "How about that problem of his being overworked or exploited that you were talking about earlier? How does that fit in this deciding business?"

"I have serious questions about that home in the sense that I expressed earlier when you and Jack were kind of hard on me—and maybe fairly so. But as of right now, I'm not sure where I stand on that issue. In view of what Jack pointed out, I would soften my view somewhat, especially on exploitation. But I think the work is too hard and beyond what John should do."

"Before this goes much further, you or somebody better talk this over with the Southerlands," Jack suggested.

"I plan to," Miss Leaf said emphatically.

Jack sensed a new atmosphere in the room. Mr. Robb had settled down and was working with Miss Leaf. Miss Leaf had given up her defensiveness and was providing some good approaches for working with John. Silence and calm faces indicated that all were satisfied and had no more questions.

"I guess that carries this case about as far as we can today," Jack suggested.

"I'll check before our meeting next week on the exact status of the legal requirements for adoption and where that whole matter is," Miss Leaf volunteered.

"Very good," Jack affirmed. "If that's it, then let's adjourn."

Pete Robb shoved his chair back, causing a break in the prevailing atmosphere of good will. A frown cut furrows in his forehead as he opened his mouth to speak. His voice contained a mixture of trust and anxiety. "We made some progress, but not very much. Not really."

He walked out of the conference room and out of the Administration Building.

. . .

10

THEY STILL DON'T GET ALONG

"Jack, I've got a personnel problem," Harold Collins said with a sigh as he sat down heavily in a chair across from Jack's desk.

"Somebody planning to leave?" Jack asked.

"No—at least not at this time," Mr. Collins answered. "But if I don't get the difficulty settled between Ken Markle and Bob Post I'll probably have a couple of resignations on my hands. Even worse, the boys' loyalties are being divided between them—some of the boys lining up with Ken and some lining up with Bob. As a matter of fact, I've seen it building for some time and it really raises Old Nick with the boys."

Jack nodded. "Any kind of staff squabble can really touch off the kids. What are Markle and Post like?"

"They are two very different fellows," Mr. Collins observed. "Markle is what I think you would call an extrovert. The psychologists might even call him self-centered because he talks so much and brags about himself. He's always telling stories; if he doesn't start out as the main character, he ends up the main character. Then he likes to play jokes on people. . . . For awhile, and you may remember, he was known among the cottage staff as 'Playboy' because he fancies himself as a ladies' man. Still does, I guess. There's nothing modest about him. He sees himself as an athlete too. He plays in the local recreational league—basketball, softball, or whatever they have going on—and he follows the big-league teams day to day. He talks about the scores of the games, the big plays, and that kind of stuff."

"So he's pretty popular with the other fellows," Jack observed.

"Yes, I think so," Mr. Collins replied thoughtfully. "Once in awhile he'll rub the other supervisors the wrong way with all of his talk, but he's got a lot of good friends among the cottage staff because he's entertaining and because he has an exceptionally kind side to him. Take for example last month when he lent about all the cash he had to Ed Jurens because he was convinced that Jurens and his wife deserved a chance to go up to the lake for a few days during their vacation. I don't know the full story, but the Jurens' situation got talked about among the fellows. The talk was that the Jurens hadn't had a chance for a real vacation for years because of a lot of family problems, so Markle figured he'd take the lead in making a vacation possible. . . . Well, Markle does that kind of thing and it's more than just show. He really feels that you should not only be interested in other people, but that you should help them.

"And he's great with the kids," Mr. Collins continued. "He doesn't operate by plan, but he'll start activities spontaneously, like a ball game, a game of cards, or a ping-pong tournament if he thinks the group needs the activity. Unlike Post, Markle takes the kids out frequently on unplanned hikes. He'll even take them in to town to the zoo or to the museum with little advance planning. You know, just enough planning to get the school bus and clear things with me . . . and he doesn't always clear with me."

"What about Post?"

"Post is quite a different guy. He's the studious type. He's friendly enough toward the other supervisors, but he doesn't go out of his way to be pals with them. In his spare time he's either reading some book or he's over at the university taking a course or two. I think he's getting near to a degree. I don't mean to say he isn't well liked, because he is. But he's more respected than liked as a buddy."

"And how is he with the kids?" Jack pursued.

"Post runs a tight ship and he's steady. When it comes to recreation, for example, he makes sure that the boys have plenty to do. He won't let kids withdraw and become wallflowers, but he's not apt to pick up the whole group and take them on an unscheduled hike or organize a trip on the spur of the moment."

"I'm getting a good picture of these two fellows." Jack said. "Could you fill me in on how long the present problem has been going on and more of what it's all about?"

"The hassle between them has been going on longer than I like to admit," Mr. Collins said with apparent uneasiness. "I'd say the situation has gotten pretty hot during the past week, maybe during the past ten days. . . . The first thing I saw was a little irritation between them over working out the kids' eligibility for home passes. You know that we have a meeting in the cottage to work out this very thing.

"Let me tell you it was slow, slow going. Every time a decision had to be made on a poor risk—a marginal kid—they would argue and argue over it instead of trying to work it out. In the past, they have settled their differences without any sweat."

"How did you handle their bickering?" Jack pressed.

"I tried to emphasize the good points concerning the boys they were arguing about," Mr. Collins replied steadily. "But they were still stubborn."

"Did you call it to their attention or ask them to do something about it?"

"I wish now that I had sat down with them in a direct fashion to get at what was going on between them, but I thought maybe it was some little thing that wouldn't amount to much and would go away on its own. . . . Then, in a couple of days when I saw they weren't talking to each other during the overlap on their shifts—you know, not giving each other information on the kids—I asked one or the other, whoever was leaving, if he had anything of importance to pass along to the other."

"How did that go?" Jack asked, hoping for some kind of breakthrough.

"Let's see," Mr. Collins pondered. "I said something like, 'The boys can't be getting along so well that we don't have something we need to talk about.' After they didn't pick up on that, I said, 'Let's take a little time to look back at what went on and plan ahead so we can move from one shift to another with greater ease.' Whoever had been on duty said something to the effect that everything was running smoothly and the other fellow said that the weekly schedule was in good shape. Their immediate mood improved a little, but their overall relationship didn't improve."

"How do you see the problem now?" Jack asked. "I get the impression things have gone downhill."

"The problem is worse," Mr. Collins acknowledged sadly. "They pass each other during the change of shifts and don't say a word. . . . And the looks they exchange are cold. Like I said earlier, these feelings have spread to the boys now and they're dividing up our unit."

"What will your next move be?" Jack asked. "You seem to have some hesitancy about bringing both of them together and talking this thing over."

Mr. Collins replied slowly, "I'm not sure about going into this face-to-face . . . so directly because I figure these guys are pretty mad, and frankly, I don't know what they might do. I'm afraid that if I bring them together and press them to deal with their problems, it will bring accusations from each about the other. And then those accusations will probably snowball into an impossible hassle, if not a fist fight. Frankly, I don't think I would be able to handle it." He looked at Jack anxiously. "Do you have any suggestions on how I ought to tackle this?"

"Well," Jack said easily, "Why not see them individually first and *then* bring them together?"

Mr. Collins nodded, relieved. "I think I'd start with Post."

"I think you should follow up on this pretty fast," Jack urged. "Otherwise, it might break wide open."

"I doubt that we'll be able to work out all of the problems between those two. Besides, whatever is going on between them right now, they're such basically different fellows—there will always be a personality conflict between them. . . . What are the prospects of transferring one of them to another unit?"

Jack shook his head. "I believe we should work out the problem in Whittier," he said firmly.

Mr. Collins nodded, then rose and said resignedly, "Let me get into this and see what's causing all of the difficulty . . ." He looked at his watch. "It's about time for change of shift now. If I get over there now, I'll be able to get to them."

Just before going out the door, Mr. Collins smiled and added, "Given the best of all possible worlds, I'll be able to pull off a truce meeting today."

Jack flashed him a thumbs-up gesture.

"Stay in close touch on this one."

As Mr. Collins was leaving Jack's office, Ken Markle entered Whittier Cottage to relieve Bob Post. Bob saw Ken without acknowledging his presence. Instead, he picked up a book from the desk in the dayroom and turned to leave the building. As he was about to pass, Ken blurted out, "Look sourpuss, you were the loser so why keep the iron curtain down? Why not be a good loser?"

Bob faced him. Ken continued, "Look, friend, you might as well get over it. It was a fair game and you lost. I should add that the best man—the best man by far—won!"

"Leave me alone, you lousy s.o.b!" Bob snarled. "And if you haven't the good sense to do that, then at least leave our personal business out of the work scene!" He looked at Ken with disgust." You know, you're a real windbag." He turned to go.

Ken rushed at him, fists formed and arms up ready to strike. Only Mr. Collins' entrance at that moment prevented a fight.

Mr. Collins rushed between them, shouting, "What the hell are you guys trying to do? Wreck this cottage? I've been watching your feuding for the past couple of weeks and I'm telling you it's got to stop! Whatever the problem is, it's not so important that I'm going to let it mess up this unit! Now, come into the office and we'll straighten this thing out! Otherwise, I'll have to find myself a couple of new supervisors!"

A combination of Mr. Collins' surprise appearance, his shouting, and his threat to discharge them quickly cooled off the combatants, and they sullenly followed him into his office.

When they were seated before him, Mr. Collins snapped, "This nonsense has gone on long enough! I want to get to the bottom of it and I want it stopped—and I want it stopped now!"

Mr. Collins' uncharacteristic toughness was paying off. Ken's and Bob's anger smoldered, but it was being replaced by a mixture of embarrassment, anxiety, and the need to regain a professional posture. After a pause, Mr. Collins continued, "Well, let's have it. Or am I to believe that you fellows were just out there getting warmed up for gym class. I expect this kind of kid stuff from some of our boys, but I didn't realize I should include you two."

Bob stared at the floor. Ken sat back with an artificial air of composure. Crossing his legs, he lit a cigarette and began to talk confidently. "There's really nothing much to it, Harold, when you get down to brass tacks. . . . We've both been after the same girl and I came out the winner. And now he's sore about it. I got engaged to her last week and he can't take it."

Bob's face became progressively more flushed as Ken talked. Finally he burst out, "Yes, and this stupid ass fed that girl a lot of lies and hot air! She doesn't see him in everyday life and know what a lightweight he really is!"

"Why you cheap—" Before Ken could charge, Bob was on his feet. Mr. Collins, with amazing agility, ran around the desk and pushed both men back into their chairs. He glowered down at them for a minute without speaking. After standing between them for several moments, Mr. Collins relaxed his stance and returned to his chair. "Now, with that out of your systems, I'd like to know if you want to talk reasonably about your girlfriend situation or whether you want to talk about your working relationship here in the cottage."

Mr. Collins leaned back in his chair, lit a cigarette, and waited for them to begin talking. He finally broke an uneasy silence by asking sharply, "Should I take this to mean you don't want to talk about either?"

Again there was a prolonged silence. Then Bob said with resignation, "I believe the girl situation is over . . . so we better talk about the work."

Watching them despise each other, Mr. Collins was struck with sadness. Obviously, Jack's suggestion that they talk out their differences was not going to solve the problem. They could not continue to work together in Whittier.

Mr. Collins, having regained his usual composure, said to them, "You two have been doing too much bickering lately and there hasn't been any real cooperation between you for weeks. The school won't stand for it and I won't stand for it. Your squaring off today was the straw that broke the camel's back. The way I figure it, one or both of you are going to have to transfer out of this cottage."

They could hear distant shouting of boys playing on the recreation field. Otherwise, the room was quiet.

Then Ken said with conviction, "I'd like to stay here in this unit. But it doesn't sound like you want me to stay."

"That's one thing about Markle," Bob said acidly. "He sure looks out for himself. If anyone is staying here, it's going to be *me.*"

"Okay, okay, you guys!" Mr. Collins snapped. He looked at them, annoyed, and said, "When I returned to the cottage from the Administration Building, I had hoped that things could be worked out to keep you both. But judging from what has happened, that won't be possible. Obviously I'm not going to pick one of you over the other. I'll talk this over with Jack. He may have a special need for one or both of you in another cottage. If he does, he can just go ahead and assign you and I won't play any part in who he picks for that assignment."

"It's unfair," Ken accused.

"Why?" Mr. Collins shot back. "It seems fair enough to me. Very simply, you fellows aren't hitting it off here together so it's either transfer to another cottage or leave the institution."

"Oh! it might be fair," Ken backtracked, "but I don't like it. It's going to make us look bad and whoever goes will be the guy who will look worse. You know that people will say things like 'He couldn't get along,' or 'He got kicked out,' or 'He's the troublemaker.' I don't like it."

"You two should have thought of that before you created this mess."

With startling sincerity, Ken asked, "Could you leave Bob and me to ourselves for a half hour or so . . . if he's willing? Maybe if we clear up some of our personal affairs, it will help clear up our work situation."

"That sounds acceptable to me, but unless you fellows really want to *talk* your problems out—instead of fighting them out—I'm not leaving."

Ken nodded his head in agreement. Bob scowled at the floor. Mr. Collins prodded him. "How do you feel about talking things over, Bob?"

Bob twisted in his chair, then, looking directly at Ken, said, "Before I get into any kind of serious conversation with you, I want to be sure you're on the up-and-up."

Ken took the rebuff, shrugged his shoulders, and commented, "There's nothing lost in giving it a try. As I understand it, nobody's hands are tied, and anyway, we don't know whether Mr. Collins will buy anything we may come up with. So you'll just have to decide." Bob hesitated. Ken raised his hand as if he were taking an oath and added, "You don't have anything to worry about with me."

Silence fell on the group. Finally Bob shrugged his shoulders. "I guess there's no harm in talking, so if Ken wants to go ahead, it's fine with me. But I don't want you," nodding his head toward Mr. Collins, "to sit in. It's our affair and I think we should try to settle it ourselves."

"That's fine with me," Mr. Collins said emphatically. "My only interest is in working things out so the cottage will run like it should." He left the room.

Uncomfortable with his own anxiety, Mr. Collins pushed the Ken and Bob problem from his mind and busied himself with various small chores. He called the laundry to complain about linens that hadn't been delivered. He hurried over to the print shop to talk about some items concerning Whittier that might be included in the school paper. On the way back, he stopped in at two of the trade training shops—carpentry, and plumbing—to visit briefly with the teachers about the work Whittier boys were doing.

Almost an hour had passed when he decided to return to the cottage. The office door was closed.

Concerned that Ken and Bob might be locked in a vicious argument, Mr. Collins knocked lightly and walked in. He was pleased to see the two men sitting quietly, their expressions less taut than before, though they appeared far from relaxed.

"Well, what did you decide?"

With a trace of bitterness in his voice, Bob volunteered, "I'll take a transfer and Ken can stay here."

"Is that okay with you, Ken? You both agree on this?"

Ken nodded his head.

Mr. Collins looked back at Bob. "Are you sure now that a transfer is really okay with you?"

Bob said curtly, "That's what I said."

"Okay, I'll talk with Jack. I'm sure he'll work out something for you, Bob." The effort to control his emotions strained Mr. Collins' voice. "I guess this resolution is the best that can be made out of the situation . . . though it's not what I would like to have happen."

The decision had been made. Only the procedural steps for transferring Bob remained. Mr. Collins said hollowly, "Okay then, I'll go up and talk with Jack and see what we can work out."

Ken and Bob only nodded their heads.

Mr. Collins walked reluctantly to Jack's office. He was worried, not only about losing Bob, but also about his failure to follow Jack's suggestion toward solving the problem between Ken and Bob. After a moment of initial friendly conversation, Mr. Collins told the story, presenting the situation to Jack from the perspective, "It seemed like the only thing to do in that situation."

Jack frowned. "I don't understand; I thought you were going to talk with them, try to work out their differences, and keep them in Whittier."

"I did," Mr. Collins defended. "It just didn't work out."

Jack hesitated a moment and said directly, "It seems quite clear—from what you've told me—that you didn't give them a full chance to talk and work out their differences."

"But I did," Mr. Collins objected.

Jack challenged, "Furthermore, you didn't allow both of them to stay in Whittier. Instead, when you pushed them with the threat of transfer or firing, you forced them into the position of asking that one be permitted to remain in Whittier and that the other accept a transfer. What's more, you don't have firing or transfer authority."

"Jack, I figure cooperation among all of us who work at Whittier is paramount—and I believe I have to be the man in charge. I can't have people challenging me. I wasn't getting cooperation from them and they weren't respecting my authority. I had to take some action."

"You're right in principle," Jack agreed. "I don't believe the conference you were having with them—at least the first part of it—violated those principles. Not at all. You were engaged in serious talk as their leader on important things pertaining to running a cottage—and pertaining to their lives. At some point in your discussion, you lost your direction."

"Okay, okay." Mr. Collins admitted. "What you say makes sense, but I wasn't getting anywhere with them, not really. And Jack, I can't go back and start over on this thing. I would lose face. I can't do that."

"How is that?" Jack asked. "It depends on how you handle it."

"Well, they'll figure you wouldn't back me up, and that's why I was returning to talk with them about their differences, and not about the transfer. . . . Jack, I can't do that."

After a long, thoughtful pause, Jack reluctantly nodded his head. "All right. Have Bob report to me tomorrow morning. I want to talk with him, encourage him, and help to launch him in a new assignment."

"Jack, I appreciate this."

After talking with Jack briefly about replacing Bob, Mr. Collins returned to Whittier and told Bob about Jack's wish to meet with him first thing in the morning. Bob listened impassively, thanked him for the information, and left the cottage.

However, when the time came the following morning for Bob to report to Jack, he did not appear. Instead, he sent a note saying that he was entering school full-time and would not be continuing at Central State.

11

THE CASE OF
THE MISSING GROCERIES

"I don't understand it, Jack, but regardless of explanations, I don't want any more staff recommendations that Hilltop Cottage boys be assigned to the Commissary. To put it bluntly, they're the thievingest damned kids I've ever seen. I'm not exaggerating when I say that I'm surprised there's anything left in the Commissary. There are more groceries stolen from that place than it would take to feed several good-sized families on a regular basis—oranges by the crate, tomatoes by the case, cabbage by the sack, even a five-gallon can of shortening!"

Mr. Eagan was about to continue with increased exasperation when Jack deterred him. "It can hardly be as bad as all that. Is the situation really bad enough to bring the educational director to the Administration Building at this ungodly hour when he ordinarily is getting his school going?"

"Sir," Mr. Eagan said with mock haughtiness, "the educational director is here because his vocational coordinator is ill and he is trying to keep the kids on their job assignments. Furthermore, the educational director has found one hell of a mess in the Commissary! And to top it off," Mr. Eagan continued, his voice rising to an intense pitch, "the educational director thinks that not only is the Commissary loaded with thieves, but that Hilltop Cottage is loaded with them, too—and that's where most of the Commissary group come from!"

"Remember, Hilltop has a greater mix of different personality types in it than the other cottages do," Jack said calmly.

"Jack, you're trying to tone me down," Mr. Eagan said wryly. "But for chrissake, give me credit for knowing that Hilltop serves as a wastebasket while the other cottages have exclusive clientele. Exclusive clientete like the manipulative kids, the aggressive kids, or the neurotic kids. But what I'm saying is that we've overloaded Hilltop with thieves!"

"So you think we should handle the Commissary problem by replacing some of the kids who are assigned there?" Jack asked.

"Right, right," Mr. Eagan responded enthusiastically. "And in addition, I'm for reassigning some kids from Hilltop."

"Well," Jack began blandly, "maybe shuffling the boys around—on the job and in the cottage—would help somewhat, but it looks to me like we've got to work on staff supervision in both places, too. The first task—handling the job assignments—is yours and the second one—handling the cottage assignments—is mine."

"I realize that," Mr. Eagan said, "but I believe we should have the staff committee reconsider both the Commissary and cottage assignments of at least three Hilltop boys—Tom Allen, Elijah Jones, and Bill Roba. I think those assignments are as basic to the problem as the supervision is."

"I'm for your bringing it up." Jack agreed. "But even if after discussing it the staff committee would recommend some transfers, I think I would feel, as I feel now, that such action would be less important than improving the supervision."

I

After closing the door to the conference room, Doc Barth took his seat to chair the weekly staff committee meeting, a meeting designed to plan newly admitted boys' programs and to consider special problems.

However, before Doc could establish his chairmanship, Mr. Eagan began to address the staff. Skilled in perfunctory courtesies, he included Doc in his preliminaries. "Doc, if you will permit me a few minutes, I'd like to bring a matter before the committee which has just come to light and is not on the agenda." Without waiting for Doc's belated and somewhat reluctant nod, Mr. Eagan continued, "A situation exists which demands our attention. We've overloaded the Commissary and Hilltop with boys who have long and well-established stealing records. These kids aren't any good for one another. All they do, in my estimation, is steal and encourage one another to steal, and lately we've had more stealing from the Commissary than we can tolerate."

"We recognized that such problems would arise before we set up the system of the cottages handling specific kinds of personalities," Dr. March, a psychologist, pointed out. "Keep in mind that our concern in placement is the particular boy's basic personality and his level of maturity. Insofar as the

Commissary is concerned, we all were participating members of the committee which carefully considered each of these boys and his needs before we assigned them to Hilltop and the Commissary."

"I recall all of that very well," Mr. Eagan reassured Dr. March. "Generally, the theory on setting up homogeneous groups in cottages and developing programs designed specifically to be thereapeutic for them—though a bit simple in conception—makes good sense and I'm for it. But the situation we're facing today shows that negative facts are running ahead of good theory, and I'm bringing this to the attention of the committee with the proposal that at least Tom Allen, Elijah Jones, and Bill Roba be reassigned out of the Commissary—and I would think that Jack would want them transferred out of Hilltop too!"

Stimulated by Mr. Eagan's presentation, Dr. March responded, "You know Hilltop has the immature kids in it . . . It's more of a mixed bag than that. But if I may, let's view Hilltop as having the immature types. . . . They see themselves as inferior to other kids their own age. And what's more, they usually feel themselves to be low man on the totem pole in their families."

"Yes," Mr. Eagan interrupted. "and they give the appearance of being easygoing, easily dominated, and lacking in a firm set of internalized standards. All of which adds up to making them prime candidates for getting into trouble, especially if somebody with clout gives them the chance."

Dr. March was ready with another point. "Keep in mind, too, that they have a great need for adult acceptance, and with homogeneous grouping the cottage staff can really help them by taking time to explain things, taking an interest in them, giving them affection, and so on."

"I know all that," Mr. Egan insisted. "I know all that. My point is that in this circumstance the kids' stealing isn't secondary. It's clear that a number of the Hilltop boys have committed themselves to stealing. Their case records and cottage statistics show it, and right now," then he corrected himself, "or during the past several weeks, they've been stealing the Commissary blind."

"Well, then, supervision of the Commissary should be stepped up to take care of this problem," Dr. March replied summarily.

"Some efforts have been made, but the boys haven't responded." Mr. Eagan said. "My contention here is that we ought to get at the source of the problem—the kids' assignments—and I think this is what the committee needs to tackle. Quite frankly, we've overloaded Hilltop and the Commissary with thieves.

"Furthermore, Mr. Stone over at the Commissary and Mr. Kline in the business office have complained loud and long about these kids. They've had it! After all, the business office has the final responsibility for running the Commissary, and Mr. Kline sees it as a place of business and a service to the institution, not as a training site for the boys. We've worked with Mr. Kline and Mr. Stone and they've accepted the boys. But let's be accurate. They accept the boys mainly for *work,* not for *training.* So I don't have a free hand to just march in there and set up the kind of supervision I think the kids ought to have and then proceed to implement it."

"I can't buy all of that," Dr. March countered. "It's quite apparent, to me at least, that some of these people are forgetting that we're here to work with kids and their problems, not to pass them off on somebody else."

"That's only partially true," Mr. Eagan challenged. "The point remains that we should be providing the right types of boys for people to work with, and I agree with Stone that assigning the Hilltop boys to work in the Commissary is a poor placement."

In a rare display of exasperation, Mr. Eagan threw up his arms and said, "I rest my case. But only after saying that to place kids with histories of stealing in the Commissary where there's all kinds of stuff accessible to steal is crazy. To insist that they stay there after they continue their stealing is absolutely ridiculous!"

A moment of silence was broken by Doc Barth's chuckle.

"I never counted on such a good meeting," he said, smiling. "All I had counted on was a mundane review of the progress or lack of it on three cases. Now Mr. Eagan and Dr. March have provided us with a lively debate on some interesting problems. I'm pleased that you brought them up—they've put just the right amount of spark into your discussion. God knows, we can use a little spark around here. Otherwise, as you know, it can get pretty dead."

This brought tension-relieving laughter.

Doc cleared his throat and continued. "We need to look into the specific problems that have been raised here and the broader issues which they are a part of. . . . It strikes me that we should break them into two or three considerations. Let me suggest that we consider the Commissary assignments of the three cases that Mr. Eagan requested, and do it this morning . . . and delay evaluating their assignments to Hilltop until next week. That is, if Jack thinks they ought to be reviewed."

"I would say," Jack put in, "that as far as Hilltop is concerned, we need as thoroughgoing a review of the cottage program and the Gill's supervision as we do of the boys we've assigned there. I would support Doc's suggestion that we take a look at the several boys Mr. Eagan is concerned with today and hold the other considerations until next week. That will give me enough time to look into the supervisory problem."

Doc scanned the group and said, "Unless I read the staff wrong, we're all ready to consider transferring Allen, Jones, and Roba out of the Commissary." With the exception of Dr. March, everyone agreed by either nodding or smiling.

Doc turned to Dr. March. "Bill, what's your position on this?"

"It's a 'yes' to consider the Commissary assignments. However ... it is a reluctant 'yes.'

"Very good," Doc said. "In this enterprising spirit, let's move ahead."

At Doc's exaggeration, the stiff demeanors of both Mr. Eagan and Dr. March dissolved. Mr. Eagan smiled bleakly and began to speak. Gone were his argumentative style and agitation. "Briefly, I spent an hour with Mr. Stone yesterday. It was one of the more candid talks I have had with anybody during the seven years I've been here.

"For those of you who know Mr. Stone, you're well aware of his kind and low-key manner, and I suppose as a part of this characteristic he finds it difficult to say anything bad about anybody—even about the kids who have literally run over him. So what he told me was related apologetically.

"Mr. Stone's got eight kids working in the Commissary. That's at least two or three too many for all the other work he has. He's overloaded and the situation is vulnerable to problems.... Specifically, and it's a sad, sad thing, he's lost control." Mr. Eagan rubbed his eyes under his glasses.

"What do you mean?" Doc asked.

Mr. Eagan explained, "The kids won't do the little work he has for them. Their stealing is flagrant. When he tries to talk with them, you know, reasonably, they put him down to his face. They hardly pay any attention to him. They are openly disrespectful, and if he tries to get them to do their work or confronts them about their stealing, they insult him with smart remarks like, 'Look, old man, you don't know the score,' or 'Hey gramps, lay off.' "

Mr. Eagan was noticeably saddened. Looking around the room, Doc saw with a mild shock that the staff's sympathy was not, as usually occurred, with the boys, but with a fellow staff member.

In a low voice, he spoke for the assembled group. "I'm sorry that things have gone so badly at the Commissary—for the kids and for Mr. Stone. If I judge the expression of this group correctly, I don't believe there would be any dissent to removing the three boys you mentioned—Allen, Roba, and Jones."

Dr. March hesitantly raised his hand.

"Bill," Doc acknowledged.

"I'd like to add something," Dr. March said softly. "Please understand that I support the removal of these three boys and one or two others, should Mr. Eagan and Mr. Stone conclude that's what is necessary to save the situation. However, I have a haunting doubt. I must admit that I don't really understand what's happening. Those kids are acting out of character. As a group they function as Mr. Eagan and I described during our argument earlier, but that doesn't include manipulating people in authority and challenging and threatening them.

"But I don't mean to hold up the group. I suggest that the boys be removed from the Commissary, that they remain in Hilltop during their customary work schedule, and that Mr. Eagan bring recommendations to the next committee meeting concerning their reassignment. . . . If that meets with everyone's approval, I suggest that we move on to the agenda we had originally set up for today."

II

After the staff meeting, Mr. Eagan decided to stop at the business office to see Mr. Kline. Buoyed up by the outcome of the staff committee meeting, yet not feeling his usual confident self, Mr. Eagan hesitated as he walked along the hallway to Mr. Kline's office. He even lingered for a few moments before the door, feeling like a businessman entering a competitor's store. He lit a cigarette and went in.

A middle-aged, somber, bespectacled man rose and greeted him with a firm handshake. Then, seating himself behind the large desk covered with orderly stacks of paper, Mr. Kline gestured for Mr. Eagan to take the chair next to his desk. Looking through highly polished glasses, Mr. Kline said flatly, "I understand you had a staff meeting this morning."

Mr. Eagan spoke directly. "The staff agreed to remove three of the boys from the Commissary. However, it was not without some soul-searching about the kind of supervision that is being provided over there." With considerable discomfort Mr. Eagan added, "Very frankly, everyone has great respect for Mr. Stone, but they feel strongly that his supervision is weak."

"What you people have to remember," Mr. Kline said curtly, "is that we're not running a vocational training site. We are running a supply depot for the institution—nothing more, nothing less. Insofar as Mr. Stone is concerned, you know as well as I that he is a very fine human being."

"Please don't misunderstand; I think Mr. Stone is a great person and I consider him a personal friend." Pushing beyond the deliberations of the staff meeting, Mr. Eagan said impassively, "I think what they had in mind was to move one of the delivery men inside, at least part-time. They believe that Mr. Stone needs additional help in supervising the boys."

Mr. Kline looked at Mr. Eagan warily, then said cautiously, "Well, that's interesting. I guess about everybody has an idea as to how something ought to be run."

"Basically the staff committee was interested in what's best for the boys," Mr. Eagan reassured him.

"I've already said how I feel about Mr. Stone," Mr. Kline said with a note of finality. "And that, it seems, about closes the matter."

Smiling, Mr. Eagan said with sunny disbelief, "Bill, you aren't going to deny a few additional boys the opportunity to learn storekeeping by keeping two delivery men on outside work? Mr. Stone is great, but he can only handle a few boys. So why not consider bringing one of your outside men in to help with the storekeeping?"

Relaxing considerably, Mr. Kline chortled, "I can do that. I can bring in Tom Hess. But hell, Clarence, you've been in this business long enough to know those kids aren't interested in a damn thing except raising hell."

"I know you've got more faith than that in the boys," Mr. Eagan suggested, "so don't rule out the prospect of giving Mr. Stone some help. Just tell me you'll think about it. In the meantime, I'll pull Allen, Jones, and Roba out of the place today."

"Okay," Mr. Kline replied flatly. "I'll think about it."

Mr. Kline telephoned the Commissary. When Mr. Stone answered, Mr. Kline announced stiffly, "Allen, Jones, and Roba are being pulled out of your shop, Alton. You may know this already. At any rate, report to me at once!"

Mr. Stone came in moments later, his face flushed but sad. Before he could sit down, Mr. Kline said sharply, "Give me the story on what in the hell has been going on in your shop. Clarence Eagan was just by to say that they're going to remove the kids I mentioned on the phone, but he also said the staff committee decided this morning that supervision has to be tightened up."

Mr. Stone's drooping expression reflected exhaustion. He began apologetically, "You're not going to like what I have to tell you, but—"

Mr. Kline interrupted him. "Just what is the situation back there?"

"To get down to the point . . . we've got too many kids and most of them are awfully tough to control."

"So what's actually going on?" Mr. Kline asked sharply.

"Stealing," Mr. Stone said guiltily.

"Can't you keep an eye on them?"

"To tell you the truth," Mr. Stone said regretfully, "I really can't. There are too many of them, and even though they're not really bad kids, they're all over the place. They're clever and slippery. But don't misunderstand me. I think they're basically good kids."

"If they're so *good*, why's all this stealing going on?" Mr. Kline asked with heavy sarcasm.

"Well, they're not angels," Mr. Stone admitted. "But you need to understand the whole picture. First, Mr. Eagan tells them that they're coming over here to learn. . . . I don't want to be accusing Clarence of anything, but I think he tries to sell the kids on taking work assignments. So he tells them—or at least some of them—that they're going to be *trained* by us, not that they're going to be *working for us.* So naturally, doing lots of heavy work around the warehouse—like unloading trucks—doesn't appeal to them."

"Clarence may be overselling the program or selling the wrong aspect. I wouldn't put either past him," Mr. Kline observed. "But how do you know that the kids aren't twisting what he tells them?"

"They may twist it; undoubtedly they do," Mr. Stone agreed. "But I've had Clarence tell me the same thing directly. So what we're expected to do and what we actually do with the kids are two different things."

"All right," Mr. Kline agreed. "So what else comes into the picture?"

"There's something wrong over at Hilltop. I don't know what, but I know the kids figure the Gills will never be upset by anything they do. When I talk with the Gills about the boys, they either take an unconcerned 'I don't care approach' or they defend the boys without any reason. Or at least for no reason that I can see. And I'm not asking them to punish the boys. All I've been asking is that they talk with them, set some standards for behavior, and back us up."

"Well, your pointing a finger at the school and the cottage doesn't impress me," Mr. Kline said scornfully. "Doesn't impress me at all. It's the kids' behavior in the Commisary that's gotten people upset. And you're the supervisor! Alton, as sure as we're sitting here, Mr. Graves will demand an inventory. He may even ask for an investigation! So what have the kids been stealing?"

"Well . . . ," Mr. Stone began.

"What, how much, and who—those are what we have to be concerned with. Someone else will have to figure out what the kids did with the stuff and how to handle them."

"I'm not sure," Mr. Stone said hesitatingly. "Some oranges, some tomatoes, some cabbage have . . . disappeared."

"What do you mean 'some'!" Mr. Kline shouted. "How much?"

"Well, it's hard to tell," Mr. Stone ventured.

"Can't you estimate?" Mr. Kline demanded. "Just give me a rough estimate."

"I figure a crate or two of oranges, a bushel of apples, maybe a couple of cases of tomatoes, a sack of cabbage, and maybe—"

"My God, where were *you* when all this took place?" Mr. Kline snapped.

"I was there," Mr. Stone asserted.

"So how did this happen?"

"Well, with seven or eight really tough kids in the Commissary, very honestly, Mr. Kline, I could have been right there when it was going on," Mr.

Stone pleaded. "I'm only one person. It's a big place. And there are seven of them. Tom's there when he's not out driving—he's only part-time. They could have carried the stuff out the back door, or even passed it out one of the back windows."

"I still don't see how you could let them get away with all that stuff," Mr. Kline maintained. "It's beyond me!"

By-passing Mr. Kline's anger, Mr. Stone added questioningly, "I can't figure out who would want all that cabbage—or a five-gallon can of lard. That can of lard really has me wondering."

Mr. Kline shook his head angrily. "Alton, you better get your house in order. An inventory and a possible investigation will be ordered. Sure as hell!" He paused, then added, "I wish you had told me more about this earlier, before Mr. Eagan got into it."

Mr. Stone pulled himself upright in the chair and said somewhat stiffly, "We talked about the situation about two weeks ago—"

Mr. Kline looked away and snapped, "I remember." He turned his attention then to the administration. "They didn't do us much of a favor when they gave *us* the responsibility to run the Commissary, but gave the staff committee and Mr. Eagan power to assign the boys to us for work. And then they change the focus from work to training—and that *really* screws us up!"

He stopped to glare at Mr. Stone "Pull Tom Hess off driving and put him to work on the inside. Full-time."

III

As Jack walked into his office following the staff meeting, the telephone rang. He picked up the receiver and Thelma, the switchboard operator, greeted him. "Jack, there's a Mrs. Adams on the phone. She wanted to talk to Mr. Graves, but he's not here. Says she's a member of the Board of the Laxton Home. She insists on talking with someone in charge. Would you take the call . . . ? Laxton is the home for dependent and neglected kids on the north side, you know."

"I hardly fill the bill," Jack pointed out, "but I guess you're right; somebody should talk to her. . . . Okay, put her on.

"Hello, Mrs. Adams," he said. "We're sorry, Mr. Graves isn't here at the moment. I'll be glad to help you in any way I can. My name is Jack Owens. I'm in charge of the cottages here."

An effusive voice bubbled into his ear so loud that he had to hold the receiver at a distance. "I'm very glad to talk with you and I do hope that you will tell Mr. Graves I called because we've been very, very tardy, even negligent about thanking Central for all you've done for Laxton."

Jack said "Yes," which Mrs. Adams plowed over in another rush of words.

"Of course, I know our staff has often expressed their thanks directly to John and Mary Gill for all of your support, especially all of that wonderful food you've been sending over. The Gills keep playing down the contribution, saying that what is being sent is only surplus and things like that. The Gills are so gracious about the giving that it does make it easier for us to accept the food. We just think so much of them! You understand, of course, that they make the gifts to the Capital City Community Church which in turn gives the food to the home. That makes it much easier for us because the Capital City Community Church has stood behind us for a long, long time!"

Jack sat motionless, stunned into silence. What could she possibly mean—'contribution'? To his knowledge, Central State did not contribute to any organization.

But before he could reflect further, Mrs. Adams continued to pour out her commentary. "I hesitate to tell you all this because we all have our dignity and the need to present ourselves to others as having the ability to handle matters. But we sincerely want to express how really grateful we are. Mr. Owens, I must say that if it hadn't been for all of those vegtables, fruits, sacks of flour, that tub of butter, and that tremendous drum of shortening, we just wouldn't have been able to make it during the past several months!"

Mrs. Adams finally paused, waiting for Jack's response. As he struggled to avoid saying something that was basically untrue or something that could be misconstrued, he sensed the woman's impatience. Figuring that friendliness was apt to be safe even in this circumstance, he began on a complimentary note. "Even though we haven't been close to Laxton's operations, we know that the staff is a dedicated group."

Mrs. Adams responded as Jack anticipated. "Yes indeed, and they are exceptionally competent too. In our estimation, the Laxton staff could have national prominence. If only we had a public relations program to push them!"

Jack diverted her from further self-endorsement by adding, "I'm sure Laxton appreciates the support that the Capital City Community Church has been giving it."

Almost frantic to form some appropriate response to Mrs. Adams' lavish thanks, Jack's imagination could only produce visions of newspaper headlines: "Central State School Overly Funded: Makes Gifts to Private Institution," "Central State's Funds Extend to Religious Sect," "Shoddy Administration at Central Leads to Unique Philanthrophy."

"Mrs. Adams," Jack finally said with intentional doubt, "there may well have been *several* sources of food flowing into the Capital City Community Church. Therefore, I think Central State ought to stay in the background in anything you are planning." He paused for emphasis. "Or even stay out of it altogether."

"Now, Mr. Owens," Mrs. Adams said coyly, "I know your type. You are just too modest to want to step forward to take any credit! Now, along with thanking you for your kindness, I want to invite Mr. Graves to a small gathering at the church on the third Friday of next month—that's January twenty-fourth. I will talk with Mr. Graves about it, but perhaps you might ask him for me in advance. I want him to make some remarks about Mr. and Mrs. Gill at the meeting. . . . And Mr. Owens, since I gather you are the Gill's direct supervisor, I'm sure you would like to say a few words on behalf of Mary and John. Perhaps following Mr. Graves."

"Mrs. Adams," Jack said, confused, "I'm not up on the volunteer work of the Gills. I'm wondering if they even know about this supper in their honor. It strikes me that they might appreciate some personal recognition, but would be apt to shy away from public recognition." He added hopefully, "You know, they're very modest."

"Oh, no!" Mrs. Adams exclaimed, "That's part of the plan—it's to be a surprise! Oh dear, please don't say a word!

"Now, about your saying that you aren't aware of the Gill's volunteer work, well, again I must say that you are just being modest. I'm sure you do know. And even if you don't know, you need not feel bad. My, with all the responsibilities you carry, you can't hope to keep up with all the things your staff is doing!

"It's not really very much," Mrs. Adams emphasized. "Not very much at all. . . . You just don't understand human nature, Mr. Owens. Even the most modest need and want recognition!"

Jack decided then to end the conversation and investigate this confusing incident. "I will tell Mr. Graves about our conversation" he said firmly. "Either Mr. Graves or someone from the School will be calling you within the next day or two. Today if possible."

"All right," Mrs. Adams said gaily. "I'm sure he'll want to be with us. And please thank him for all that wonderful food."

No sooner had Jack replaced the receiver than the full force of what Mrs. Adams had said penetrated the confusion in his mind. He suddenly felt blood mounting in his cheeks. Perspiration broke out across his forehead and on the back of his neck. In his imagination Elijan Jones was lifting a crate of oranges through an opened Commissary window to Al Roba and Tom Allen who waited anxiously outside to receive it. Mr. and Mrs. Gill were greeting the boys with smiles when they delivered their shipment to Hilltop.

Jack snatched up the phone.

"Thelma, is Mr. Graves in?"

"No, he's not. You know he's been working late preparing for the legislative hearings on the budget," Thelma reminded him. "But he left me a note telling me that he would be in around one-thirty. Would you like to have him give you a call when he comes in?"

"If you would, please," he said shakily, then replaced the receiver slowly and wiped perspiring hands on his shirtsleeves.

IV

Seated before Mr. Graves, Jack noticed the man's tired and discouraged expression. However, Mr. Graves recovered himself with a deep breath and a smile.

"Well, Jack, how are things going?" he asked. "Thelma said you wanted to talk with me."

"Yes," Jack started slowly. "What at first looked like a program problem— a bit nasty but nevertheless still manageable— has become much more complicated."

"Tell me more," Mr. Graves suggested. "This is the place where complicated problems find their way—and hopefully get untangled."

Jack took a breath. "I'll try to make it brief and stay with the facts, but since it's such a mixed-up story—more than a few unfounded opinions are a part of it—I'll probably be unable to separate them. So you'll have to check me so I don't mislead you. . . . And as I can, I'll try to point out the opinions as I go along."

"Okay," Mr. Graves responded with a chuckle. "Just remember that you're not in a courtroom."

Relaxing a little, Jack described the decision to remove several boys from the Commissary because of their stealing, the discussion about the criteria and procedures for assigning the boys to cottages and work assignments, and finally the phone call from Mrs. Adams.

The last part of the narrative brought back Mr. Graves' grim and weary look. His hands tightly grasped the arms of his chair.

"How long has food been going to Laxton?" he asked angrily.

"I figure about two months," Jack said uneasily.

Mr. Graves' face flushed and then turned greyish-white. "I can take almost any kind of behavior from the kids, but if there's one thing I cannot tolerate and will not tolerate, it is criminal behavior from the staff!"

He rose from his chair and walked to the window, where he stood staring out at the grounds. Finally he spoke in a fierce whisper, "And with the legislature in town, this we don't need!"

Mr. Graves returned to his desk.

"Have you talked with anybody about the possible tie between the Gills and the stuff that was stolen from the Commissary?" Mr. Graves asked sharply.

"No," Jack responded. "This problem is explosive. I thought we ought to talk before I make any moves."

"Excellent. I'm going to have Mr. Kline run an inventory of what's in the Commissary. That is, what's left in there. I also want to know what food the kitchen has received from the Commissary and what they actually have on hand. In the meantime, you'd better talk to the Gills and see what you can learn from them."

"Right," Jack agreed. "How do you plan to handle the situation with Mrs. Adams?"

"I don't know for the moment," Mr. Graves answered. "From the way it looks now, I doubt that it can be handled very smoothly. . . . I really don't know. It's going to be messy any way we do it. . . . I'll just have to think it out and play it by ear."

"Maybe there'll be a break in the situation someplace," Jack said hopefully.

"Let's hope so," Mr. Graves responded. "Though that seems like a very unlikely possibility." He picked up the telephone and asked Thelma, "Would you please have Mr. Kline come to my office?" After replacing the receiver he told Jack, "I want to get going on this."

"Okay." Jack rose. "I'll see the Gills right now."

Mr. Kline entered Mr. Graves' office alert and tense.

"Sit down, Bill," Mr. Graves began. "We've got a bad situation that includes the Commissary. To get at the problem, I want an inventory made of that place. I want to know how much food has been moved in and out during the past two months and how much you have on hand right now. And I want to know what the kitchen has received. In other words, I want a check on what was sent to them and what they actually got. I know you've been working on a new record-keeping system. This is a good time to see how well it works."

"We'll get right on it," Mr. Kline said crisply.

"Concentrate on foodstuffs," Mr. Graves added. "I need the report tomorrow. If you lack receipts from the kitchen, I want a firm opinion from Mr. Slocum as to what he's actually been getting during the past two months."

"One other thing on this inventory," Mr. Graves pressed soberly, "which I can only put in blunt language. I want this inventory to be absolutely honest. I won't stand for any nonsense on this."

Mr. Kline agreed heartily, "It's really long overdue. Once we get the inventory done and our records system in shape, I'd appreciate your support in straightening out the relationship between the school and the Commissary."

"I gather it's been undefined," Mr. Graves acknowledged. "But let's get on with the inventory." He nodded dismissal. "Come in and see me tomorrow afternoon at two-thirty with a full report."

When he was alone again, Mr. Graves left his desk with its pile of papers and walked to a window at the far end of his office that gave him a full view of the campus. As he looked over the grounds, Mr. Graves pondered his situation. He was aware that he had accepted the superintendent's job at Central State with an exceptional reputation and demonstrated skill in developing and managing complex programs for troubled youth. Further, he realized that this reputation, plus considerable hard work, had won him the support of Central's staff, the bureaucrats at the State House, and key members of the legislature. But Mr. Graves was a realist. He recognized the tenuous quality of his position. If he were to be attacked by the newspapers or members of the legislature concerning an activity that smacked of incompetence or dishonesty, his reputation would not see him through. Boys' stealing from the Commissary could be explained to the press and to state officials on the basis of the cliche "boys will be boys" or by describing Central's population and the boys' life-long records of stealing. However, that the staff was involved in the boys' stealing, indeed that they encouraged the boys to steal goods they then used for their own enhancement, would be impossible to explain.

Mr. Graves returned to his desk. Fatigued, he dropped into his chair and swung around to view the grounds again. He stared fixedly across to the Educational Building at the other end of campus. Somebody, he thought, had to talk to the kids—Allen, Jones, and Roba. If the Gills had been putting pressure on them to steal, and it surely looked that way, then how in the world could Central hold its head up when the boys had been committed to the institution specifically to learn just the opposite behavior and way of life? . . . And in connection with Mrs. Adams, should he call her right back as a courtesy or to probe for more information on the Gills, or should he wait until he had more facts from his own people? He decided to wait, judging that the advantage of his knowing his own situation far outweighed any annoyance she might feel for having to wait a day or two for a return call.

V

Jack walked over to his office after leaving Mr. Graves, checked his telephone messages, and then started toward Hilltop. The last of the cottages on the far side of the mall, the colonial design of Hilltop Cottage and its ivy-covered walls gave it a peaceful, secure appearance. Crossing the grounds, he tried to plan the most effective way of getting information on the boys' stealing, and the possibility that the Gills had encouraged the boys to steal.

It had all seemed so clearcut, so certain during the discussion in the Administration Building. But as Jack walked toward Hilltop to confront the Gills, his certainty dissolved. The only firm pieces of information were that the Hilltop kids were stealing from the Commissary and that Mrs. Adams had named the Gills in connection with contributions of food. While nasty, those were far from incriminating. Besides, who among the boys at Central wasn't involved in stealing from time to time? . . . And even though the Hilltop boys' stealing was allegedly substantial and done blatantly, no one had solid proof of what they had actually stolen, or how much, or what they had done with the stolen goods.

As he walked, Jack recalled that John Gill had come to Central as a carpenter's helper and general repairman four or five years ago. There had been a temporary layoff at the aircraft plant in Flight City. Despite an opportunity to return to the plant, John had decided to stay at Central. In his interview with Jack, he had not only mentioned his dislike for the continuous uncertainty about plant employment, but also had talked at some length about his interest in the school. Mr. Gill had hesitantly revealed that he and Mrs. Gill were unable to have children and consequently would very much appreciate the opportunity to work closely with the boys. Because there were no vacancies in the cottages for a man-and-wife team at the time, Mr. Gill was hired as a general repairman. After a year of good work, the Gills had been placed in charge of Hilltop when Jack found an opportunity to make a change in cottage personnel. In spite of Mr. Gill's fine work record as a repairman, including supervising the boys in his charge, the Gills performed only marginally well in their cottage assignment. After their initial enthusiasm wore off, they handled their job perfunctorily. They traded their authority to the more aggressive boys, who paid for the delegated authority by keeping the rest of the boys in line. To the staff Mr. Gill was cooperative, but only superficially so. Though friendly and agreeable during meetings and conversations, Mr. Gill often failed to carry out the decisions reached in those staff situations. Often his own approaches ran counter to specific supervisory policy.

Mrs. Gill posed additional problems. Jack had thought that having a woman in the unit would improve the character of the place, ranging from the boys' language to cottage decoration. However, like John, her initial burst of enthusiasm had dissipated, and she had settled into a pattern of avoiding supervisory duties—especially sustained contacts with the boys. She commented with a lack of propriety to members of the Employees' Wives Club during her second meeting that she couldn't stand the boys' repulsive smell and foul language. Seeing to it that the boys made their beds, did some cleaning chores, brushed their teeth, and followed through with the chores to be done in a daily-living situation was not for Mrs. Gill.

Jack walked up the front walk to Hilltop, through the door, and into the dayroom. It was unoccupied, as were the library-reading room and the toilet-shower area.

In the dayroom he noticed that the telephone had been adjusted to ring in the Gill's apartment on the second floor. He turned and went back out through the hallway to the door that opened onto the stairway leading to the second floor. He rang the bell just to the right of the door. An obviously new card, "Ring only in case of an emergency," was posted above the bell.

Just another indication of the Gill's poor work—of their avoiding the boys to protect their own comfort, Jack thought with annoyance. He let his finger rest on the button until Mr. Gill called down, "Who is it?" in an irritated voice.

"John, you're being paid to be on duty. When I come by, I expect to find you on duty and not up in the apartment!" Jack shouted.

"I'll be right down," Mr. Gill answered hurriedly.

Now bristling with anger, Jack walked back into the dayroom but did not sit down. Mr. Gill appeared in a couple of minutes, looking ill at ease. He began, "I'm sorry; I just went upstairs for a few minutes to change my clothes before the boys come in from school."

"I didn't come over to talk with you about staying on the job, but since it's come up, I see no point in avoiding the subject," Jack said firmly. "You and Mrs. Gill are going to have to stay out of the apartment when you're on duty. I've talked with you about this before. Your record of staying on the job is so poor that it's gotten to be common talk among the staff. Even Mr. Graves commented on it the other day!"

"I know it looks bad," Mr. Gill said apologetically. "Really though, there are many times when we're on the job straight through. At other times we do use the apartment to catch up on our rest. You have to admit that we put in a lot of overtime."

"John you're over-playing your overtime. Besides that, Mary just does not work the required work week. These are matters of fact!" When Mr. Gill did not say anything, Jack continued angrily, "Let's get into what I came over about."

"Okay," Mr. Gill said.

"You were off yesterday and may not have gotten the word about the discussion that took place at the staff committee meeting. The Hilltop boys' stealing from the Commissary came up." Jack, watching Mr. Gill's face, saw his expression change from mild interest to shock. "It started when Mr. Eagan charged that the Commissary and Hilltop are getting more than their share of boys with long records of stealing. And let me tell you that the meeting really got into that.

"There was even more concern, however, about the lack of supervision at both the Commissary and Hilltop. How do you see it?"

Mr. Gill had regained his impassive look. He shrugged, but did not respond. "Well?"

After a few moments' delay, Mr. Gill hedged, "Well, it's hard to tell. We get our share of kids who have a history of stealing, but since most of the kids come to the school because of that problem, it's pretty normal to get more than a few thieves."

"Your view is important because a number of people believe that you're being saddled with more than your share of them," Jack said mildly.

Mr. Gill smiled blandly.

"The staff committee removed Allen, Jones, and Roba from the Commissary," Jack went on. "We'll consider new assignments for them at next week's meeting. . . . So, if you have any preferences as to where you would like to see them work, be ready to bring them up then."

"If they need to be reassigned, why doesn't Mr. Eagan just go ahead and do it?" Mr. Gill asked anxiously. "Why assemble a committee to do that?"

"Because it's the committee's responsibility to reassign them and you carry a part of that responsibility. Besides the reassignment of the boys, I'm sure that meeting will get into the bigger issue. The boy's stealing is only part of the problem. There's not only concern about the stealing from the Commissary, but there's a bigger concern about keeping places of service to the institution like the Commissary open to train the boys. . . . And of course the committee is concerned with the supervision of the boys in the Commissary—and here."

"So why does that mean we have to have a staff meeting?" Mr. Gill reiterated.

"Because we've got some serious problems," Jack repeated with obvious annoyance, "and the staff committee provides us with one way of working on them."

Mr. Gill looked uncomfortable.

"You'd better be there just to protect your own interests," Jack suggested firmly. "Remember that the committee talked about transferring Allen, Jones, and Roba out of your cottage."

"It's nice to know everyone's thinking of me," Mr. Gill said with a forced laugh, "but I don't really go for all this sudden attention." Then he added anxiously, "I don't want any of our boys moved to some other unit. I don't see any need for it. I don't mean to say that these boys don't have their share of problems, because they have plenty. At the same time, they aren't all that bad."

"Maybe I'm not telling this right," Jack said concisely. "The staff figured that you might not have the right mix in your unit. They don't want to move them because they're such bad kids. It's just that you've got too many who are alike. . . . And speaking in all honesty, the committee—and I—are questioning your supervision."

"I can't buy that," Mr. Gill said defensively. "My supervision is all right. It's just that the boys organize themselves like gangs, and try as we will to control them and their stealing, we just can't."

"And speaking of not controlling them adequately, some of the staff think that you seem to be relying too heavily on an organization of boys in Hilltop that may be pushing stealing," Jack charged. "The question becomes, 'What are you going to do about it?' "

"Well, I'll be glad to go to the meeting, but I don't see any need to move any boys out of here," Mr. Gill insisted.

"Then there's the matter of cottage supervision that I need to talk with you about. Besides the failure to cover the cottage, I don't think you have a real sense of where the kids are."

Mr. Gill gave him a beseeching smile. "Jack, you're beginning to bug me. You know what the work situation is here and yet you keep at me. In spite of all of the problems and the lack of help, I'm supposed to be on top of everything."

"Let me put it to you straight, John," Jack responded irritably. "Why aren't you on top of the kids' stealing?"

Contempt which had shown itself only slightly before now fully surfaced in Mr. Gill's tone. "Look, Jack, I feel good if I can keep up with the kids' stealing here in the cottage and I have to admit that I can't always. Now you ask me to try to control their stealing in the Commissary too. . . . Be reasonable, man! That's just too much. And you haven't even given me any convincing evidence that my boys have actually *done* any stealing in the Commissary. The only evidence I've heard is 'staff talk' and there's always a lot of that. Some of it's okay and then some of it . . . well . . . I just don't buy it."

"Look, John, the information we have is that not only have the Hilltop kids stolen a great deal of stuff during the past two months, but we know that some of it has been moved into *this cottage.*"

Mr. Gill digested that for a moment, then mumbled, "That could be the case. *If* they're stealing and *if* they're bringing some of the stuff into Hilltop, my guess is that they're probably trading it for favors. You know the racket—favorite food from the cafeteria workers as they go through the line, or for freshly pressed pants and shirts from the laundry boys every day instead of the twice-a-week change they they're allowed, or for cigarettes . . .

you name it. You know it goes on all the time throughout the whole institution. This is nothing new!"

Jack said pointedly, "But I want to know what the situation is in *Hilltop*."

Mr. Gill slowly raised the palms of his hands and shrugged.

Jack stared at him angrily. "John, I was hoping you'd choose to talk more candidly with me about this matter. But since you haven't, let me ask you how I am to interpret a phone call from Mrs. Adams in behalf of Laxton?"

Fear flashed across Mr. Gill's face. For the first time in their cat-and-mouse conversation, Jack sensed Mr. Gill was ready to open up. However, he pressed on. "She told me that you and Mary have given them a considerable amount of foodstuffs over the past couple of months and that you have represented it as being surplus from Central!"

Mr. Gill laughed nervously and exclaimed, "Now, what do you make of that! We've given them a little food, yes. Helped them collect a lot of stuff from the state outfit that handles the surplus food program and from every other kind of place, too. But giving them food from Central—no. Absolutely not!"

"She named items and amounts, John, and the way she tied things down, I don't believe she was exaggerating."

Mr. Gill shrugged. "I don't know what she's talking about."

"Then describe to me what you and Mary have given to the Capital City Community Church."

Mr. Gill shrugged again. "It wasn't much, really."

"Mrs. Adams mentioned a number of things—including a five-gallon can of shortening, fruit, vegetables, a tub of butter—all received from us. That's not all. I made a list as she mentioned the items on the phone, but I'm not going to try and recall them all now."

"Well, Jack," Mr. Gill said tensely, "I can't say any more than I've already said." His eyes were wide and he looked frantic.

"You haven't said much," Jack said wryly. "I just want you to be sure that you don't have anything additional you want to say to me. We obviously will be checking this out with other people—and in great detail."

"No," Mr. Gill exclaimed. "I'll . . . no . . . I'll have to think this over!"

"All right, think it over," Jack said calmly. He turned to leave, then added, "If you have anything to add, John, you better be in touch with me today because the matter is moving fast."

He walked out the door.

VI

When Jack entered the Administration Building, Thelma called out from her small office, "Mr. Graves would like to see you." Jack turned into Mr.

Graves' office, but before he had a chance to sit down, Mr. Graves fired the first question.

"How did it go?"

"He's playing it close to the vest, awfully close," Jack analyzed. "Of course, the fact that I had to chew him out for being up in the apartment instead of down in the unit didn't start us off on any great note of harmony."

"Are they up to that again?" Mr. Graves asked irritably. "Those damned apartments in the living units are the best excuse for staff goofing off on their jobs that I know of."

"Oh, he explained why he was up there," Jack said.

"I'm sure he did," Mr. Graves laughed sarcastically. "It must have been that he needed a break because he's put in so much overtime."

Jack nodded and shrugged. "But back to the main part of our conversation. John disclaims any knowledge of the boys' stealing or any carrying of foodstuffs into the cottage, and of course he acknowledged nothing about his own involvement."

"How did he explain Mrs. Adams' call?" Mr. Graves asked eagerly.

"Well, he said that she tends to exaggerate people's contributions and that he gave very little food, but helped collect a lot of it."

"A likely story," Mr. Graves scoffed.

"When I pressed him on specifics—a five-gallon can of shortening, fruits, vegetables, and so on—he flatly denied everything."

"How did you end up?"

"He seemed really shook up and I told him that if he had anything to tell me about the matter, he'd better get in touch with me *today*."

"All right, let's see what, if anything, develops with John," Mr. Graves said. "Maybe he'll decide to talk. I've already asked Kline to move ahead with a complete inventory. That will take time, but it's important. Check me on this: I want to press Mr. Stone for what he knows and what's missing. At the same time I want you and Mr. Eagan to talk to the boys from Hilltop—those three who have been removed from the Commissary. If after talking with them you feel that you ought to talk to others, please go ahead. Don't wait on Mr. Stone and me.

"I've decided to delay calling Mrs. Adams back until late tomorrow afternoon. Thelma knows what to tell her if she calls. I've left instructions for whoever is on the switchboard to be cordial to Mrs. Adams and to tell her that I'll be telephoning her tomorrow."

VII

Immediately after Jack left his office, Mr. Graves buzzed Thelma. "Please have Mr. Stone come over from the Commissary. You might tell him that I know he's swamped with work but I still need to see him. Then please phone

Mr. Kline and tell him that since I'm going to be talking with Mr. Stone, he may want to drop by. Please make it clear, though, that he's not required to be here, and that the decision is up to him."

A few minutes later Mr. Stone entered the office, obviously upset. His furrowed brow was beaded with perspiration and his eyes were narrowed to a squint.

Mr. Graves motioned to a chair. "How's the inventory going?"

"We're working at it," Mr. Stone responded with a weak smile. "Actually we're just getting a good start."

"Can you work on it tonight?" Mr. Graves asked.

"Of course," Mr. Stone said without hesitation.

"I'm trying to do two things at once . . . and I need your help," Mr. Graves continued. "The one thing is the inventory which you're already working on. The other is that I need a clear, straightforward estimate from you about how much food the Hilltop boys have been taking, how long they have been taking it, and what they have been doing with it."

"Mr. Graves, I want to cooperate with you," Mr. Stone began sincerely. "You've been right with me in my job here and I appreciate it. What I have to say won't be as strong factually as I'd like, but I'll try to tell you what I know and what I think. . . .

"First, on how long the boys have been stealing . . . I'd figure for about six weeks, maybe for as long as two months. Now I might be making the problem bigger, but I just learned this afternoon in a roundabout way from one of the kids, not a Hilltop boy, that they've been getting into the root cellar for about a month now in addition to the stock in the Commissary. That's where some of the garden stuff, especially potatoes, is stored." He paused, frowning. "What else . . . oh, yes, you want an estimate of how much has been stolen. . . . I don't really know, but I'd say it would run like a crate or two of oranges, maybe a bushel of apples—I'm more aware of the fruit because we keep a close eye on it—a couple of crates of vegetables, like Brussels sprouts, a sack of cabbage, maybe a bag of sugar . . . and a funny thing, a can of shortening is missing. . . . For now, that's my best estimate. I think some of this stuff will show up missing on the inventory. Some of it won't because the kids probably didn't deliver what was checked out of here to the kitchen. And then, too, the kids have been stealing from the kitchen. I've talked to Mr. Slocum over there. These figures are the ones we've come up with together." He handed a sheet of paper across the desk.

"Have you actually seen the kids do any of this stealing?" Mr. Graves asked sharply, surveying the page.

"No, I haven't actually seen them stealing," Mr. Stone answered slowly.

"Then how did it happen?" Mr. Graves pressed. "Can't you keep an eye on them?"

"Well, I'm the only one there all the time. Tom Hess is there only part-time—when he's not out on one of his runs . . . and there are eight of those kids."

"So they work around you," Mr. Graves said. "Would you agree?"

"That's exactly right," Mr. Stone nodded. "Tom will be inside with me full-time starting tomorrow. Then we'll be in better shape."

"But the kids you've been getting are pretty slick?" Mr. Graves suggested. "Pretty hard to deal with?"

"They aren't bad. They just haven't had any real care," Mr. Stone modified. "At least, that's one way of putting it. One thing they do, as they put it, is to 'keep their cool.' . . . Now, I've really gotten on them sometimes about their not working and their irresponsible attitude, but what I say runs right off their backs. They just laugh." His face saddened. "You know, Mr. Graves, when I really put the screws on them, they laugh at me and call me names. Then, to rub my nose in it, they say that I can't tell them what to do. They claim that Mr. Gill 'calls the shots.' "

"Why didn't you report these things to Mr. Kline or somebody?" Mr. Graves inquired.

"Right now I ask myself the same thing," Mr. Stone said with candor. "But Mr. Graves, now is now and then was then. When these things were happening, they didn't really seem like such a big thing. Annoying enough, but no big thing. Now it has turned out to be a big thing. We have stuff like this or just about like this happening every day. Maybe we're too tolerant and we pass over too much bad behavior that ought to be corrected, and corrected but good. . . . Maybe it was because the boys' stealing didn't take place all at once so I didn't get excited. Maybe . . ."

"What you say makes good sense," Mr. Graves agreed. "We usually encourage our people to be tolerant in the way they live with the boys, not setting themselves apart from them, and now we're turning the tables—at least somewhat. I'm not sure that's fair. And I'm not sure that we've quite gotten across the precise mix of tolerance and strictness that we want our people to apply."

Restraining his annoyance, Mr. Graves said, "What I can't figure out in all of this is why you didn't talk with Mr. Kline, Mr. Eagan, Jack, or myself about the situation. Alton, I am just amazed that you would let this slide the way you have."

Mr. Stone looked away in shame and did not answer. After a few moments he looked directly at Mr. Graves and sadly said, "I know I haven't handled it right. The only thing I can say is that I was trying to go easy on the kids and in the process I turned my back on too many things . . . and there were too many kids for me to keep up with."

Though dissatisfied with Mr. Stone's explanation, Mr. Graves accepted it and moved ahead. "Where, in your opinion, has all of this food been going—that is, beyond the usual trading the kids do?"

Mr. Stone looked down at his hands. "I hate to say this because . . . well, you'll see in a minute. . . . I think much of the stuff has been going over to Hilltop, and what's more, I think the Gills are mixed up in it somehow."

"I don't quite read you," Mr. Graves prompted.

"Well," Mr. Stone responded more bravely, "to say that another staff member is stealing or involved in stealing without much evidence is bad business in my book. Since I don't really know for sure about where the food has been taken, I thought I would be out of line to say anything."

"Then what gave you the impression that the food was being taken to Hilltop and that the Gills were involved?"

"From bits and pieces of talk among the Hilltop boys," Mr. Stone said uneasily. "They made out like Mr. and Mrs. Gill were using it for parties. That didn't make much sense to me though, because I couldn't really see anybody throwing much of a party with the kind of stuff the kids were taking . . . and the kids would say things among themselves like, 'We've got to get some grub over to the man or he'll be on us.' "

"And who did you think 'the man' was?" Mr. Graves asked.

"Mr. Gill."

"How did you decide that?"

"Just from the way the kids talked. When Hilltop boys talk and say 'the man,' they couldn't be talking about anybody esle."

"Then why didn't you report this to someone?" Mr. Graves demanded.

When Mr. Stone did not answer, Mr. Graves shook his head in disbelief.

His next chore, he thought grimly, was to find out if any of the other staff members suspected the Gills of being involved.

"Does anyone else feel the way you do about the Gills?"

At Mr. Stone's quiet "No," Mr. Graves continued, "And you say that you haven't discussed this with anybody?"

Mr. Stone shook his head.

"Okay, let's leave it that way. I'll ask you to keep this discussion under your hat. I had invited Mr. Kline to sit in with us if he wanted to, but he must have gotten tied up. Feel free to talk with him if you like, but have him understand that the matter is confidential. I think you realize that along with clearing up this matter, we also have a responsibility to keep our dirty linen from public view."

Mr. Stone nodded emphatically.

"I want you to go ahead with the inventory," Mr. Graves went on. "Do a thorough job. Go over your work with Mr. Kline. Try to finish it so that you and Mr. Kline can come in and see me after lunch tomorrow, about two-thirty."

Jack and Mr. Eagan had agreed to meet that day in the conference room of the Administration Building to plan their interviews with the boys.

Jack said, "I don't think we should bring them together in a group. Besides their sticking together, Tom Allen, who is strong and cagey, would try to take over."

"You're right," Mr. Eagan said. "I agree."

"Elijah Jones is probably the one who will talk," Jack predicted. "He's tough, but without Tom he loses his confidence. I think he'll tell us what we need to know. I'm going to ask you to talk to Bill Roba. I'll talk to Elijah. I want each of us to go after information to establish their stealing, what they stole, and where the food has been going."

"Right." Mr. Eagan nodded.

"Okay, so we're together on that," Jack reaffirmed. "Now I'm going to have Thelma call Hilltop and have the Gills send Bill over to see you here in the conference room and Elijah to see me in my office."

"Better have her stagger the phone calls five or ten minutes apart so the boys don't get organized on their way over," Mr. Eagan suggested.

Thelma called Hilltop. "Hello, Mr. Gill. This is Thelma. Would you please send Elijah over to see Jack?"

"Elijah to see who?" Mr. Gill asked, startled.

"Elijah to see Jack," Thelma repeated, and added, "and to see him right away."

"It's getting late."

"Jack said *now*," Thelma said firmly.

"Okay," Mr. Gill relented. Thelma detected a note of protest in his voice.

As soon as she saw Elijah coming up the steps of the Administration Building, she telephoned Mr. Gill again. "Here's another request," she said crisply. "Would you please send Bill Roba over to the staff conference room to see Mr. Eagan? And while we're making appointments," Thelma added with mock formality, "send Tom Allen over five or ten minutes after Bill leaves Hilltop. I'll watch for them coming across the grounds."

"But it's late," Mr. Gill protested. "We'll be leaving for supper in about ten minutes."

"I know," Thelma said. "But you are to send the boys over."

"The reason I'm so uptight about this is that my kids are hard enough to manage under ordinary circumstances," Mr. Gill explained with forced pleasantness. "Now, if several of them—and several of our tougher ones at that—are going to miss supper, it's going to be even harder to control the rest of them tonight."

"I'll call the dining room and ask them to hold three big plates for the boys," Thelma reassured him. "I'll take care of it. Don't worry. Just send them along."

Mr. Gill changed his tactics. He asked in a confidential tone, "Thelma, what in the devil is going on? Have these kids gotten into some kind of trouble?"

"I don't have the slightest idea," Thelma responded neutrally. "I suppose if they have, Jack will sure find out and then he'll be talking with you about it." She paused. "Maybe you already know something and could fill me in."

She was disappointed when Mr. Gill did not respond to her probe.

"I'll send Bill and Tom over." After a brief pause, Mr. Gill asked coyly "Thelma, can't you let an old friend in on what's happening . . . ? Can't you?"

Thelma rose to the appeal. "I don't know for sure what is going on," she whispered "but things have been jumping up here this afternoon, let me tell you. People have been in and out of Mr. Graves' office like it's headquarters or something. The little that I *have* been able to learn makes me think that there must have been some trouble in the Commissary. That's all that I've been able to pick up. I think it's got something to do with some stealing over there. The one thing I know for sure is that Mr. Graves is mad. I don't think I've ever seen him so mad. Never! Look . . . Mr. Gill, I've got to open up this line in case somebody really needs it."

"Thanks," Mr. Gill said lifelessly.

Thelma disconnected the lines while muttering under her breath, "Well, that's a strange way of saying thanks after I put myself on the spot by telling him something I probably shouldn't have."

Elijah Jones entered Jack's office wide-eyed, wiping perspiring hands on the inside of his pockets.

Jack waved him to one of the chairs in front of his desk. Elijah stood by the chair for a moment and then sat down hesitantly. Jack looked at him a moment in silence. He began quietly, "Running a place like this sometimes gets to be more of a job than the staff can take care of, at least take care of right. That's why I asked to see you even though it's your supper time. That's my situation. I don't know yours, but I expect you're trying to find your way or make your way in a pretty rough world."

Elijah looked at him warily, then nodded.

"Now, I've gotten reports from people who know your work in the Commissary firsthand. They say you're a fair worker, really a good worker when you want to be . . . so that's on your side. . . . But I also know that you and some of the other Hilltop boys have been stealing from the Commissary. Stealing quite a bit."

When Elijah did not answer, Jack said crisply, "Isn't that right? The evidence is clearly against you. . . . There's no doubt about it. . . . But I want to hear it straight from you."

Elijah blinked his eyes and tightened his grip on the arms of his chair. Finally he nodded.

"What in the world did you and the other fellows do with all of that food? You took more than anyone could possibly eat. Besides, much of the stuff you took had to be cooked, and you fellows aren't in a position to do any cooking. Yet it all must make sense in some way. But I must say that I can't figure it. . . . Tell me, Elijah, what have you fellows been doing with all that food?"

Elijah fidgeted in his chair, wiped his brow with the back of his hand, and then wiped his hand on his shirt. He began, "Mr. Gill . . ." but stopped.

"Go on about Mr. Gill," Jack pressed.

"When we brought oranges, apples, and that kind of stuff into the cottage, he passed them around, you know, like after supper when the guys get hungry," Elijah explained.

"Who's 'he'?" Jack asked with heightened interest.

"M—Mr. Gill," Elijah stammered.

"Yes, but what about the vegetables, the shortening, and the rest of the stuff?" Jack asked. "I know you didn't eat that. . . . Did you give that to Mr. Gill? And what did Mr. Gill do with it?"

"Mr. Gill took it all right," Elijah said scornfully. "He took it all right. . . . That's mainly what that crazy man was interested in. At first we thought he might be giving parties, but that didn't make sense, unless he was giving them someplace outside of Hilltop. . . . We never saw no parties here."

"I don't think it makes sense either," Jack agreed.

"So we asked him," Elijah continued, warming to the story, "because he kept pushing us to bring whatever looked like surplus to us. He told us that he was giving the food to a place for orphans who really needed it. He said that if they didn't get the food from us, they probably wouldn't have very much."

"Didn't you fellows stop to think that we needed the food, too?" Jack asked, astonished. "Didn't you think it was a little strange to be stealing your *own* food?"

"We always have plenty," Elijah reasoned. "Mr. Gill said that there will always be more coming into the Commissary, that the state never runs out. From the way he explained it, it just seemed okay."

Jack shook his head soberly, "Who all have been in on this deal?"

"Well, pretty much everybody from Hilltop," Elijah said vaguely.

Jack nodded. "Bill and Tom are being talked with now, so you don't have to feel that you're the only one we've picked on or that you've been tattling on anybody."

"To tell you the truth, we three were the main ones," Elijah confessed. "There were three others—Ed Wills, Herm Stay, and Ray Schneider. But Mr. Gill was putting pressure on us. He's always doing that. Especially this afternoon."

"Why this afternoon?" Jack queried.

"Well, Mr. Gill said he didn't want us to say anything, and if he heard that anybody was doing any talking, he was going to hold up our paroles. And he said he was going to make it hell for us in Hilltop!"

"If that's the case," Jack mused, "then I'd be interested to learn why you *did* talk."

"I don't know," Elijah answered softly. "I guess I didn't count on having to see somebody like you. I didn't think it was that important. . . . Besides, Mr. Gill was rotten. First he put pressure on us to steal. That wasn't right. I didn't mind stealing when we divided up the stuff when we got back to Hilltop so everybody could have some fruit to eat or something like that. That stealing was all right, but I didn't like this other stealing. . . . Now he's threatening us if we squeal. . . . So I'm for getting back at him."

At that moment Mr. Eagan appeared at the door and motioned to Jack, who joined him in the hall.

"Bill has told me all I think we need to know," Mr. Eagan said quietly. "John Gill has put pressure on the kids to steal and Bill claims John has been giving the food to a church group. How is it going with Elijah?"

"Identical stories," Jack said. "Would you have Bill wait in the reception area while you go ahead and talk to Tom? Then we'll send them over to supper together. I'll finish with Elijah shortly."

Jack returned to his desk, lifted the receiver, and buzzed Thelma. "If you haven't done so already," he told her, "Please have the dining room save three plates of food. The boys will be over in about a half-hour. Also, please call the infirmary and have them set up to sleep three extra boys tonight. And, I want to know who's on duty over there tonight. Please let me know when you find out."

Elijah was watching him anxiously. "What are you putting us in the infirmary for?" he protested.

"You told me just a few minutes ago," Jack reminded him, "that Mr. Gill told you not to talk. So, if we return you to Hilltop without our talking with him first, you fellows will surely come under some pressure from him. . . . Don't you want to avoid that?"

Elijah nodded quickly. "What are you going to do to us?" he asked defensively. Implicit in his question, it seemed to Jack, was 'What are you going to do to Mr. Gill?'

"From the looks of the clock," he said calmly, "I would say that Mr. Eagan or myself and maybe Mr. Graves will talk with you boys about that tomorrow morning. It will be a staff decision. I think you know how we handle these things."

Another knock on the door interrupted them. Mr. Eagan entered. "I've only talked with Allen a few minutes, but he's given me essentially the same information as Bill did. So, unless you want to talk to him, I suggest we take them over to the dining room and then on over to the infirmary."

Jack nodded his head. "Can you see to that for me? I need a little time to firm up the infirmary arrangements, but there shouldn't be any problem."

"Okay," Mr. Eagan agreed with dispatch. "Elijah, if you'll come with me, we'll pick up Bill and Tom and get on our way."

VIII

Jack completed the infirmary arrangements and telephoned Mr. Graves. "Just reporting in," he said. "All three boys—Allen, Jones, and Roba—admit to the stealing, taking the goods to the Gills, and most important, they claim the Gills put pressure on them to steal. Bill Roba says John has been giving the food to a church group. Elijah reported that the food went to a place for orphans."

"Everything we knew pointed to the Gills," Mr. Graves responded. "What a sad mess. . . . Jack, would you follow up and see John? Get his resignation immediately. If he won't resign, we'll have to place him on leave pending a full investigation."

Jack answered, "Okay, I'll follow through." However, after putting the receiver down, he procrastinated in calling Mr. Gill, debating with himself how he should confront him. He recognized his own uneasiness about making the call and reprimanded himself for putting it off. Finally, with a pang of anxiety, he asked Thelma to telephone Hilltop.

"I'll try," Thelma offered, "but I'm afraid they're still over at supper."

Listening to the Hilltop phone ring, Jack tried to imagine what the Gill's defense would be. He was about to hang up when someone answered. "Mr. Gill here," said an uncertain voice.

"Look, John, I must talk with you later this evening about the stealing from the Commissary," Jack said seriously.

"Let me beg off until tomorrow morning," Mr. Gill pleaded. "I'm tired to the bone. Let's hold off on a meeting until then."

"John, this can't be put off," Jack pressed.

"Jack, I'm bushed," John repeated. "I'm groggy. Quite plainly, I just can't do any more today . . . no way. . . . let's make it first thing in the morning. We'll both be fresh then. What do you say?"

Jack was tired too. He sighed. "All right. Be in my office at eight."

"Okay," Mr. Gill said appreciatively. "I'll be there at eight sharp and we can talk this whole thing over."

Feeling ambivalent, Jack hung up, thought a moment, then picked up the phone again.

"Thelma, please get Mr. Graves at home for me."

"Jack, what's up?" Mr. Graves responded.

"I'm sorry to report that John begged off on meeting me tonight," Jack said dejectedly. "But we have an appointment for eight in the morning."

"Too bad," Mr. Graves responded. "It would have been preferable to see him tonight, to get his resignation, or at least press to get it. Why wouldn't he meet?"

"He said he was 'bushed.' I believe he really was. Actually, so am I."

"All right, push ahead with the resignation in the morning," Mr. Graves directed. "If he won't resign, put him on leave, pending an investigation."

"Okay," Jack answered. "I have the pitch."

"Fine," Mr. Graves reassured him. "If there's anything new, please let me know."

"Okay. I'll see you in the morning."

Feeling slightly buoyed by Mr. Graves' support, Jack straightened his desk and left the Administration Building.

As he passed Hilltop on his way to the staff apartment building, Jack noticed that the Gill's apartment was brightly illuminated. "Looks like they've got every light on in the place," he mused. "What in the world can they be doing?" But unable to justifiably investigate, he continued walking toward his apartment.

After a fitful night, during which he thought he heard the deep growl of a truck engine, Jack arose at six-thirty to settle what had now become to him the "Gill problem.'

Following breakfast, he left the apartment for the office. Walking by Hilltop, Jack observed a peculiar quiet, appropriate considering the boys were at school and the staff was busy with their unit work. Yet it seemed exceptionally quiet. He walked on to work. As he entered the Administration Building and headed for his office, Thelma called out, "Jack, I have an envelope addressed to you that was on my desk when I got here."

Jack took the envelope and continued on to his office. Unmindful of its contents, he sat down at his desk and in a businesslike manner opened it, unfolded the message, and began to read. As he read he was gripped by mounting tension:

Jack:

By the time you read this, Mary and I will have been off the grounds for several hours. We have taken our belongings from Hilltop. Bill will be on duty today. Everything should be in order. I am sorry things didn't work out any better. Consider this a letter of resignation.

John

12

TOO HOT
IS TOO HOT

It was on a very hot day in August, the thirteenth day in a row during which the temperature had risen to one hundred and ten degrees, that Len Hall ran into real trouble. The previous days had been hot and dry, and with the help of a little breeze, Len Hall and his boys had been able to survive. But two days of high humidity combined with the high temperature were too much. Signs that this particular day was going to be a bad one began to show at daybreak.

Several boys woke up in foul moods, refused to make their beds, and when pressed to do so, cursed and threatened to beat up the night man. It was only after Len Hall came on duty a half-hour later that the altercation was worked out—but not before the whole cottage was upset by the angry and potentially violent eruption. Delays in getting to breakfast intensified the agitation.

Having to eat what was left—cakey oatmeal, hardened toast, and warm fruit juice—added to the boys' frustration. On their return to the cottage, only through patient encouragement, some gentle prodding, and an occasional sharp reprimand could Len Hall get the boys off to their varying schedules: work, summer school, or recreation.

The boys who remained in the cottage were those currently not "making it" in the regular program: Elliot Fread because of his irritability; Carl Sturger and Alfred Fredrick because of their laziness; Roger Barrien and Richard Delder because they were considered dangerous by some staff who were concerned about their volatile anger and histories of assault; and Tom Lester and Lee Pearson because they had just been returned from running away. As a practical way of keeping them occupied and also punishing them, these boys were organized into the House Force, a crew that did janitorial and yard work.

After the game room was swept, the toilet and shower scrubbed, and the entryway and hallways swept, Mr. Hall called out, "Okay fellows, let's move out and tackle the lawn. It's a week overdue."

The boys had scattered themselves around the dayroom. Several were lying on the floor. A few were sprawled across the furniture. Two were leaning on the windowsill staring listlessly out at the grounds.

Mr. Hall's direction impinged on them from a world they were trying to shut out. Not only did they abhor the exceedingly hot weather and the vast expanse of lawn—especially the front, which ran all the way down to the highway—but they also reacted negatively to the prodding.

"Let's move out," Mr. Hall said again. No one moved. "Okay, okay! Let's get out there and take care of that lawn." The boys ignored him. "Come on, I'll take the first mower and the rest of you can follow. We let it go last week with the agreement that we'd do it this week. That's *today*."

Recognizing their agitation, Len acknowledged, "Okay, I know it's miserable outside but we have to do it . . . and we can look forward to a swim this afternoon."

His empathetic urging reached them and they began to get up slowly. Grumbled complaints, not clearly audible to him at first, became more pronounced as they filed out the door, and a flow of vulgarities was climaxed by Roger Barrien's "Hall runs Achor like a goddamn slave ship!"

Hall's position at the tail end of the line may have prevented an immediate confrontation. Roger's comment stimulated a wave of anger that passed through Len like a bolt of electricity and its resulting tension pitched him forward ready to strike. His first impulse was to shove his way through the line of boys, grab Roger back by the collar, spin him around, and slap him across the face. But the bright impact of a stream of sunshine transformed his violent urge into nervous sweat.

As they trudged out the door into the oppressive weather, he wiped his forehead and the back of his neck with an often-used handkerchief and reassured himself that his authority had not been destroyed. Yet, his anger smoldered.

Mr. Hall deliberately ignored Roger's insult. When everyone was out of the cottage, he moved to the head of the line, led the boys to the institution's tool shed, and checked out eight mowers.

As the boys pushed their assigned mowers back toward Anchor, Roger pointed to the hand-driven mowers and observed with disgust, "This goddamn institution still operates in the dark ages! Other people use power mowers! Central State uses hand mowers and slave labor!" Then, facing Len Hall directly, he added with a sneer, "And you're the one who drives the slaves."

Two great strides carried Hall's two-hundred-thirty-five-pound frame to within a foot of Roger. This behavior had proved helpful in the past—not only in helping a boy to recognize what he would be up against if he decided to get physical, but also in giving Mr. Hall several moments in which to reflect. Usually this served as a brief cooling-off period for both parties.

He planted his feet wide apart and said tensely, "Roger, you've just said all you're going to say this morning."

None of the other boys moved. Some opened their mouths in shock.

All of his natural, good-natured tolerance had been driven out by anger. His face was flushed and drawn. The muscles at the edge of his right eye twitched.

The boys watched, frightened at the change in their supervisor.

"Wipe that surly look off your face!" Hall demanded.

Roger twisted his face into an ugly smirk.

"I said wipe that surly look off your face!"

Suddenly Roger unleased a powerful blow aimed at Len Hall's mouth.

Though caught by surprise, Len ducked, but not fast enough. Roger's fist cut across his forehead, leaving an ugly red streak.

The genial flexibility that had characterized Len Hall during his ten years at Central State snapped. Though he subsequently referred to the episode as "the straw that broke the camel's back," in no way was that an adequate explanation for the reckless explosion that swept away his self-discipline and defied Central State's rule about corporal punishment and the common-sense rule of not responding to a boy at his own level of behavior.

With a cry of rage, Len Hall swung a blow to Roger's head. Seizing the boy by the collar of his shirt as he recoiled, Hall began striking him about the head and face with an open hand.

The other boys in the group stood by, cringing. Finally Roger broke away and bolted madly for the cottage.

He did not get more than five yards, however, when Len, charging in pursuit, caught him by the collar and threw him onto the ground. Before Roger was able to respond, the supervisor had grabbed two fistfuls of shirt and skin, jerked him to his feet, slapped him across the face several times, and finally shoved him in the direction of his mower.

And still Hall pursued him. Alfred Fredrick, the most amiable among the boys, seemed to realize that the matter had gotten out of hand, and ran between Roger and Len Hall trying to grab Hall's arms. Len easily shook him off and shoved him to the ground.

Roger sprang away.

As Len was about to renew his pursuit, he twisted his ankle and fell to the ground. The sharp pain and the jarring impact of the ground brought him partially back to his senses. Still seething with anger, he slowly and painfully pushed himself up off the ground and, in spite of the pain, forced the full weight of his body onto his injured ankle.

With the exception of Alfred Fredrick, who was still on the ground several yards behind Len Hall, the other boys had circled to protect Roger, who cowered next to his mower.

Len Hall, gritting his teeth and squaring his shoulders, felt the anger drain from his body. Silence hung around the group like the muggy air. He glanced briefly around at the group of subdued boys, tucked his shirt into his trousers, and said grimly, "Now let's get at that damned lawn. I'm going up to the Administration Building." Before turning to go, he added, "If there's any more nonsense from any of you, you've got a good idea of what you'll get!"

Len Hall waited until the boys began to push their mowers, then turned abruptly toward the Administration Building. The grossness of his act began to sweep over him as he walked. Yet he mumbled to himself justifying his attack: he was fed up with the extraordinarily long work hours, the poor pay, and having to absorb the boys' hostility. At the best of times, after all his maneuvering, they didn't even meet his *lowest* standards of how adolescent boys should behave!

Variations on these themes ran through Mr. Hall's mind a number of times before he got to the front door of the Administration Building. But as he started down the hall toward Jack's office, all of his justifications began to sound weaker the farther he got from the scene of the violence. Numbness overtook him as he stumbled through the door.

Nodding mutely at Jack and seating himself in the chair before his desk, Mr. Hall sat with limp hands on his knees, staring at the wall behind Jack like a person in shock. In an uncharacteristically soft voice, very nearly a whisper, he said, "Jack, I'm going to quit. And if it's all right with you, I'd like to leave sooner than the usual two weeks' notice that you usually need."

Taken aback by Len's mental state, Jack responded gently. "Len what are you talking about? You've been one of our mainstays during the past ten years or so—we'd be lost without you. What does this mean?"

"That may be the trouble," Len answered almost inaudibly. "I've been here too long. I'm worn out. I've started to act just as bad as the people I used to criticize."

"You'll have to explain," Jack said softly, "I don't follow you."

"I've had it," Len responded. His voice picked up as he repeated, "I've had it. I've had it."

After several attempts to get him to explain further, Jack shifted his tactic. "Look Len, I . . . think we should go over to the dining room, have a cup of coffee, and see if we can't work this thing out, whatever it is."

Len Hall shook his head.

Jack tried again. "You've obviously been working too hard. . . . I'll tell you what. I'll get Harold Collins to fill in for you for a couple of days and you go home and rest. You know how capable Harold is; you won't have to worry about a thing. I'll come by and see you day after tomorrow. By that time I'll bet you'll have thought it over and decided to stay! I'll get in touch with Harold now. Leave everything to me."

Suddenly Mr. Hall looked up at Jack with focused eyes. "I remember so well, in fact like it was yesterday, when you and I first talked about my coming to Central. . . . Well, it's been like you said it would be."

Speaking with fond recollection, Len talked for twenty minutes, tracing back his experiences at Central State. Jack listened with a puzzled smile. After a pause, Len Hall's face paled. He looked at Jack with anguish. "Jack, I can hardly bring myself to tell you this. I just beat up Barrien pretty badly. I couldn't take him any more."

As Mr. Hall described the incident, tears rolled down his cheeks and several times his whole body shook. Though Jack hoped the man might be able to give way completely to his emotions to release the tension, Mr. Hall fought for control. When he seemed calmer, Jack asked, "How badly is Barrien hurt?"

"He isn't really hurt, but that's not the issue, Jack. The issue is that I know now I've had it. And when a person gets in that frame of mind, he should get out. . . . Besides, I can't face people after having knocked Barrien around."

They argued, but Mr. Hall persisted in his decision to quit. Finally he got up from his chair, took a deep breath, and squared his broad shoulders.

"Jack, I've had it and I'm through," he announced firmly. "I'm getting out of here."

"Len, you can't just turn your back on this whole thing. Not after all we've been through," Jack countered. "It just doesn't make sense. Besides, I still don't really know what you've had too much of."

Len Hall sat down heavily and burst out, "I just beat the hell out of Roger Barrien. . . . No other words for what I did. Just beat the hell out of him."

"He provoked you. You let him have it and now you want to quit," Jack challenged.

"That puts it in a nutshell," Len acknowledged forcefully, but then softened. "Jack, I'm not staying on. . . . There's no way."

"Why not?" Jack asked sharply. "You're not going to chicken out on us, are you?"

Mr. Hall did not rise to the provocation.

"Jack, you can say what you will. I've had it. This Barrien thing just brings it all to a head. That kid has been asking for what he got for a long time, but I'm not trying to justify my beating the hell out of him. What I am trying to tell you is that the Barrien case tells me I've had it and it's time for me to leave."

Jack swallowed with an effort. "Let's leave it this way," he proposed. "Harold Collins will cover for you during the next two days. I'll be over to see you day after tomorrow and if you decide then that you really want to quit, then I'll agree. Of course, if you decide that you want to continue, it will be the best news I could get."

"Jack, I want to tell you now—"

Jack cut in. "Let's just leave it this way."

Without agreeing, Len Hall got up and walked out of Jack's office.

Jack sat almost stupefied by what felt like the rejection of an old friend, as the broad back disappeared behind his door.

13

JACK'S EXIT

Jack closed the door, walked blindly back to his chair, and crumpled into it. A pall of depression which had been dogging him for several months now descended. Having grown more gray and grim during recent years, with lines deepening in his forehead and around his eyes, he had aged dramatically during fifteen years as Director of Group Life at Central State. Gone were the customary steadfastness of purpose, the quiet confidence, and the sparkle of enthusiasm that characterized his early years.

He tried to analyze why this depression hit him so hard. He had been accustomed to brief periods of it before, but those had not affected him so deeply. Certainly there were enough causes: the many problems posed by the boys, their parents, the staff, the community, and problems he had in dealing with the state offices and the legislature. It must be an accumulation of all those things, he thought. It seemed to him that after his mother's death a great weariness had set in. But then he shook his head. That didn't make sense. After all, he reasoned, she was ninety-three when she died, and she had lived a full life and had experienced a relatively painless death.

In spite of all his efforts to buck himself up, the overwhelming sense of discouragement had persisted day after day. Regardless of its cause, the depression hung on, and Jack could not shake it. He had found himself avoiding work situations that required negotiation of staff differences and decision-making.

Jack leaned back in his chair. The contour of its cushions responded to the form of his body. It was used to him. Yet the chair had not always been Jack's. It had been sent to the school as a reject from the State House when the State modernized some of its offices. The high back, topped by a headrest, looked incongruous with his other furnishings. But he had grown used to its odd appearance and its reliable comfort. Though he rarely used the headrest, this evening he leaned back and let his head recline on the cushion and stretched his arms over the upholstered arm rests.

Jack sat for awhile in the darkness and looked out the window of his office to the empty yard outside. A single light next to a gnarled cottonwood burned dimly. The stillness, the utter quiet of the scene, further depressed him. Tears welled up in his eyes. He wondered whether he could continue. The pain that he had been intermittently experiencing during the past several weeks stung him once again in the upper-left section of his chest, and he wondered whether he might be developing what Doc Barth would call a "psychosomatic disorder." The pain reminded him of the time he had cracked some ribs, but that had been a long time ago. After a thorough examination by his physician the previous week, the doctor had shrugged and said, "From all indications you check out all right. Though, at your age, you'd better maintain a reasonable work schedule and let somebody else handle the pressures." Though the suggestion seemed reasonable to Jack, he had continued to follow his regular heavy routine.

Jack closed his wet eyes tightly. He began to feel protected, even invulnerable from his troubles in the big chair, and he settled deeper into its security.

His mind wandered from the pressures of his work. Intuitively his thoughts sought the refuge of his childhood memories. There, within the confines of their simplicity and order, Jack might find the peace he so very much needed. He fell into an uneasy sleep.

. . . "Hello son."

Jack turned to where the husky voice had called.

"How're you doing?"

Jack saw his father standing at the end of the trailer.

"Good God son! You're not even half-way finished!"

Jack eyed the stacks of crates that filled the trailer.

"This trailer's got to be unloaded by six, boy, six o'clock! What's the hold-up?"

Jack tried to speak, but he couldn't.

"Six o'clock, boy, six o'clock!" The voice echoed louder and louder through the trailer.

Perspiration covered Jack's brow as he attacked the crates with new vigor.

A sharp pain in his chest shifted Jack from the trailer to a white room where his mother sat alone on a bed, crying.

"Your father's dead. . . . Now it's up to you," she moaned. "You've got to find a job!" Jack stood facing his mother. A wave of anxiety overcame him. He ran from the house repeating, "I've got to find a job. I've got to find a job."

Jack ran to a hardware store. Behind a counter a huge stern man answered his plea in a deep voice, "No job here. No job here."

Jack turned to see a room filled with more huge stern people who shouted in unison, "No job here! No job here!"

Jack ran from the store in wild panic . . .

He was breathing heavily. The pain tugged at his chest.

Jack opened his eyes and looked around his office with a peculiar need to draw it close to him. Then he shut them again and reality faded away.

Almost at will, he fell back to sleep.

. . . He heard bells ringing softly in his ears. The bells rang louder and louder, as if he was getting closer to them. They are church bells, Jack decided. It must be close to ten.

Jack began to run. I mustn't be late, he thought. I mustn't be late.

The bells rang louder still as he ran across a field toward the church. Yet, he felt that he was hardly moving.

After reaching a deafening crescendo, the bells stopped. Jack knew that church would start immediately, and that his mother would have given up waiting for him and entered the sanctuary . . .

Jack awoke with a start. His heart was beating wildly. He was looking straight out of his office window, and saw the light play on the shimmering leaves of the cottonwood. Then it faded from his vision. His breathing became increasingly labored. He cleared his dry throat and tried to wipe the sweat from his brow. He twisted and turned to relieve the tightness in his chest and the pain in his left arm.

Jack's breathing became heavy gasping. Panicking now at the realization of imminent catastrophe, he leaned back in his chair, gripping its arm rests desperately.

Jack sensed that someone was entering his office. But before he was able to turn his chair around, three knife-sharp pains ripped through his chest in rapid succession. He saw his mother drift in front of him. He tried to reach out to her, but pain forced him to double over. As he strained, Jack saw his mother smiling peacefully at him. He straightened back up, but in doing so he was gripped by violent convulsions. Finally, he lay still in the chair. Expressionless eyes stared across the dark office. Jack was dead.

THE WORKSHOP

The Workshop has an explicit instructional objective: to put the vignettes to use as curriculum material. To assist readers who are pursuing this instructional aim, materials are provided in four areas: (1) orientation to residential settings for youth having problems, and information on roles that youth care workers play; (2) procedures and techniques for interpreting the vignettes; (3) an illustrative vignette analysis; and (4) questions to assist in discussion of the vignettes.

The vehicle for formal study of this curriculum material can vary from university course or community college unit to inservice educational sessions, or any format that fits the needs of the participants and the setting. Whatever the vehicle, the vignettes can be used most effectively as curriculum material in enabling learners to gain some insight into the human relations involved in working with delinquents, while at the same time providing them with intellectual information about the field. Aspects of this insight include the learner acquiring a conception of the necessary skills of social interaction for working both as team members and individually with delinquent youth. And further, the learners—be they actual or potential—can enhance their own working and attitudinal skills by utilizing the curriculum material in organized discussion or in the private process of mental rehearsal. However, the vicarious experiences of discussion or individual analysis need to be supplemented with actual experience in a job environment, and one that is conducive to ongoing professional growth. Finally, when the vignettes are used as curriculum material, their discussion needs to include an atmosphere of exploration, freedom of expression, respect for divergent ideas, and a spirit of cooperation among members whose common goal is learning more about and acquiring skills to deal with the problems of delinquent youth.

RESIDENTIAL SETTINGS AND YOUTH CARE WORKERS

A variety of facilities serve adolescents who are experiencing psychosocial problems. Those required to accept court-committed delinquent youth are typically called "training schools," "industrial schools," or some similar title. Those accepting emotionally disturbed youngsters who may or may not be adjudicated as delinquent are usually referred to as "residential treatment centers." Residences accepting dependent and neglected young persons are often designated as "group homes." The term "half-way house" indicates an organized residence in the community with less structure than a formal institution serving young persons whose variety of problems do not require that they be institutionalized.

These several types of facilities vary in regard to criteria other than the special population they serve, including the following aspects: the *size of the population*, with training schools tending to be larger than other facilities; the *program*, with training schools tending to have less highly developed programs than other institutions; the *staff/youth ratio*, with training schools usually having fewer staff in relation to the youth than other facilities; and the *professional training* of the staff, with training school staffs tending to be less highly trained than those in other settings. Treatment in these facilities can be defined in several different ways. In a limited sense, treatment can refer specifically to individual or group psychotherapy. In a broader sense, it can be viewed as a suitable program for an individual that is based on a diagnostic evaluation of his particular needs. In this definition, the proper utilization of the environment constitutes a basic tool in treatment.

Innovative facilities encourage youth care workers to play—sometimes simultaneously—a variety of work roles, including those of *program planner* and *administrator, supervisor, care giver, advocate, activity leader, counselor,* and *educator.* As a *program planner* and *administrator,* the youth care worker designs and administers an overall cottage program that provides recreation, work, and other activities for the group while giving appropriate attention to individuals. As a *supervisor,* the worker monitors and controls a youth's behavior, particularly as it relates to rules and routines. As a *care giver,* he is concerned about and is responsible for an adolescent's well-being; in addition to providing affection, the worker sees to it that the young person is provided with food, clothing, and other essentials. As an *advocate,* he recommends special services for a teenager and, if necessary, intercedes by breaking through red tape to obtain those services. As an *activity leader,* he organizes and leads formal or informal recreational and leisure-time activities, particularly during late afternoons, evenings, and weekends. As a *counselor,* he helps youth cope with difficult and crisis situations: specifically, he listens empathetically; encourages anxious, shy, and sad young persons; monitors the behavior of manipulative youngsters; confronts them with their behavior; and encourages them to attempt changes. Finally, as an *educator*, the youth care worker gives instructions, information, and advice concerning the interpersonal skills of daily living.

Along with these more formal roles, youth care workers also play the roles of *colleague*, in which they encourage and support their fellow workers or are supported by them; and *counselee* or *supervisee* when being advised by another person.

INTERPRETING THE VIGNETTES

Phases in the Process of Interpretation

First. Read the vignette carefully.

Second. Identify concerns important to you as a youth care worker or as a prospective one. For example, a vignette may deal with (1) the complicated problems of a teenager, (2) a worker's lack of motivation to work in a residential setting, (3) a worker's lack of skill in working with teenagers who are having psychosocial problems, (4) the complexities of relationships within and between agencies, (5) a youth care worker's relationship to his supervisor, (6) the influences from outside the agency which affect the work situation, or (7) the emotional reactions of the youth care worker to the problems of the youth he works with.

Third. After you have identified the concerns in the vignette which you believe are important, think through the approach you are going to take to those concerns—your decisions and actions. You may find it useful to begin by breaking the vignette into beginning, middle, and end sections.

Next, analyze the vignette from various perspectives. Consider at least five possibilities. One is the perspective of the *individual*—that is, a person's feelings, hopes, aspirations, needs, thoughts, and roles. For example, a youth care worker can function specifically as a *care giver* by serving as a parent substitute in providing physical and mental health care; as a *counselor* by providing a youngster with one-to-one reality testing and help in problem-solving; and as an *educator* by providing cultural and technical information and a mature model of how to approach a task or situation.

A second perspective, the *interpersonal* perspective, concerns what happens between persons. Here you will be looking for instances of mutual support, competition, aggression, dominance, and submission. For example, you may find that a staff member is competing with another staff member for a new assignment, or that a male teenage resident may behave aggressively toward the new boy in the unit in an attempt to define their roles.

The *intragroup* and *intergroup* perspectives involve what is happening inside or between groups. Here you will be looking for actions which contain support or threat, such as struggles for status and leadership, competition for available rewards, and loyalty or suspicion toward a leader or outside group.

Two final perspectives to be considered are those from the *intrainstitutional* and *institutional-community* standpoints—that is, what happens within a given institution, and between an institution and a community. Intrainstitutional perspective involves looking at such matters as the style of the agency's top leadership and supervisory staff, institutional policies for dealing with its staff, how the institution divides up its work, and the mechanisms of communication within the institution. Institutional-community perspective has to do with the relationship that exists between the two—how they get along, and where their interests and concerns join. In using these perspectives, you will be looking analytically at competition, conflict, cooperation, dependence, and interdependence.

At this point it will be necessary to recall the previous discussion on roles in order to identify those roles assumed by the characters in the vignettes. Again, they can be one or any of the following: *program planner* and *administrator, supervisor, care giver, advocate, activity leader, counselor,* or *educator.*

Fourth. Now you are ready to begin a more detailed analysis, applying the perspectives that you selected in the previous step. Remember that even though the terms you will be using to label these perspectives are abstract, they really refer to particular things that are happening in the vignettes.

Fifth. Relate the elements of analysis to one another. For example, check a teenager's sadness against his peer relations, his earlier life, and his relationships with youth care workers and other staff. Or consider a youth care worker's behavior toward a teenager in terms of the worker's skill, his feelings about his workload, and the quality of communication within the residential setting. In this phase of your analysis, you will want to step back and try to see the vignette in its entirety. Look for more complex connections as well as the simpler ones. For instance, be on the alert for recurrent cycles of events, typical behavior of staff and/or residents, and the consequences that result from the interaction among the elements of a vignette.

Sixth. Now you are ready to explain not only the connections, patterns, cycles, and effects of the vignette's elements, but you are also ready to explain *why* they occur. This explanation may be in terms of past incidents or elements having to do with the more immediate situation, or some combination of the two. For example, a youth care worker's actions can be explained in terms of his earlier work experiences or his immediate residential work situation, or both.

Seventh. At this point, take a careful look at the concepts and terms that have been used. Decide how adequate they are in relation to a particular vignette. Perhaps you will need to consider others or revisions of the ones you have used. For example, you may find that a teenager's anxiety is inadequately explained by the immediate living situation, and that you will need facts from the adolescent's case history to shed some light on what is actually affecting his feelings. Or, you may find that a particular vignette contains an exception to an assumption about human behavior. For instance, a young person may not respond negatively to what appears to be poor staff handling, but instead may be highly motivated by it.

Eighth. Pause to consider how the staff decisions and action sequences in a vignette could have been improved. Begin by defining for yourself the objectives you think the main character was trying to achieve and his means of achieving them. Then think about what *you* believe the appropriate objectives should have been and how *you* would have gone about achieving them. For instance, did the youth care worker in the vignette work to overcontrol a teen's behavior and, in the process, take on the role of an enforcing *supervisor*? Putting yourself in the place of the youth care worker, might your objective have been instead to encourage the teen's expression, a goal that might have led you to play the role of a *counselor*? On the other hand, you may find that you agree with the vignette's objectives and processes.

Techniques of Interpretation

First. After you have finished reading the vignette, think it over. Let your imagination roam with the material. Be realistic, but don't limit what you allow yourself to think about.

Second. Look carefully for additional meanings in what the characters say—try to read between the lines. As you know from experience, people sometimes mean something considerably different from what they actually say. Or you may find that what is said has more than one meaning. For example, a young teenager expressing dissatisfaction with a residential program may not only mean what he says, but also may be suggesting that he wants to return home or that he is considering running away. Compare what people say with that they do. Sometimes there is a substantial difference! As you note the differences between a character's words and his deeds, examine whether something happened during the course of the vignette to change his intentions or whether the character simply never meant to do what he promised in the first place.

Third. Now concentrate on carefully sorting out those concepts in a vignette which seem reasonable to you from those that seem less plausible. Be aware of the difference between facts and the absence of clear evidence; also separate facts from assumptions, inferences, and conclusions. Remember that facts include only actions, thoughts, and statements. None of the vignettes contains *all* of the facts necessary to understand precisely what is happening, what led up to it, and what the outcome is. Consequently, the burden falls on you to make some assumptions and judgments. You may have to add "facts" that you consider reasonable, elements which you infer but which are not reported in the vignette.

Fourth. As you synthesize the several parts of a vignette and interpret them, pin down the concrete facts in the vignette to which the abstract terms apply. If a vignette is complicated and involves several episodes and a considerable number of characters, you may find it helpful to: (1) break up your overall analysis and synthesis and begin with individual episodes of the vignette, and (2) withhold pulling the related parts together until you have thoroughly examined them separately.

Pitfalls in Story Evaluation

First. Take your time in developing the summary of a vignette. Be sure to identify the important events and think about the concepts or terms that seem to relate usefully to the particular situation.

Second. Be careful not to pass premature judgments of approval or disapproval on the behavior of a resident or staff member, most especially concerning a staff member's techniques for working with young persons. Moral or ethical judgments tend to block or bias understanding rather than aid it. Therefore, value judgments have no appropriate place when you are in the analytic phase of vignette evaluation. To the extent that you do make value judgments, be aware that you are making them and either go ahead cautiously or discard them and start over. (You *will* be making value decisions when you are thinking about what future steps ought to be taken concerning a vignette.)

Third. Do not let yourself be sidetracked by some striking episode or event in a vignette that will lead you to jump to a conclusion about the overall situation. Instead, be sure that your conclusion is a balanced one which is relevant to all aspects of the vignette.

Fourth. You may come across a vignette that does not "ring true" for you. Do not play down or rule out its possible reality simply because it reports material that is inconsistent with your own experience or preconceived ideas. The fact that the vignette may present material new to you or that you consider incomplete or vague allows you the opportunity to examine it, work it over, and increase the dimensions of your experience in the process.

Fifth. Never assume that you are out to find one correct interpretation or solution to a given situation or problem. Every vignette involves a complicated interaction of people, events, and circumstances that can be analyzed and interpreted usefully in a number of ways.

AN ILLUSTRATIVE VIGNETTE ANALYSIS

"Nobody Likes Me or Wants Me," Chapter 3, is analyzed below to exemplify the application of the vignettes as instructional material, using the process of interpretation just presented.

First. Reread "Nobody Likes Me or Wants Me" carefully.

Second. Indentify what it is about Chapter 3 that is important to you. Develop a list of these concerns, using a passage from the chapter to illustrate each one.

A. The perplexing problems concerning Larry:

- "I've had him [Larry] over to see Doc a couple of times this week. You know he's thin, his shoulders sag, and with that tall frame of his, he looks like a scarecrow. He keeps complaining about his stomach. Doc's given him all kinds of tests, but all he can find is a nervous stomach."

B. Mr. Blake's lack of skill to work effectively with Larry, particularly his counseling skill:

- "Do you think these things will really help?" Mr. Blake asked with doubt in his voice.
"It's hard to know," Jack acknowledged. "As I said, they make good sense. But you seem doubtful."
"They do make sense," Mr. Blake agreed. "But I don't know if I can make them work. I really don't."

C. Mr. Blake's emotional reaction to Larry's problems.

- "Now that's a tougher thing for me," Mr. Blake pointed out with half a smile. "But I've been mulling it over. There are a couple of things that I know of that tend to upset me. One is that I can't stand one kid bullying another one. So when that starts happening, I've got trouble with myself . . . and . . . the other one is when a kid looks like he's about to cry. Somehow that really gets to me."

D. Jack assisting Mr. Blake through supervision.
   1. Jack listening to Mr. Blake:

- "Is it serious?" Jack asked with concern as they sat down to eat.
- "I'm interested to know what you picked," Jack said eagerly.

   2. Jack attempting to assess the problem:

- "What does the Doc have to say about that?"
- "What do you know about his background?"
- "So, instead of everyone being full of sympathy, the world turned on Larry," Jack suggested.

   3. Jack exploring techniques for approaching the problem:

- "How about Miss Smith—does she have any leads?" Jack inquired hopefully.
- "On that other thing, about changing how you ordinarily handle what the kids talk about, well . . . you may want to add other techniques to your ways of handling [the problem]."
- "Right. You don't want a whole cottage of kids around, and neither would Larry."

   4. Jack helping Mr. Blake with his feelings:

- "You know," Jack said, "you may not have to brace yourself as much as you think. You can share the feelings that Larry is having and still not get carried away by those feelings. In fact, your willingness to tune in to him may help the boy to sense you're really on his side."
- "Who knows," Jack shrugged. "It seems to me you were doing fine."

5. Jack offering encouragement and support:

- "Look," Jack pointed out with deliberate lightness, "don't sell yourself short."
- Sensing that Mr. Blake was feeling he somehow fell short, Jack said, "I know exactly what you are saying."
- "Sounds like you were right on target," Jack responded enthusiastically.

E. Mr. Blake's concern and desire to help:

- Mr. Blake began, "You recall the other boy I wanted to talk with you about was Larry Higgins."
- "Right. And I've been looking for something in the unit that might be causing Larry pressure ever since Doc mentioned it . . . but for the life of me, I can't see anything that might be doing it."
- "At any rate, after our earlier talk, I was determined to get to the bottom of Larry's complaining—to see what, in addition to his stomach trouble, was bugging him."

F. The dilemma of Jack and Mr. Blake.
1. How Jack helps Mr. Blake deal with his personal feelings, particularly as they relate to Larry's feelings:

- "Well, you may have to change that habit with Larry," Jack chuckled to ease Mr. Blake's anxiety.
- "Sure," Jack said confidently. "The other thing to work on is what we talked about yesterday. You're going to have to get a hold on your own feelings about listening to the boys' troubles."
- [Jack] reproached himself for neglecting to provide Mr. Blake with a chance to talk further about his response to the sad feelings expressed by his boys.

2. How Mr. Blake copes with his feelings as they relate to Larry's feelings:

- "I get your point and it makes sense. I guess I'll just have to try it." Mr. Blake continued to reflect silently on the point for a minute, his eyes becoming misty. After what may have been some resolution of the problem in his mind, he nodded his head and in an appreciative tone said, "Jack, I think if I feel right along with the kid, it might help. It seems like a natural thing to do."

- "Things were moving pretty fast, but I got control and made myself look at all of the stuff he had said—at least all that I could remember—and I tried to pick out the most important thing he'd been shouting so I could ask him about it."

3. The continuous and final problem of sadness:

- "Figuring he wanted to be left alone, I told him that I would be glad to talk with him further whenever he wanted to."
"Has he come back to you?"
"No," Mr. Blake answered softly.

Third. Think through the approach you are going to take in relation to the concerns that you have identified as important and in relation to the overall vignette.

Initially break the story down into its three major sections: the beginning, middle, and end. In reviewing the youth care worker's concerns in each of these portions, it becomes clear that they fall mainly into the categories of *individual* and *interpersonal* perspectives. An *intragroup* perspective is likely to be useful in only a minor way; for example, in looking at the situation in which the boys tease Larry about his illness. Further, the concept of roles assumed by the youth care worker, as discussed in the introductory section, should assist the reader considerably in understanding the behavior of Mr. Blake, Larry, and Jack.

Fourth. Begin the more detailed analysis by applying the perspectives selected in the previous step to the characters and by identifying the roles they assume in the vignette. The analysis below employs an outline that may be helpful to you. It begins with the topical heading of *Initial Concern,* which states the particular problem that will be analyzed. This heading is followed by *Phase,* which refers to the specific section of the story. The next heading, *Roles,* refers to the variations in function assumed by the staff, as defined and discussed in the introductory section. The headings *Individual* and *Interpersonal* refer to the categories of perspective relevant to this particular vignette. After analysis of the beginning has been completed, the outline is repeated to provide an analytical framework for the other portions of the story.

The beginning of "Nobody Likes Me or Wants Me" includes up to the point where Mr. Blake stopped by Jack's office a week and a half after they had discussed Larry during supper. The middle portion of the vignette runs from that point to Jack's question, "How did you end it then?" The end is all that follows, including Jack's image of Mr. Blake's sadness.

1. *Initial*

Concern:	Perplexing problems concerning Larry.
Phase:	Beginning.
Roles:	Concern is reflected through the interplay of roles: Jack as *supervisor* listens and advises while Mr. Blake as *supervisee* reports on his work with Larry. Also, Jack indirectly plays the role of *educator* and Mr. Blake that of learner. In Mr. Blake's work with Larry, he assumes the role of *advocate* in relation to Doc Barth, Miss Smith, and Mr. Long, and also that of Larry's *care giver*.
Individual:	In the aforementioned interactions, Larry is viewed as depressed, deprived, tearful, irritable, and as having psychosomatic problems.
Interpersonal:	Larry's interpersonal relations with his parents and significant others are unsatisfactory: his mother did not nurture him, his father was not in the home, and others close to him rejected him. His relationship with Mr. Blake is dependent and complaining.
Phase:	Middle.
Concern:	Larry's problems are evident during this portion through the interplay of the roles described below. Further light is thrown on Larry's problems during the last phase as Jack and Mr. Blake talk. We learn that Larry withdraws when memories and feelings about his mother and his home are touched on by Mr. Blake.
Roles:	In their second discussion about Larry, Jack again plays the roles of *supervisor* and *educator*. He listens, clarifies, and advises Mr. Blake who is a *colleague* and *supervisee*. Mr. Blake presents his efforts to function as a *counselor* in order to help Larry.
Individual:	Again, Larry is a sad boy with psychosomatic complaints. However, this phase of the vignette adds a new dimension to Larry's personality—that of explosive anger. Larry's feelings of rejection which are apparent in the first phase of the vignette are emphasized during this portion by Larry's exclamation, "Nobody likes me or wants me!"
Interpersonal:	Mr. Blake's report about Larry's interpersonal relations indicate that Larry's relationship with Doc is demanding and angry; with his peers, disruptive; with his parents and with Mr. Blake, stormy. The interpersonal relations between Mr. Blake and Jack are amiable, intense, and cooperative.
Phase:	End.
Concern:	Larry's basic condition is unimproved. He has become more sad and has withdrawn.

Roles:	Jack and Mr. Blake conclude their conference with their earlier roles intact.

Individual
and
Interpersonal: Larry is basically unchanged, though he may be more sad and withdrawn than he was earlier. Some aspects of his problem are more clearly understood than previously.

2. Initial
Concern: Mr. Blake's lack of skill to work effectively with Larry, particularly his counseling skill.

Phase: Beginning.

Roles: The problem is seen through interplay of the same roles presented in the beginning phase of *Initial Concern 1.*

Personal
and
Interpersonal: Mr. Blake's lack of skill is revealed in his quandry over how to approach Larry. He does take several commendable actions; he contacts Doc, Miss Smith, and Mr. Long, and is supportive of Larry. However, he is perplexed by Larry's behavior—he feels Doc's instructions are not sufficiently detailed to cope with the problem. Among other things, Doc's suggestion that Mr. Blake encourage Larry to confide in him does not provide Mr. Blake with the "cookbook" instructions he feels he needs to approach Larry. So, when he comes to see Jack, he is in a dilemma: he recognizes the need to listen to Larry's problems, to explore and attempt to work them out, yet he is highly uncertain about actually making such an effort.

Phase: Middle.

Concern: Mr. Blake demonstrates considerable expertise in working effectively with Larry, reported in his second interview with Jack.

Roles: Mr. Blake is *supervisee* and *colleague,* and *counselor* to Larry. Jack is *supervisor,* and *educator.*

Individual
and
Interpersonal: Mr. Blake listens to Larry closely and, moreover, understands the significance of what he says. Mr. Blake's techniques in working with Larry are sound: he encourages him to express his thoughts and feelings, gently asks important questions, makes matter-of-fact comments about Larry's reports, and is sympathetic. However, Mr. Blake fails in over-encouraging and

stimulating Larry, who then expresses more problems and feelings than either Larry or Mr. Blake can handle.

Phase: End.

Concern: Jack and Mr. Blake continue to discuss Mr. Blake's counseling skills.

Roles: Same as in *Initial Concern 2.*
Individual and
Interpersonal: Jack suggests that Mr. Blake continue to be very much available to Larry, yet respect his need for privacy. Mr. Blake is discouraged and saddened by his experience.

3. *Initial*
   Concern: Mr. Blake's emotional reaction to Larry's problems.
   Phase: Beginning.
   Roles: Same as in *Initial Concern 2.*
   Individual and
   Interpersonal: Mr. Blake is annoyed by listening to the complaints of "manipulators" and is made anxious and sad by his boys' sadness and crying. In discussing Larry's sadness, Mr. Blake is deeply touched. He knows he is wrong in discouraging the boys from presenting their complaints and expressing their negative attitudes, and that Central State disapproves of that practice. Yet, he is embarrassed by his own responses. Jack asks Mr. Blake about his feeling "upset" by sad youngsters and assures him that it is appropriate to emphathize with them. However, Jack chastises himself for failing to explore Mr. Blake's reactions in any depth.

   Phase: Middle Portion.
   Concern and
   Roles: In addition to Mr. Blake's sadness, his emotional reaction to Larry's problems include here an enthusiasm to help, pride in his work, and an attempt to steel himself against his own negative feelings.

   Roles: Mr. Blake continues to play the roles of *colleague,* learner, and *supervisee,* while Jack continues his roles as *supervisor, educator,* and *colleague.*

   Individual and
   Interpersonal: When Larry's sadness about his mother comes to the fore and he begins to cry, Mr. Blake becomes distressed and sad. In relating the story to Jack, the roles they play are interchanged, with Jack as *counselor* and Mr. Blake as *counselee.*

Phase:	End.
Concern:	Mr. Blake's emotional distress in reaction to Larry's problems continues during the last phase of the story.
Roles:	Jack and Mr. Blake continue in their roles of the previous phase; however, Jack's strong, supportive posture now concentrates his effort even more noticeably in his role as *counselor,* while Mr. Blake's behavior increasingly casts him into the role of *counselee.* However, this interpretation must be applied tentatively because the evidence is sketchy.
Individual and Interpersonal:	In spite of Jack's assistance and Mr. Blake's efforts to pull himself together, Mr. Blake's mood remains gloomy.

4. *Initial*

Concern:	Jack assisting Mr. Blake through supervision.
Phase:	Beginning.
Roles:	The substance of this concern is played out through interactions between Jack as *supervisor* and *educator,* and Mr. Blake as *supervisee.* Jack seeks to understand Larry more clearly and Mr. Blake reports on Larry in the manner of a *colleague.* In this process, Jack affirms Mr. Blake's efforts and encourages him to work with Larry as a *counselor.*
Individual and Interpersonal:	Jack reassures and jokes with Mr. Blake attempting to relieve his anxiety. He suggests that Mr. Blake drop certain of his practices and adopt others. He clarifies the various motivations youngsters can have for complaining; suggests that Mr. Blake counsel Larry in the privacy of his office; and after indicating that Larry may cry if given the opportunity, he suggests that Mr. Blake prepare consciously for that possibility. He maintains that it is natural to feel sadness in response to another's sadness, but warns Mr. Blake not to get "carried away." Even though Jack helps Mr. Blake in many respects, Mr. Blake's despondency at Larry's crying remains unresolved.
Phase:	Middle.
Concern:	Jack listens carefully to Mr. Blake as he reports on his interaction with Larry, stimulates Mr. Blake to explain his reasons for using particular techniques with the boy, accepts Mr. Blake's expression of emotion, and compliments him on his techniques.
Roles:	Same as in *Initial Concern 4.*

Individual
and
Interpersonal: Jack's secure manner is generally unruffled. Despite his anxiety over the combination of Larry's intensity and Mr. Blake's limited training for in-depth counseling, he maintains a gentle, steadfast approach which eases Mr. Blake's strain and increases his understanding of Larry.

Phase: End.

Concern: Jack's efforts to assist Mr. Blake through supervision conclude with Jack gently but persistently asking Mr. Blake about Larry's current condition.

Roles: Same as in *Initial Concern 4.*

Individual
and
Interpersonal: Jack seeks to raise Mr. Blake's spirits by encouraging him, complimenting him on his work, and advising him to observe Larry carefully and make himself available in case the boy needs him.

5. *Initial*
   Concern: Mr. Blake's concern and desire to help.
   Phase: Beginning.
   Roles: Mr. Blake is primarily a *learner,* and *counselee.* Doc is an *educator,* as are Miss Smith and Mr. Long. Again, Jack is *counselor.*

Individual
and
Interpersonal: Mr. Blake is highly motivated to help Larry. He seeks information from Doc, Miss Smith, and Mr. Long. He contacts Jack for counsel on how to proceed with Larry. Further, Mr. Blake admits his own limitations in the interest of learning to improve his helping skills.

Phase: Middle.

Concern: Mr. Blake continues his high level of motivation to help Larry, to improve his skills, and to relate to Jack in the manner of a colleague.

Roles: Same as in *Initial Concern 4.*

Individual
and
Interpersonal: Mr. Blake is still persistent, even though his interview with Larry had been stormy and his discussion with Jack, though congenial and supportive, proves to be demanding.

Phase: End.

Concern: Blake leaves Jack's office promising to continue his efforts to help Larry.

Roles: Jack remains the affirming *supervisor, counselor, colleague,* and *educator.* Mr. Blake is still *supervisee, counselee,* and *colleague* to Jack's roles; and *supervisor* and *counselor* to Larry.

6. *Initial*
Concern: The dilemma of Jack and Mr. Blake.

Phase: Beginning.

Concern: Jack's dilemma is how to encourage Mr. Blake to attempt an innovative approach to Larry, one that is within his capabilities. He is also faced with the problem of exploring Mr. Blake's feelings about Larry's sadness or leaving them undisturbed. Mr. Blake's dilemma is less clear; however, it appears that on the one hand he is interested in maintaining his routine approach to Larry, while on the other hand he is strongly motivated to change that approach. Mr. Blake is aware of the reactions—anxiety and sadness—that a boy's crying precipitates in him. He copes with these feelings by holding them in abeyance and working in spite of them.

Roles: Jack's roles are *supervisor* and *colleague* to Mr. Blake's *supervisee* and *colleague.*

Individual and Interpersonal: Jack is strongly interested in having Mr. Blake work more intensively with Larry. Mr. Blake is also interested in pursuing that course, but he is uncertain about the adequacy of his skills and is disturbed by Larry's sadness. The relationship between Jack and Mr. Blake is congenial and friendly in spite of the knotty problems they are working with.

Phase: Middle.

Concern: Most of the vignette's middle portion does not pose dilemmas for either Jack or Mr. Blake. Mr. Blake reports effective work with Larry, in spite of his feelings. Jack listens closely, asking questions and supporting him. However, at the end of the middle portion the problem of what should be done about Larry's distraught condition is clearly apparent—should Mr. Blake pursue Larry actively, or should he wait for Larry to approach him?

Roles:	The specific roles that come to bear on the concern of how to approach Larry are *supervisor, colleague,* and *educator* (for Jack) and *supervisee, colleague,* and *learner* (for Mr. Blake). Jack to a limited extent also assumes the role of *counselor* and Mr. Blake the role of *counselee.*
Individual and Interpersonal:	The men's relationship is serious yet friendly, one in which there is a joint regard for Larry's problems and for his improvement. While both Jack and Mr. Blake are encouraged by some aspects of Mr. Blake's work, they are also anxious about Larry breaking off communication with Mr. Blake.
Phase:	End.
Concern:	The dilemma of "what to do" to help Larry becomes a stark reality at the close of the vignette.
Roles:	In this process, Jack works as a *supervisor* and *educator* while he is educated in the process. Mr. Blake plays the role of *supervisee* and *learner.*
Individual and Interpersonal:	Jack advises Mr. Blake and Mr. Blake is an anxious listener. Though Jack maintains considerable overt optimism, he shares some of Mr. Blake's gloom. Jack's problems remain: how to help Mr. Blake come to terms with himself and how to help him in his efforts with Larry. Mr. Blake's problems remain coping with himself and Larry.

Fifth. Relate the elements identified in the previous steps of the analysis to one another. Examine the content of the topical headings in relation to one another as you develop more general statements about how the elements fit into patterns. The synthesis below is an illustration of this process.

We find Larry to be a chronically irritable, demanding, discouraged, depressed boy with psychosomatic complaints, which emotions he vents by crying.

Mr. Blake is strongly motivated to help Larry. Moreover, he is tolerant, patient, and innovative. While he is generally in good spirits, Larry's moodiness, complaining, and crying upset him. Yet, he struggles to understand Larry more thoroughly, to handle his feelings about Larry's crying and complaining, and to improve his helping skills.

In regard to roles, Mr. Blake functions mainly as a *counselor* with Larry and occasionally as an *educator, care giver,* and *program planner.* Larry plays the role of troubled child. In relation to Jack, Mr. Blake plays primarily the roles of *supervisee* and *colleague*. Under conditions of great stress, he becomes a *counselee*; however, since Mr. Blake and Jack do not deal intensively with Mr. Blake's emotional reactions, the counselee role is limited.

Jack's personality is characterized by steadiness, helpfulness, and availability.

From the standpoint of *interpersonal* perspective, the relationship between Mr. Blake and Larry is generally cooperative, one in which Mr. Blake is dominant in a parental sense, nurturing and supporting Larry. Larry is initially submissive, yet demands to be nurtured in a childlike way. As the vignette progresses, Mr. Blake refers Larry to Doc, asks Miss Smith and Mr. Long about him, and talks with Jack. Moreover, he directly engages Larry in order to learn about the sources of his stomachaches and related complaints. Although Mr. Blake is not able to identify the exact sources of Larry's stomachaches, he learns a great deal about his problems. In the interplay between them, Mr. Blake attempts to get Larry to consider some of his more basic problems and to see himself in a realistic light. However, Larry continues to believe that others fail to nurture him. The struggle between Mr. Blake and Larry comes to a climax in an interview in which Mr. Blake seeks to help Larry get to and bring out some of the sources of his emotional disturbance.

Continuing to view the vignette from its *interpersonal* aspects, the relationship between Mr. Blake and Jack is important as a way of learning what happens between Mr. Blake and Larry (at least from Mr. Blake's point of view). Jack serves as *supervisor,* confidant, *colleague,* and *counselor.* Although Jack is the dominant person in the relationship, Mr. Blake is by no means passive; he initiates meetings with Jack, contributes ideas to their conversation, questions Jack, and occasionally challenges his ideas. Moreover, Mr. Blake feels free to express his thoughts and feelings, and only concerning his most sensitive feelings—his discomfort and sadness stimulated by the boy's crying—does he hold back.

Sixth. Explain not only the connections, patterns, cycles, and effects resulting from the interrelatedness of the vignette's several elements, but also try to explain why they occur.

Larry's behavior—complaining, crying, accusing, demanding—is influenced by those with whom he interacted: Doc, the boys on the sidewalk, and Mr. Blake. They did not nurture him as he wanted and in the manner they had in the past. Further, Larry's current upset state is very closely related to the lack of nurture in his home life. In the interview with Mr. Blake, Larry's reactions are intensified by Mr. Blake's probing the sources of his problems. His disturbance becomes most apparent when Mr. Blake asks him about his anger toward Doc and the boys who teased him and when he displays deep sadness about not having received a letter from his mother.

Jack's work with Mr. Blake is influenced by his desire to help the boys solve their personal problems through assisting Mr. Blake to develop his skills and handle his feelings. However, Jack is unable to fully assist Mr. Blake with his strong feelings about Larry's crying. This leaves all three distressed.

Seventh. Carefully evaluate the concepts and the relevant details relating to *individual, interpersonal,* and *role.* These terms take on additional helpfulness when they are considered within the framework of *concerns* or issues facing the youth care worker.

Three additional concepts should be specified which will help in studying the other stories. The first term is *process*—what happens in the Jack-Mr. Blake contacts and the Mr. Blake-Larry contacts. Each step in the *process* affects the following steps. For example, the initial contact between Jack and Mr. Blake about a plan of strategy for working with Larry is related to Mr. Blake's earlier consultation with Doc and his own experience with Larry. Likewise, Mr. Blake's dramatic interview with Larry follows as a result of and according to prior consultation with Jack.

The second term is *case history,* which includes such background material as earlier family-life experiences and school experiences. The case history should be set forth for use by the reader in understanding current situations.

Third, examining *expectations* between or among the vignette's major characters can be helpful in understanding their behavior. For example, Jack expected Mr. Blake to be thoughtful about Larry and to explore new ways of working with him; Mr. Blake expected Jack to be interested in and to listen to what he reported; and Larry expected Doc and Mr. Blake to be sympathetic to him. In some instances these expectations become reality; in others they do not and so result in frustration.

Eighth. Consider how the decisions and actions in the vignette could have been improved. Several questions are set forth below to encourage your further thinking about the vignette's major action sequences, issues, and objectives.

A. Questions within the framework of the way in which the problem was handled:
   1. Should Jack have inquired further about Mr. Blake's feelings of uneasiness and sadness concerning Larry's crying? How might such an inquiry have been made? What might its effects have been?

   2. Assuming that Mr. Blake's interview with Larry was only one of a number of contacts that he will continue to have with Larry, what might Mr. Blake do next, particularly to help Larry with his anguish over his mother?

   3. Recognizing Jack's concern about Mr. Blake and his belief that Mr. Blake was very sad as a result of his work with Larry, what might Jack do next?

   4. What might Mr. Blake do to deal with his own sadness?

B. Questions outside the framework of the way in which the problem was handled:

1. If Mr. Blake had played mainly the role of an *educator* instead of that of a *counselor* in relation to Larry, might that have changed his approach and tactics? What would his approach and tactics have been? What do you think might have followed from his intervention in an *educator*'s role?

2. Might Doc have spent more time with Larry and, in so doing, might he have talked with Larry (to the extent that Larry would have participated) about the psychological aspects of his problem? How might such an effort have affected the situation?

3. Might Mr. Blake or Jack have referred Larry to Miss Smith, the social worker? What differences might that referral have made in the vignette?

4. Should consideration be given for Larry to make home visits at the point at which the vignette ends? If so, what specific aspects should be taken into consideration? If not, why not?

5. Should Jack and Mr. Blake confer with Doc in planning the next steps for dealing with Larry? If so, what questions might they ask him?

DISCUSSION QUESTIONS

Chapter 1
"Jack's Entrance"

1. Describe the roles of the several members who made up the informal group that met in Mr. Owens' store. How did these roles contribute to the group's activities and the town's interests?
2. Consider the personalities of Mr. and Mrs. Owens and the roles they played in their family. How, for example, did they mutually support each other? How did their roles contribute to the family's solidarity?
3. Identify the values of Lawnwood and of the Owens. How were these related to the Owens children's upbringing?
4. What in Jack's early training and experience inclined him to accept the position as Director of Group Life?

Chapter 2
"He Keeps Asking the Same Questions"

1. What roles was Jack playing and what techniques did he use in talking with Mr. Blake about Dick Jones?
2. Though Jack and Mr. Blake had a thorough planning session concerning Mr. Blake's approach to Dick Jones, what else might Jack have included?

3. Why might Jack have made a specific appointment with Mr. Blake to consider the next steps in working with Dick?

Chapter 3
"Nobody Likes Me or Wants Me"

1. Should Jack have explored more thoroughly with Mr. Blake his deep and intense reaction to boys' crying? If so, how?
2. Might Mr. Blake have been too direct in suggesting to Larry: "Larry, the feeling that 'nobody likes you or wants you' is terribly important to you."? Explain your answer.
3. In view of Mr. Blake's sadness, should Jack do any follow-up work with him? If so, what might he consider?
4. What do you believe Larry's prospects are for developing a therapeutic relationship with Mr. Blake? Consider in your analysis the roles required in such a relationship.

Chapter 4
"Where There's Smoke"

1. What roles did Mr. Collins play with his boys in trying to work out the marijuana smoking and pushing in Whittier?
2. Describe Mr. Snell's relationship with and technique for working with the boys in Venture. Would those techniques be equally applicable to boys with other kinds of problems? Explain your answer.
3. Describe Mr. Hall's relationship with and technique for working with the boys in Anchor. Might other techniques be useful in working with them?
4. Consider Mr. Alderman's job of improving the cottage program. How might he best distribute his time and effort among: direct work with the boys; teaching recreational skills to cottage staff; consulting with cottage staff about the implementation of cottage recreational programs?

Chapter 5
"Seminar for Lunch"

1. What would you suggest to Jack about designing a plan to orient new boys to Central State?

2. How do you understand Central State's lines of communication among the cottage supervisors, social workers, psychologists, and psychiatrists? What effect did those lines have on the supervisors' work?
3. What is your impression of the impact on the cottage supervisors of giving the boys psychiatric labels? Impact on the boys?
4. How do you feel about John Waldo's comments on the importance of respect for the boys' dignity?

Chapter 6
"What Makes Rick Run"

1. What were the several ways in which Mr. Wellman worked with Rick? How would you assess the impact of his efforts?
2. At what points do you believe Mr. Wellman and Mr. Blackburn let their own individual expectations and standards come into play in respect to Rick?
3. What were Jack's plan and techniques for dealing with Jack Wellman's overconcern? Did they change during the course of the vignette? If so, how and why?
4. What should Jack do with the information he abstracted from Rick's file?
5. Drawing from Jack's notes, relate various aspects of Rick's life to his experience at Central State.

Chapter 7
"Sex Education"

1. What factors do you see as contributing to the difficulties of Central State and Upper State staff members in talking directly to one another about sex and sexual problems among their respective residents?
2. How might the discussion have been different if the participants had stopped to analyze their roles as *care givers, educators, counselors,* and *supervisors*? What aspects of dealing with sexual concerns and problems might have been included in each role?
3. Assuming that Jack, Doc, and the others at Central State have an effective program functioning to control homosexuality, what can they be doing to insure the program's continuance and the avoidance of a relapse?
4. What roles should staff in an institutional setting play in regard to sexual morality and standards of conduct?

Chapter 8
"Is There More Than One Way To Get Out?"

1. Analyze each person's report at the staff meeting regarding Sam Walker. Do you observe any blind spots in the staff evaluations?
2. What do you think were the basic differences between Jim Watson's and Bill Wilson's appraisals of Sam? Do you see any way in which these differences could be brought together to form a total picture of Sam?
3. What was Cal's basic appraisal of Sam's progress?
4. What image of himself was Sam trying to convey to Cal? How did he try to convey it: what did he say and how did he say it?
5. In view of the several appraisals of Sam, how would you describe him, both in terms of his self-concept and his relationships?

Chapter 9
"Timmy's Hung Himself"

1. Analyze the role that Jack played in relation to Mr. Wilton and Mr. Robb. What alternatives were available to him?
2. Might other people have been involved in Timmy's complex placement problem—Mr. Graves, the superintendent, for example? If so, how might they have influenced the decision-making?
3. Besides the advantages of using routines to place Timmy, what other factors contributed to hardening Mr. Wilton's line that procedures must be followed?
4. What might Jack do after Timmy's suicide to pull the pieces back together? What might Mr. Wilton and Miss Leaf do?

Chapter 10
"They Still Don't Get Along"

1. Analyze the possibility that, after Mr. Collins prevented a fistfight between Bob and Ken, he might have concluded too quickly that he could not salvage them for work at Whittier. What alternatives were open to Mr. Collins?
2. What might have happened if Jack had rejected Mr. Collins' work with Bob and Ken and had required him to pursue resolving their differences and retaining them in Whittier?
3. Should Jack have taken over for Mr. Collins when he failed to follow their agreement to work out the differences between Bob and Ken? Should he

have met with Bob and Ken in his office? If he did so, should he have had Mr. Collins sit in on the session?

Chapter 11
"The Case of the Missing Groceries"

1. Evaluate the interpersonal relations among the staff at the meeting when Mr. Eagan presented the problem of the Commissary being overloaded with Hilltop boys.
2. How might the two conflicting ideas of the Commissary's function—training site versus supply depot—be resolved in order to preserve the Commisary in its function as a training site?
3. What tasks faced Jack after reading John Gill's note? In relation to the boys at Hilltop? In relation to the supervisors of the other cottages? To Mrs. Adams? To Mr. Graves? To the staff committee?

Chapter 12
"Too Hot is Too Hot"

1. Recognizing Len Hall as an experienced and level-headed worker, do you think he either failed to note or rejected signs—the especially hot day, bad mood of the boys—that serious trouble was imminent? Why do you think so?
2. Given the escalation of the problems associated with mowing the lawn, at what point might Len have caught himself and changed his approach? What approach might he have shifted to? How might he have implemented it? What impact might it have had?
3. Evaluate Jack's efforts to retain Mr. Hall at Central State. Should he have made the effort? Why or why not?
4. What follow-up work will be necessary with Roger Barrien, Alfred Fredrick, and the others in the lawn-mowing group?

Chapter 13
"Jack's Exit"

1. Consider Jack's mental and physical condition and the regime he had followed for fifteen years at Central State. How might he have altered his

work style to rid himself of the chest pains? What might Mr. Graves have done to sustain Jack?

2. What connections do you find among the several topics dealt with in Jack's dreams?

3. What relationship do you find between the topics of the dreams and Jack's impending death?

ABOUT THE AUTHOR

George H. Weber is currently Deputy Director, Division of Special Mental Health Programs, National Institute of Mental Health (NIMH)—a division which administers research and training programs in seven areas including crime and delinquency, child and family problems, prevention and control of rape, metropolitan problems, minorities, aging, and natural disasters. In addition, the author's background includes: Deputy Chief, Center for Studies of Crime and Delinquency, NIMH; Executive Secretary to President Kennedy's Committee on Youth Employment; U.S. Children's Bureau Consultant to training schools and juvenile institutions (while in this position Dr. Weber consulted in over one hundred institutions throughout the United States and Puerto Rico); Head of Minnesota's institutions for delinquents and youthful offenders; and senior staff member of Kansas Boys' Industrial School.

Dr. Weber has coedited two books, *Residential Treatment of Emotionally Disturbed Children* (with B.J. Haberlein, 1970), and *Social Scientists as Advocates* (with G.J. McCall, 1978), and has published over 40 articles and reviews. He holds a Ph.D. in sociology and has had training in psychology, including psychoanalytic therapy training with the late Dr. Otto Fleischman of the Menninger Clinic (who had worked with August Aichhorn of Vienna, author of *Wayward Youth,* 1935, and a pioneer in the application of psychoanalytic principles to the milieu treatment of delinquents).

Though the author's career has been in "applied work," he has taught part-time at a number of universities, including Washington College of Law of American University, Georgetown University, Catholic University, and the University of Minnesota.